CHOP CHOP

CHOP CHOP

Cooking the Food of Nigeria

Ozoz Sokoh

PHOTOGRAPHY BY JAMES RANSOM

ARTISAN | NEW YORK

Library of Congress Cataloging-in-Publication Data

Names: Sokoh, Ozoz, author. | Ransom, James (Photographer), photographer.
Title: Chop chop : cooking the food of Nigeria / Ozoz Sokoh ; photography by James Ransom.
Description: New York : Artisan, 2025. | Includes index.
Identifiers: LCCN 2024029815 | ISBN 9781648291890 (hardcover)
Subjects: LCSH: Cooking, Nigerian. | LCGFT: Cookbooks.
Classification: LCC TX725.N6 S65 2025 | DDC 641.59669—dc23/eng/20240701
LC record available at https://lccn.loc.gov/2024029815

Design by Nina Simoneaux

Artisan books may be purchased in bulk for business, educational, or promotional use. For information, please contact your local bookseller or the Hachette Book Group Special Markets Department at special.markets@hbgusa.com.

The publisher is not responsible for websites (or their content) that are not owned by the publisher.

The Hachette Speakers Bureau provides a wide range of authors for speaking events. To find out more, go to hachettespeakersbureau.com or email HachetteSpeakers@hbgusa.com.

Published by Artisan,
an imprint of Workman Publishing,
a division of Hachette Book Group, Inc.
1290 Avenue of the Americas
New York, NY 10104
artisanbooks.com

The Artisan name and logo are registered trademarks of Hachette Book Group, Inc.

Printed in China on responsibly sourced paper

First printing, February 2025

10 9 8 7 6 5 4 3 2 1

Lagos Lagoon at Epe Fish Market

PREVIOUS: *Red palm oil*

To my mum and dad (RIP), who persevered in my first nine years of not eating because I hated food. How things change, and for the better, too! Thank you.

To my family, especially my sisters, who were my first partners in our make-believe kitchen at the back of 7 Ramos Close—you laid the foundation for my curiosity and confidence as a cook.

To my children—your thoughtfulness and willingness to explore food fill me with joy. I'm proud of you.

To Nigerians the world over, I offer this celebration of our heritage, with love.

And to you, dear reader, who might be encountering Nigerian cuisine for the first time, I dedicate this book to you. I hope you find joy and delight in these pages, and a flavorful glimpse into the world of Nigerian food culture.

A PARTY IN YOUR MOUTH

SMALL CHOPS *33*

WHEN YOU WAKE UP IS YOUR MORNING

BREAKFAST *58*

KNEE CHOP

SALADS *90*

ALL DAY, EVERY DAY

MAINS AND SIDE DISHES *114*

THE MAIN, THE MAIN

RICE AND BEANS *134*

ASSORTED

OF MEAT AND MORE *160*

ALL-TIME FAVORITES

STEWS AND SAUCES *187*

MORE THAN JUST FUFU

LUNCH AND DINNER
OF CHAMPIONS
(SOMETIMES BREAKFAST, TOO)

THINGS TO KEEP
THE MOUTH MOVING

SWEET MOUTH

QUENCH YOUR THIRST

CUISINE BASICS *326*

A bunch of palm nuts

PREFACE

Chop Chop celebrates classic and traditional Nigerian cuisine, mostly through dishes made by home cooks, and the ingredients, flavors, and textures that make it not only beloved but delicious. Through this book, you might find similarities with dishes, drinks, and snacks from your own culture and cuisine.

In Nigerian pidgin and across West Africa, the term *chop* is about food and feasting, used as both noun and verb. A "chop chop" is a food lover or an overeater. When we say "Come chop," it is an invitation to sharing and community. "I wan chop" means "I want to eat."

Many of my memories of growing up in Warri, on the southern coast of Nigeria, involve food and family. Both my parents worked full-time—Dad as a marine engineer and Mum as the proprietor of her own nursery school and elementary school. We gathered for family dinners at 6 p.m. almost every day, and enjoyed weekend meals, especially Sunday lunch. Even though I didn't eat much as a child, I was surrounded by love and lessons around our Nigerian table.

My parents—Mum the recipe collector and crafter and Dad the gadget explorer—were obsessed with making things from scratch. They taught me and my siblings to be handy in the kitchen, and to shop for, prep, and cook our meals. We learned how to make red stew, bright in color and flavor, a pot always present on the stove, and vegetable stews with sautéed greens like èfọ́ rírò; to pound yam; wrap mọ́ínmọ́ín elewe (think tamales filled with pureed black-eyed peas); clean snails; and cook great jollof rice.

Today, I'm very much like my parents (who would have thought!), gathering my children around me not only to cook, eat, and celebrate Nigerian food but to learn its history and heritage, its connections with other West African cuisines, and the edible traces and trails it has left in the diaspora, from Brazil to the American South.

My nine-year-old self would be surprised at me now, an expert on Nigerian cuisine, focused on celebrating and documenting our food. Since 2009, when I started my food blog, *Kitchen Butterfly*, I've been invested in sharing the faces and facets of our foodways, and intersections with geography, history, culture, heritage, legacy, politics, economics, colonization, decolonization, movement and migration, language, religion, origins, erasure, representation, and everything in between.

Those early years in Warri shaped my plate and palate, giving me a well-rounded taste of Nigerian cuisine, and it is my privilege to share it here. This is my invitation to you to explore and experience Nigerian cuisine.

I know some of it may be new to you—the recipe names, ingredient compositions, and serving combinations. I hope I can court your patience and encourage and inspire you to travel by plate, to taste Nigeria with curiosity, at home, embracing the joy of discovery in all the ways we are similar despite our differences.

Yellow Danfo buses, Obalende, Lagos

THE FOODWAYS OF NIGERIA

◇◇◇◇◇◇◇◇

Nigerian cuisine is a mosaic of soups, stews, sauces, swallows (soft doughy, glutinous starches), and more. The flavors are multilayered and the aromas sweet, spicy, and pungent. Nigerian food is based on predominantly fresh produce, as well as dried and preserved ingredients.

Though food in Nigeria varies regionally, there are many similarities on the plate. For instance, bean fritters are often paired with smooth, fermented puddings and porridges of Guinea corn (sorghum), corn, and/or millet for breakfast, at home, and sometimes street dinners. Across the country, the pairing reflects the different languages and foodways.

In the South West, South South, and South East, the fritter is known as àkàrà while the pudding goes by many names, including pap (which is similar to South African mieliepap). In the South South and South East, it is commonly known as àkàmù, made from white or yellow corn, while in the South West, it is known as ògì, when made with corn—or ògì baba, a version combining corn, millet, and red Guinea corn. In the north, the fritters are known as kosai and the pudding, koko, is made from millet, Guinea corn, and/or corn, with or without spices.

Many of the dishes we eat are surf and turf, combining the best of sea and land. Dried krill, shrimp, and prawns, known locally as crayfish, bring a depth of flavor, paired with smoked and fermented elements like nuts and seeds.

Since precolonial times, West African yams, millet, Guinea corn, and African rice (*Oryza glaberrima*) have been staples for dishes and drinks, as have products of the African palm tree, from palm oil to palm wine, and others like coconut and date. Spices—such as alligator pepper, Guinea pepper, and uda (grains of

Selim), from the region known as both the Grain Coast and the Pepper Coast—were abundant, and remain popular today for soups, stews, and sauces, along with Indian spices that came to the country via Indian and British colonialists.

Fermented nuts, seeds and legumes, vegetable salts leached from wood ash, and rock salts were popular seasonings until the colonial imposition of bouillon cubes, which dominate today. This shift, driven by politics, was not a benign exchange; it disrupted agricultural practices, driving people away from the diversity of customs and practices of their ancestors and focusing instead on monocultures and food as commodities. This diminished the value and documentation of traditional foods. And though we live with bouillon cubes today, the way they came to us cannot be forgotten.

Chattel slavery brought cassava via the Portuguese, and global events brought the peoples and cuisines of Lebanon, China, and India here at various points, making shawarma, spring rolls, and samosas staples. The Nigerian love of protein—meat, seafood, tofu, and everything in between—however, is homegrown. Nothing goes to waste, and animal cuts from nose to tail are prized and feature in delicacies like Nkwobi (page 179).

In addition to embracing elements of other cuisines, there is a culinary bridge between the cuisine of Nigeria (and the West African region) and that of the African diaspora, across

Dried bonga fish

which dishes and drinks have traveled, in both directions. From the African coast to Central and South America, the Caribbean, the American South, and Europe, you'll find intellectual contributions of enslaved West Africans largely due to chattel slavery as well as ingredients they brought with them: rice, black-eyed peas, okra, indigo, coffee, and sugarcane.

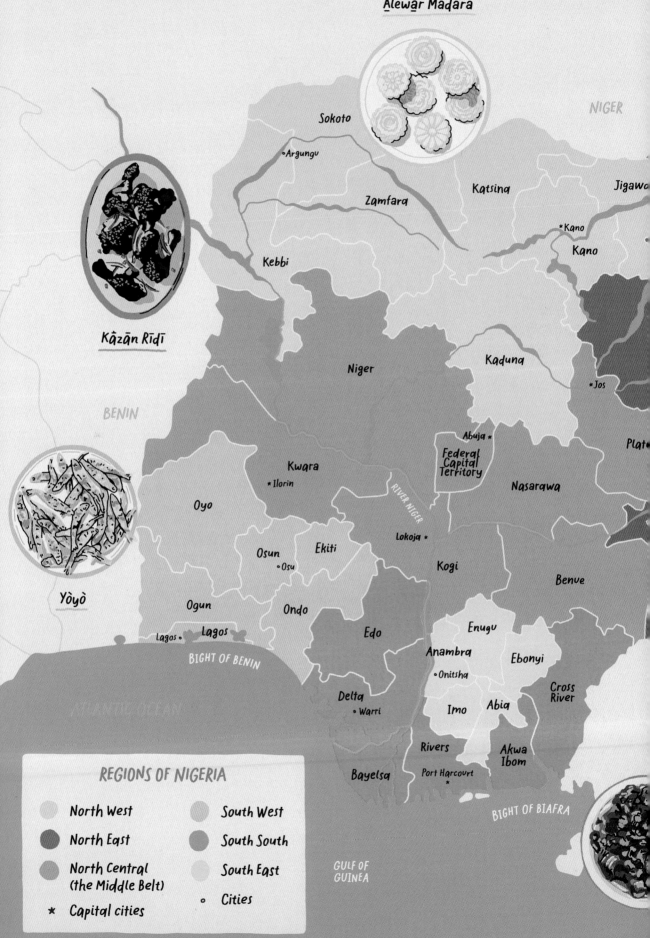

Alēwar Madara

Kâzān Rīdī

Yòyò

REGIONS OF NIGERIA

- North West
- North East
- North Central (the Middle Belt)
- ★ Capital cities
- South West
- South South
- South East
- ○ Cities

Map labels

NIGER

Sokoto
Argungu
Zamfara
Katsina
Jigawa
Kebbi
★ Kano
Kano

BENIN

Niger
Kaduna
★ Jos

Kwara
★ Ilorin
Abuja ★
Federal Capital Territory
Nasarawa
Plat

Oyo
River Niger
Osun
Ekiti
○ Osu
Lokoja ★
Kogi
Benue

Ogun
Ondo
Edo
Enugu
Lagos ○
Lagos
Anambra
Ebonyi

BIGHT OF BENIN
Onitsha
Cross River

ATLANTIC OCEAN
Delta
○ Warri
Imo
Abia

Rivers
Akwa Ibom

Bayelsa
Port Harcourt
★

BIGHT OF BIAFRA

GULF OF GUINEA

Māsà

CHAD

LAKE CHAD

Yobe

Borno

× Maiduguri

Gombe

Adamawa

araba

CAMEROON

mbilla Plateau ○

Nkwobi

Edikang Ikong

THE REGIONS OF NIGERIA

◇◇◇◇◇◇◇◇◇◇

Nigeria is one of sixteen countries in tropical West Africa, a subregion of the continent, south of the sandy, dusty Sahara. It is a relatively young country of many geographies, ethnicities, and languages, broadly divided into north, south, middle belt, east, and west. Regional foodways are shaped by geography and what the land and waters support—various waterways traverse the country, and communities around them engage in fishing activities. Religion and belief systems, whether Christian, Muslim, or traditional Nigerian, also play a role in the foodways. Though the north is predominantly Muslim and the south predominantly Christian, you will find Muslims in the Middle Belt, South West, and South South; and Christians in the north.

Nigeria, named after the river Niger, is the most populous country on the African continent, with a population of more than 200 million people, and the most populous Black nation on the planet. It encompasses 356,669 square miles (923,768 km²)—roughly three times the size of Italy.

A federal republic, independent from Britain since 1960, Nigeria shares land borders with predominantly French-speaking countries, from Niger in the north, the republic of Benin in the west, and Chad and Cameroon in the east. To the south, its curved coastline meets with two bends in the waters, the Bight of Benin and of Biafra (also known as the Bight of Bonny), part of the larger Gulf of Guinea swath in the eastern Atlantic Ocean.

The geography of the country is a network of rivers, streams, mountains, plateaus, swamps, deserts, and more. The two main rivers are the Niger, the third longest river on the continent, and the Benue. They form a Y at the south-central river port of Lokoja and continue all the way to the southern end of Nigeria, where the coast and swamps meet the Atlantic in the Niger Delta, the third largest delta in the world.

Above the rivers' confluence, the northern region is split into three of the country's six zones: North West, North East, and North Central (the Middle Belt). Below the confluence, the region splits into three regions to the west and east of the dividing Benue River—South West; South South, a U-shaped region around the Niger Delta; and South East. These geopolitical regions are broken down into thirty-six states, with the country's capital in Abuja, in the Federal Capital Territory.

The weather impacts agricultural patterns, growing seasons, the variety of crops, and ultimately what ends up in the kitchens and on the tables across the country.

Each region has unique rainy and dry seasons, with higher dry season temperatures than during the rainy season. In the south, the rainy season runs from March to October with a spell of dry weather in August known as August Break. In the central regions, the rainy season is shorter, from April to September, and in the north, the rains kick off in June–July, peak in August, and end in September. In the south, the dry season begins in November, which is marked by harmattan across West Africa. This season of dry, dusty, hazy, and chilly winds lasts until March.

The North West

This region is home to the Hausa, Fulani, Nupes, Gwaris (Gbagyis), Kambaris, and many others. The geography is dominated by sudan savannas and high temperatures. It is one half of the Arewa Kitchen (*Arewa* from *areoun*, meaning north, and *wa*, meaning people, in Hausa). Seafood, particularly fish, and the waterways are celebrated here almost every year in grand style at the Argungu Fishing Festival in Kebbi state, first hosted in 1934 as a peace-making endeavor between the Sokoto Caliphate and the Kebbi Kingdom. Today, with peace established, the festival kicks off the fishing season and marks the end of the farming season. Groundnuts (peanuts) and ginger are some of the region's products, alongside a variety of greens, millet, and Guinea corn (sorghum). There's also rice and cowpeas, which are featured in Garau Garau (page 157); sugarcane; and commercial livestock.

The North East

The other half of the Arewa Kitchen, this region is home to the Fulani, Kanuris, Jukuns, Hausas, and other peoples who are spread across semi-arid sahel and sudan savannas with hills and mountains, plains, and plateaus. Millet, Guinea corn, maize, sesame, cowpeas, sugarcane, tomatoes, onions, tatashe peppers, tea, coffee, and commercial livestock are key agricultural products. Sweet porridges, savory pottages, drinks, and sweet treats are made from cereals and grains, some traceable to West Asia and North Africa. You'll find a variety of dairy products, from soft cheeses to fermented milks and cultured butters like mân shānū (page 18).

The North Central

Named for its central location, North Central, also known as the Middle Belt, extends from east to west and is the location of Nigeria's capital, the Federal Capital Territory of Abuja. It is home to the Tiv, Igala, Berom, Igbiras, some Yorùbás, and others. A variety of crops thrive in the tropical savanna, including rice, beans, tea, coffee, potatoes, sweet potatoes, Guinea corn, and millet, used in Ibyer (page 78). The yams and mangoes of this region are second to none in flavor and size. The Plateau region and its capital city, Jos, give us everything from great tomatoes to the most delicious strawberries you'll ever have; pomegranates; passion fruit; apples; white, brown, and black sesame seeds; and fruity atili oil, the latter two enjoyed in Kàzān Rīdī (page 171). It's no surprise considering the region is home to the confluence of the Niger and Benue rivers, and thus some of the richest soil in the valley.

The South West

Also known as the West, this region of the Yorùbás stretches from the coastal Atlantic regions inland, thus it is no surprise that seafood is popular, from Yòyò (page 54) to Ìmóyò Ẹlèja (page 107). Corn, cassava, yams, coconut, cocoa, rice, plantain, a wide variety of leafy vegetables and greens, and seafood are abundant. It is home to Lagos, Nigeria's most populous and most cosmopolitan city, sometimes referred to as mini Economic Community of West African States (ECOWAS) for the sheer diversity of people from across the West African subcontinent and beyond. The people of this region are known for their love of partying and parties, known as owambes. Huge fans of hot chiles, they believe that "the one who shies away from eating peppers is a weak soul"—Ẹmi ti o jẹ ata, ẹmi yẹpẹrẹ ni.

The South South

The cuisine of this U-shaped region, also known as the South, reflects its proximity to the Atlantic coast, and the extensive network of waterways in the Niger Delta—welcome to seafood central! It is home to a diverse group of people, including the Urhobos, Isokos, Edo people, Ijaws, Itsekiris, Rivers, Ibibios, Efiks, and a group of the Igbos, who are spread across mangrove forests, freshwater swamps, and rain forest. The abundance of fish and shellfish—fresh, dried, smoked—shows up in Banga Soup (page 257) and more. Crops like cassava, yam, and plantain, along with a variety of spices and vegetables, from leafy greens to herbs, are abundant in dishes like Edikang Ikong soup (page 249). Though pepper soup (see page 241) is enjoyed across the country, the version made by the people of the South South is the absolute best, made with a host of spices, yielding a complex, delicious blend. Some of the tastiest pineapples call this region home, along with a variety of palms, from oil to coconut palms and those that delight us with their sweet fermented palm wine.

The South East

Also known as the East, this region is Igboland. Cassava, yams, maize, breadfruit, cocoyam (taro), Bambara beans, and rice are staples, as are palm nuts and glorious red palm oil. The love for cassava is evident in everything from Àbàchà Ǹcha (page 103) to fufu. Vegetables are prized, from leafy ones like ọkazī, used in soups and salads, to garden eggs. Yams play an important cultural role in society, and are celebrated in festivals like the New Yam Festival, where Ofe Nsala (page 237) and Pounded Yam (page 226) make an appearance. Specialty meat dishes like Nkwobi (page 179) and its compatriot, isi ewu, also have their origins here.

THE LANGUAGE AND LEXICON OF NIGERIAN CUISINE

◇◇◇◇◇◇◇◇◇

Nigerians have unique descriptions for food, the result of multiple influences. We say "this pepper soup is hot" meaning spicy or peppery. Here are some notes to help you understand Nigerian English.

Nigerian food is often thought of as peppery, but it's more about spice than heat. In Nigeria, "pepper" is a word used to describe everything from a chile to a level of spice. To me, "peppery" speaks to one instance of flavor, mostly fiery heat, while "spicy" embraces a plethora of warming flavors and fragrances, including floral, earthy, nutty, caramelly, sometimes with heat.

So, when you first hear of Nigerian pepper soup, which is sometimes more spicy than peppery, I would not blame you for thinking it was all about heat as the name suggests. I encourage you not to be put off by "pepper" in recipe titles.

In Nigerian Pidgin English, delicious food, whether sweet or savory, is described as sweet. "Mehn, this soup sweet o" translates to "Wow, this soup is delicious." Never mind that the soup is savory and, in fact, a stew.

By global agreement, most soups are liquid and easy to drink. Stews, on the other hand, are thickened by combinations of vegetables and protein and require some utensil to eat. Yet in Nigeria, the majority of the dishes that fit the stew description are called "soups"; for example, ègúsí, okro, ògbòṇò, and banga feature nuts, seeds, and other thickeners, along with protein

and vegetables. When we say "stew," we're referring to a specific orange-red tomato- or pepper-based dish (Classic Stew, page 193).

This may be confusing, but in the end, none of the descriptions impair the deliciousness, the sweetness that is our cuisine.

NIGERIAN WORDS AND PHRASES

- **"Cook it until it is done."** The stew or soup is "done" when the flavors are rounded and developed, and oil, if used, appears on the surface.
- **"Dry pepper"** refers to ground dried chiles.
- **"Frying the stew"** is all about cooking the tomato or pepper mix in oil until it splits and reduces, and oil coats the surface.
- **"Pepper"** could mean fresh pepper or stew base, raw or cooked, used in a variety of ways.
- **"Pick"** as in "Have you picked the beans?" refers to cleaning grains and legumes to remove chaff and other inedible parts.
- **"Wash"** could mean rinse, wash, or skin. "Washing the beans for àkàrà" is all about skinning the beans, while washing rice refers to rinsing it. Washing can also mean removing bitterness from greens and mucilage from spinach and waterleaf through soaking and pressing.

A seller and her selection of trays, racks, and other utensils; Makoko, Lagos

THE NIGERIAN STORE

◇◇◇◇◇◇◇◇◇

The Nigerian pantry, known as the store, is the heart of many kitchens. The store embraces the entire array of ingredients—in the fridge, freezer, and dry pantry. Some kitchens have separate stores; others have cupboards, counters, and shelves that hold food treasures. Fresh and dry ingredients showcase influences from local and regional exchanges, deep-seated legacies of colonialism, and transatlantic chattel slavery. As expected, no two stores are the same, but these are some common ingredients stocked within them, as well as suggested substitutions for some.

Beans and Legumes

There are many varieties of beans and legumes, of which black-eyed peas and other cowpeas are the most common. Used fresh and dried, made into flour, and fermented for seasonings like irú (see page 25), they are essential in a variety of recipes.

Fats and Oils

Fats and oils come from a variety of animal and plant sources, and include mân shānū, tallow, palm oil, coconut oil, shea butter, atili oil (African olive oil), sesame oil, soybean oil, groundnut (peanut) oil, and a host of others. Unlike North American peanut oil, Nigerian groundnut oil is not neutral in flavor or aroma. North American peanut oil is used in these recipes.

ANIMAL FATS

Mân shānū ("oil of the cow") is popular in the north and comes in two forms: raw, thick, and slightly fermented, like Moroccan smen and cultured butter; or spiced and clarified, similar to Ethiopian niter kibbeh, cooked with aromatics like onion and ginger. The goal is flavor, a high smoke point, and preservation. These butters likely have similar origins, perhaps the result of cultural exchanges in the Middle Ages by pastoral nomads who ate, cooked with, and traded butter.

CLARIFIED MÂN SHĀNŪ

MAKES 1 CUP (200 G)

8 ounces (230 g) raw mân shānū or room-temperature unsalted (cultured) butter
1 small red onion, sliced into rings
3 slices dried ginger, or 1 (2-inch) piece fresh ginger (20 g), smashed or thinly sliced
12 whole cloves

Put the mân shānū in a 2-quart (1.9 L) pot and add the onion, ginger, and cloves. Set the pot over low heat and cook until the mân shānū has liquefied, about 20 minutes.

Stir well and increase the heat to medium. Cook until the milk solids rise to the top and the mixture froths and bubbles, about 5 minutes. With a fine-mesh sieve or spoon, skim off and discard the milk solids. Continue cooking until the mixture is aromatic with hints of sweet, caramelized onion, the liquid is golden, and the onion is fried, 15 minutes more. You might see additional milk solids accumulate around the sides and bottom of the pot—if so, skim and discard them.

Take the pot off the heat. Cover and let cool, about 30 minutes. Strain through a fine-mesh sieve or cheesecloth into a jar. Seal the jar, allow to cool completely, another 30 minutes, and refrigerate for up to 3 months. Use as desired.

Tallow, or kakide, is made from rendered beef or ram fat. Muslims make it after Ramadan for the Eid celebrations, when meat is plentiful.

PLANT FATS

Two of the most common oils in Nigeria, and the first to be commercially produced, are:

Red palm oil. Also known as unrefined palm oil or simply palm oil, this is the bright orangey-red, alpha- and beta-carotene-rich oil expressed from the fleshy pericarp of the red palm fruit, native to the African continent. Rich and thick, there is nothing quite like it. It is not to be confused with highly industrialized palm and palm kernel oil, also described as white palm oil. While you can approximate the color of red palm oil (by steeping annatto seeds in neutral oil, for example), the floral, smoky, slightly fermented vegetal flavor is hard to replicate.

Groundnut oil. Nutty and fragrant with the flavor of roasted groundnuts, this is available in plain versions, known as mân gyàdā, and spiced ones, known as mân kulī from the kulīkulī extraction process (see page 277). This is a great option for dressings.

Flours and Meals

There are many flours and ground meals of indigenous ingredients—yam, millet, Guinea corn (sorghum), beans—and introduced ones—wheat, cassava, and corn, forms of which include corn flour, cornmeal, and grits.

Greens and Herbs

An abundance of herbs and leafy vegetables—from soft, spinach-like waterleaf to hardy leafy vegetables like ugu (pumpkin leaves) and herbs like scent leaf and uziza leaves—are used fresh, dried, frozen, or in combination.

Frozen greens like spinach and kale from the grocery store work well as substitutes in dishes like Ẹ̀fọ́ Rírò (page 250), ègúsí (page 253), and others.

Kulīkulī

Kulīkulī (page 277), a specialty of the Nupe people in North Central Nigeria, are hard, crunchy, deep-fried snacks made from defatted groundnut (peanut) butter, a by-product of expressing groundnut oil. The dough is shaped into crackers, sticks, and more. If kulīkulī are soft, dry them out in a warm oven at 300°F (150°C) and let cool completely before using.

Meats

Sustainability is a pillar in Nigerian cuisine, and whole-animal cooking, aka nose-to-tail cooking, is a common practice. Beef, poultry (especially chicken), goat, and ram are common alongside a variety of offal and muscle cuts known as "assorted." For everyday cooking, chunks and stewing cuts are used more commonly than steaks or whole birds.

ASSORTED

Also known as offal, variety meat, organ meat, inu eran or orisirisi (Yorùbá), afo anu (Igbo), or kāyan ciki (Hausa), "assorted" refers to an array of meats and offal from poultry, cows, goats, and rams. This includes skin, gizzard, heart, intestine, lung, liver, kidney, tripe, oxtail, cow leg, goat head, and tongue. Popular in street food, stews like Omi Ọbẹ̀ (page 194), and some versions of pepper soup.

SUBSTITUTES FOR LEAVES, LEAFY VEGETABLES, AND HERBS

If you can't find the greens or herbs listed in a recipe, refer to this chart for substitutes. I've listed the primary function of the greens; they may have different purposes in other Nigerian recipes, like in soups where the herbs act as pot herbs.

Leaves, Leafy Vegetables, and Herbs	Used	Function in These Recipes	Flavor or Texture	Suggested Substitutes
BẸLẸNTIẸNTIẸN	Dried	Herb	Earthy	Dried tarragon
BITTERLEAF OR UTAZI	Fresh or dried	Herb	Bitter	Any bitter greens, such as chard, chicory, collard, dandelion, kale, mustard, turnip
ẸFÓ SỌKỌ (cockscomb amaranth, celosia amaranth, edible celosia)	Fresh	Greens	Soft and silky	Spinach, baby or mature
ẸFÓ TẸTẸ (amaranth greens, alayyahu, callaloo)	Fresh	Greens	Firm	Ugu (pumpkin leaves), sweet potato greens, curly kale
EWÉDÚ	Fresh	Greens	Viscous	Combination of okra and spinach
MÓÍNMÓÍN LEAVES	Fresh or frozen	Wrappers	Imparts light sweet taste	Banana or plantain leaves, Vietnamese dong leaves
MORINGA	Fresh	Greens	Sweet, earthy, and bitter	Lacinato kale
ỌKAZị	Fresh	Greens	Earthy	Baby kale or collard greens
SCENT LEAVES	Fresh	Herb	Herby—fresh, slight citrusy	Clove basil, African blue basil, Japanese shiso, Korean perilla
UGU	Fresh	Greens	Firm	Lacinato kale, curly kale, amaranth greens, sweet potato greens
UZIZA	Fresh	Herb	Spicy and aromatic	Scent leaves, clove basil, African blue basil, Japanese shiso, Korean perilla
WATERLEAF	Fresh	Greens	Soft	Spinach, baby or mature
YAKUWA	Fresh	Greens	Sour and tangy	Green sorrel

Intestines. Cow, goat, and ram entrails are part of the "assorted" meat selection. Both small and large intestines are turned inside out and thoroughly cleaned prior to cooking; the small intestines (similar to pork chitterlings) are often braided. Intestines are also known as roundabout, for their circular shape. Buy them already cleaned from South and Central American markets, where they're known as chinchulines, or ask your butcher.

Pomo. Also known as ponmo, canda, or kanda, this is cowskin that has been passed through fire to singe off any hairs, resulting in a light smoky flavor. The skin is then parcooked and sold fresh or dried. Pomo has a chewy-crunchy texture with some rubberiness and absorbs the flavors of whatever it is cooked in. In cooking, it is sometimes cut into small pieces or left in rolls (which look like cinnamon sticks).

Shaki. Also known as tripe, stomach lining used in Nigerian cuisine comes in three main types: towel (aka blanket or plain), which resembles a fluffy towel; honeycomb, with a raised network of hexagonal walls; and bible (or book), with a spine holding several thin sheets of tripe. Tripe must be cleaned and prepared before you add it to soups, stews, and sauces. In North America, you can find it already cleaned, blanched (dull, light brown-green tripe with a meadowy smell), or bleached (bright, white-cream tripe with a distinct chlorine smell, which strips the tripe of a lot of flavor, so buy this as the last resort).

To clean tripe, rinse it in cool water in a large, heatproof bowl, then drain and cover with boiling water. Change out the water two or three times to rid it of the smell. You can also do this in a pot on the stovetop: Cover the tripe with cold water, making sure it is submerged, and cover the pot. Bring the water to a boil, then remove from the heat. Drain, rinse with cold water, and repeat the process once or twice more.

Cook the tripe in a pot appropriate for its size, and one that can hold twice the volume of water. Season lightly with salt and cook over medium heat until cooked with a touch of resistance, 20 minutes (or in the pressure cooker, about 10 minutes at normal pressure, with quick release).

BEEF

Stewing and grilling are popular methods of cooking beef in Nigeria.

Stewing (and braising) cuts. A lot of the beef cooked in soups, stews, and sauces comes from tough working cuts from the animal's shoulder, flank, and hip. Cuts like back ribs, blade, brisket, chuck, flank, knuckle, neck, round (eye of round and inside round), sirloin tip, and shank are good choices. Meat is often boiled or braised in water or stock, then used as is or fried, grilled, roasted, or smoked, depending on the desired outcome.

Grilling cuts. Typically from the midsection of the cow, with some from the shoulder, flank, and hip, these include cuts like flank, flat iron, filet, outside flat, petite tender, round, sirloin tip, skirt, tenderloin, and others. These cuts are great for recipes like Beef Sūya̱ (page 173).

"Biscuit bones." Many Nigerians call the collagen-rich cartilage from the cow's chest area "biscuit bones," not brisket bones. Part of bone-in brisket cuts, these are a treat for their soft but crunchy chew, and are great in soups, stews, and pottages. Use them to replace some of the stewing beef in recipes like Classic Stew (page 193) and Omi Ọbẹ̀ (page 194).

CHICKEN

Available whole and in parts, commonly bone-in, two types of chicken are popular: stewing hens (known as old layers), and broilers/fryers/roasters, which are younger, more tender birds with shorter cooking times. Stewing chickens are tougher, leaner, and tastier birds, great for everything but especially for long, slow cooking in soups and stews, while broilers/fryers/roasters work well for shorter cook times and stand-alone recipes like Kàzān Rīdī (page 171).

Onions

Red or purple onions are most commonly used. You'll also find white and yellow onions, as well as spring onions (scallions) and shallots.

Peppers (Chiles)

The wide variety of chiles available fresh or dried are all known as "peppers." Some can be hot, so adjust the quantity and type used according to your preference. These are some common types.

DRIED PEPPERS

Barkono. Dried African bird's-eye or peri-peri/piri-piri chiles (also known as spur peppers). This is hotter than dry pepper (see below), so should be used with care. Substitute dried Tabasco peppers.

Dry pepper. Single or multiple varieties of dried hot red peppers, including cayenne, bird's-eye, and others, ground into fine and coarse blends. Although its flavor is closer to cayenne, dry pepper is used like black pepper in Nigerian kitchens. Even when fresh chiles are used in a dish, you'll find us sprinkling a pinch of dry pepper over it.

FRESH PEPPERS (HOT AND SWEET)

Scotch bonnets and habaneros. These hot, aromatic peppers are available in a variety of colors, from red (the most common) to green to yellow, which can be used interchangeably. The seeds and membranes may be removed to temper the heat, though this isn't common

practice in Nigeria. Scotch bonnet peppers are named after the Scottish tam-o'-shanter hat, immortalized in the eponymous 1790 poem by Robert Burns—the scalloped top side of the pepper resembles the segmented hat. The Scotch bonnets and habaneros available in North America—and used in this book—are much hotter than those in Nigeria. And though not traditional, you can use Caribbean seasoning peppers instead; they have great flavor and aroma without heat.

Sombo. Long, hot red cayenne peppers. Substitute Holland red peppers or Thai red peppers.

Tatashe. Thin-skinned peppers with pointed tips, on average 4 to 5 inches (10 to 12.5 cm) long and 2 to 3 inches (5 to 7.5 cm) wide at the base. They come in green and red, and resemble Hungarian Beaver Dam peppers. Mild to medium hot, they have a sweet and fruity flavor

Dry pepper

with a slightly spicy finish and deep color. Some people use them for a deep red-orange color instead of tomato paste in stew, jollof rice, etc. Substitute one 10-inch-long (25 cm) red shepherd pepper, Italian sweet pepper, or medium bell pepper for every two tatashe peppers.

Rice

Rice is essential in the Nigerian kitchen, and is sold in a variety of sizes, including 55- and 110-pound (25 and 50 kg) bags, a testament to how much rice we eat. I keep 17-pound (8 kg) bags of parboiled long-grain and Indian Golden Sella basmati rice on hand.

Salt

Alkaline (rock), lake, table, and sea salts are abundant. Lake, table, and sea salts, sometimes iodized, are used in most cooking. Here is a conversion chart if you use different salts.

Fine Lake Salt, Sea Salt, or Table Salt	Morton Kosher Salt	Diamond Crystal Kosher Salt
1 teaspoon	1½ teaspoons	2 teaspoons
1½ teaspoons	2¼ teaspoons	1 tablespoon
1 tablespoon	1½ tablespoons	2 tablespoons

Seafood

Many kinds of dried seafood are used in Nigerian cuisine as seasoning and protein, including crayfish, prawns, "dry fish," (Scandinavian) stockfish, oysters, periwinkles, and whelks.

CRAYFISH AND PRAWNS

While we call this mix of crustaceans from krill to pink and brown shrimp "crayfish," they are completely unrelated to the North American crawfish. How the name emerged is something of a mystery.

Crayfish are often sun-dried, sometimes smoked, then used whole or ground. Ground crayfish is used in much the same way fish sauce and shrimp paste are used in Southeast Asian and East Asian cuisine. It brings that sweet, fermented funk and seafood essence that many Nigerian pots would be lost without. Substitute dried shrimp or prawns from Thai, Chinese, and other Asian grocers, or Thai shrimp paste, made from krill; dried ground mushrooms or ground nori sheets are suitable plant-forward options.

On average, 1 cup whole crayfish weighs about 1.4 ounces (40 g). When ground, 1 cup whole crayfish yields ½ cup plus 1 tablespoon.

Prawns, also known as red crayfish, oporo, okporo (Rivers), and ede (Yorùbá), are large and often dried, and are used whole, broken, or sometimes ground like crayfish.

DRY FISH AND SMOKED FISH

Dry fish as a category covers a variety of fish, including catfish and sole, with varying degrees of residual moisture, from barely to fully dried. The fish is cleaned, typically preserved by sun, air, oven heat, smoke, or a combination of these methods, and sold. It is used as a protein, delivering rich flavors, and also for seasoning. If your dry fish comes in pieces too large for your recipe and doesn't break down easily, clean it and soak it in hot water for 5 to 10 minutes, until it is easier to divide.

You can buy dry fish powder or make your own: Clean the fish or fish parts; whole dried bonga fish (also known as shad—small, flat, super-bony fish) and catfish heads work well. Rinse the fish, place them on a baking sheet, and dry them in the sun for up to 1 hour (covered with cheesecloth) or in a 300°F (150°C) oven for 20 minutes, turning halfway through, until dry on the outside and a touch oily. Fill a spice

A seller of stockfish; Oyingbo Market, Lagos

STOCKFISH

Prized for its flavor, nutritional benefits, and ability to withstand Nigeria's hot, humid climate, stockfish has been imported from Norway since the 1890s. Stockfish is cod, haddock, saithe, or tusk that has been suspended from wooden frames called stocks and air-dried until super dry and hard. It is also known as panla (Yorùbá) or okporoko (Igbo), onomatopoeia for the sounds it makes in the pot. It is sold whole; cut into pieces (from head to tail, often by machine or with heavy-duty knives); or in bits or flakes.

Rehydrate stockfish before using. Rinse the fish, put it in a bowl, and add cold water to cover by 2 to 3 inches (5 to 7.5 cm). Let stand until the fish plumps up and softens enough that you can flake the flesh with a fork, about 15 minutes for flakes (longer for larger pieces), then drain. Use as directed or freeze in an airtight container for later use, defrosting before using.

Seasoning

The range of seasoning used in Nigerian cooking has many regional variations made from different bases. The resulting products, however, are similar: salty, earthy, and pungent, with intense savoriness and distinctive aromas. They are available on the shelf or frozen.

LOCUST BEANS

Not to be confused with carob or locust bean gum tree, these long beans in pods produce two food ingredients: sweet powder from the mealy yellow or orange pulp known as dorawa (Hausa), and the seeds beneath the pulp that go into small-batch ferments for dàddawā.

Dàddawā, also known as daudawa (sometimes erroneously called dawadawa, which is a grass), are fermented dried locust beans or soybeans. Popular in the north of Nigeria, the beans are processed and commonly shaped into small,

grinder three-quarters full with the dried fish and grind it as smooth as possible, starting on low speed and gradually working up to high, stopping periodically to scrape down the sides. Shake the bowl for easier blending. Let the ground fish rest for a minute, then pass it through a fine-mesh strainer and, if need be, regrind any large pieces; discard any leftover bits. Transfer the fish powder to a dry jar with a lid and store at room temperature (away from light and heat) for up to 1 month or in the refrigerator or freezer for up to 3 months.

On average, 1 dried bonga fish weighs about 1 ounce (30 g); after grinding, it yields ⅓ cup (30 g) fish powder.

Smoked fish is most often different species of mackerel, soft and moist with golden skin after smoking.

You can freeze cleaned dry fish and smoked fish, so they keep well regardless of how long they were smoked or dried.

1-inch (2.5 cm) balls or flat discs, like Burmese tua nao.

Irú. The name for locust beans in the South West. The beans are processed fresh to make irú woro, which has firm, distinct split beans; and irú pete, a soft paste that readily dissolves in sauces. You'll also find dried split beans (rehydrate them by soaking in hot water until plump and doubled in size) and powder made from dried beans.

OGIRI

Also known as ogili, these fermented pastes are made from oil seeds like castor, ẹ̀gúsí, and sesame. The seeds are cooked until soft, then left whole or processed into a paste. They are then wrapped in leaves—banana, plantain, mọ́ínmọ́ín, or others—and left to ferment. Some are combined with alkaline-rich ashes before fermentation. Once fermented, if the seeds were left whole, they are pounded into a paste, then wrapped again in leaves, and, traditionally, kept on the hearth to smoke slowly. The results are pungent, savory, gray-colored pastes often sold packaged by the teaspoon. Store frozen or refrigerate in glass jars.

Ogiri Igbo. Also called ogiri isi, this gray paste made from castor oil seeds, or a combination of castor oil and ẹ̀gúsí seeds, is common in the South East.

Ogiri Ijebu. This version, made from ẹ̀gúsí seeds, is popular in the South West.

SEASONING CUBES AND POWDERS

Stock or bouillon cubes and powders come in a variety of flavors, including beef, chicken, and crayfish. Much like soy sauce and other umami-rich seasonings, they can be very salty. If using, consider reducing the amount of salt in the recipe, and be sure to taste and adjust the seasoning as you cook. In the north, seasoning cubes are sometimes served on their own as a condiment. Substitute homemade stock (see page 333) or Basic Yaji (page 26).

Spices and Spice Blends

A wide variety of herbs and spices are used on their own or ground into blends. They fall into two main groups: traditional Nigerian seasonings and legacy British seasonings.

Ehuru, also called calabash nutmeg, are seeds of *Monodora myristica*, and come in a (sometimes shiny) calabash-like shell. The seeds are sold shell-on or shelled. To toast and grind shelled seeds, spread them over a dry pan and toast over low to medium heat, shaking the pan often, until the seeds become aromatic, begin to pop and cackle, and develop brown spots and patches. Transfer the toasted seeds to a plate to cool before grinding. The result is a fragrant blend, the texture of almond meal. Use as required.

For unshelled seeds, 1 teaspoon (4 or 5 seeds) weighs about 3 grams and 1 heaping tablespoon (12 to 15 seeds) weighs about 9 grams; ¼ cup shelled seeds (48 to 60 seeds) weighs about 1.3 ounces (36 g), and yields ¼ cup plus 1 tablespoon (32 g) ground ehuru.

Nigerian-style curry powder is an aromatic, turmeric-heavy blend of spices, with mild flavors and hints of sweetness. This legacy of British colonial times is made with ingredients rooted in Indian culture and cuisine. Substitute Jamaican, West Indian, or Japanese curry powder.

CURRY POWDER
MAKES 1¼ CUPS (110 G)

Although it takes more time, you can toast the whole spices individually or in groups by seed size for more control. You can also toast them all together, if you must—just add the large spices first, then the smaller ones later. They are ready when aromatic and golden or brown in spots.

½ cup (40 g) whole coriander seeds
1 tablespoon whole fenugreek seeds
1 tablespoon allspice berries
½ teaspoon whole black peppercorns
½ teaspoon whole white peppercorns
1 tablespoon cumin seeds
1 tablespoon green cardamom seeds
½ teaspoon fennel seeds
4 whole cloves
3 tablespoons ground turmeric
1 tablespoon ground ginger
1 teaspoon yellow mustard powder
1 teaspoon freshly grated nutmeg
½ teaspoon dry pepper (see page 22)

In a small stainless-steel or cast-iron skillet, combine the coriander, fenugreek, allspice, and black and white peppercorns. Toast over low to medium heat, stirring and swirling the pan often, until fragrant, 2 to 3 minutes. Transfer the spices to a bowl.

In the same pan, combine the cumin, cardamom, fennel, and cloves and toast over low to medium heat until fragrant, 2 to 3 minutes. Add the spices to the bowl with the coriander mixture and stir to combine. Let cool to room temperature, about 10 minutes.

Transfer the toasted spices to a spice grinder and grind into the smoothest powder you can. (You may need to do this in batches.) Empty the ground spice mixture into a bowl and add the turmeric, ginger, mustard powder, nutmeg, and dry pepper. Stir to combine, then transfer to a jar with a lid. Seal the jar and set aside to rest for 2 to 3 days, then regrind and pass through a sieve. You can regrind the larger bits if you like, or discard them.

Return the spice blend to the jar and store at cool room temperature, away from light and heat, for up to 6 months, or store in an airtight container in the freezer for up to 12 months.

Yaji, meaning "pepper," is an umbrella name for a Nigerian dry spice blend with rich, spicy flavors. In its basic form, it is a combination of dry pepper, ginger, cloves, salt, and often stock cubes, a set of ingredients known collectively as kāyan yaji. Its name comes from Ali Yaji Dan Tsamiya,

the first sultan of Kano, a fourteenth-century ruler who had a fiery temper.

BASIC YAJI

MAKES 1 SCANT CUP (100 G)

1 tablespoon barkono (see page 22)
1 tablespoon alligator pepper seeds (see page 235)
4 whole uda pods (see page 164)
3 ehuru seeds (see page 25), shelled
3 whole cloves
½ teaspoon whole uziza peppercorns (see page 95)
3 tablespoons sweet paprika
2 tablespoons ground ginger
1 tablespoon onion powder
1 tablespoon dry pepper (see page 22)
1½ teaspoons fine sea salt
1 teaspoon garlic powder
1 teaspoon sugar

In a spice mill, combine the barkono, alligator pepper, uda, ehuru, cloves, and uziza peppercorns. Grind the spices as fine as possible (you may need to do this in batches).

Empty the ground spice mixture into a bowl and add the paprika, ginger, onion powder, dry pepper, salt, garlic powder, and sugar. Stir to combine, then transfer to a jar with a lid. Seal the jar and set aside to rest for 2 to 3 days, then regrind and pass through a sieve, discarding any larger bits.

Return the spice blend to the jar and store at cool room temperature, away from light and heat, for up to 6 months, or store in an airtight container in the freezer for up to 12 months.

YAJIN KULI

MAKES ABOUT 2 CUPS (175 G)

Use yajin kuli (also known as yajin tsire or sūya pepper) as a spice, dip, or part of a dressing for salads. Kulīkulī forms the base of this blend. To save your home spice mill/coffee grinder, crush the kulīkulī bits with a mortar and pestle (or put them in a zip-top bag and smash with a heavy object) before grinding them. About 125 grams kulīkulī bits makes 1 cup ground kulīkulī.

NOTE: *You can substitute 1½ cups (125 g) raw (defatted) peanut flour or peanut powder, which is available at grocery stores as well as bulk and health food stores, for 1 cup (125 g) ground ƙulīƙulī. If using raw peanut flour or powder, toast it in a dry pan over low to medium heat, stirring continuously and making sure you're stirring to the bottom of the pan, until its color changes from beige to brown, 5 to 6 minutes. Spread the toasted peanut flour over a plate to cool. Note that yajin kuli made with peanut flour will be finer-textured compared with that made with deep-fried ƙulīƙulī.*

1 tablespoon alligator pepper seeds (see page 235)
4 whole uda pods (see page 164)
3 ehuru seeds (see page 25), shelled
3 whole cloves
½ teaspoon whole uziza peppercorns (see page 95)
1 cup (125 g) ground Ƙulīƙulī (page 277)
2 tablespoons sweet paprika
2 tablespoons ground ginger
1 tablespoon onion powder
2 teaspoons garlic powder
2 teaspoons dry pepper (see page 22)
2 teaspoons sugar
1½ teaspoons fine sea salt

In a spice mill, combine the alligator pepper, uda, ehuru, cloves, and uziza peppercorns and grind. Add the ƙulīƙulī and grind again, as fine as possible. (You may need to do this in batches.)

Empty the ground spice mixture into a bowl and add the paprika, ginger, onion powder, garlic powder, dry pepper, sugar, and salt. Stir to combine, then transfer to a jar with a lid. Seal the jar and set aside to rest for 2 to 3 days, then regrind and discard any larger bits.

Return the spice blend to the jar and store at cool room temperature, away from light and heat, for up to 6 months, or store in an airtight container in the freezer for up to 12 months.

VARIATIONS: There are many versions built on the basic yajis, with different textures from fine to coarse and varying quantities of certain spices or additional ingredients like coriander seeds, cumin seeds, turmeric, green cardamom, anise seeds, curry powder, and protein. Herbs are not a common addition. Here are a few examples:

- Yajin citta, a warming, ginger-forward version (made without the garlic), often added to pap or kunu, drinks and porridges from cereals.
- Yajin dàddawā, also known as local yaji, made with dàddawā (fermented locust beans).
- Yajin gauta, made with dried pea eggplant.
- Yajin kifi, made with dry fish powder.
- Yajin nama, a meat-heavy version made with Dambun Nama (page 172) or deep-fried beef.
- Yajin tafarnuwa, with a greater proportion of dried garlic, used in rice and stews.

Stocks

There are two main types of stock: Curry Stock (page 333) and traditional Nigerian stock with onions, peppers, and sometimes crayfish or dry fish powder, like in the base of È̩gúsí Soup (page 253). Both have flavor profiles different from European- and American-style stocks. Consider flavor adjustments if substituting.

Technically falling somewhere between stock and broth, Nigerian stocks are often made with an assortment of meats on the bone. The liquid forms the basis for a pot of soup, stew, or rice, and the cooked pieces of meat are reserved to be used in soups, stews, or sauces, or are fried, grilled, or sauced and served alongside other dishes—an efficient, no-waste strategy. If the meat is not needed for another dish, make the stock with beef bones and chicken carcasses instead, which you can find in a variety of Asian grocers. When time and freezer space allow, make a large batch of stock, portion it into smaller containers, and freeze it for later use.

Most stocks end up with a bit of fat. Once the stock has cooled, the fat solidifies on the surface and can be removed and used in cooking or discarded.

SHOP LIKE A NIGERIAN

◇◇◇◇◇◇◇◇◇

Many Nigerians shop for ingredients in a mixture of places, from small neighborhood shops where you can find all the basics, in small quantities—a half dozen eggs, a small pack of sugar, sachets of salt or tomato paste, a few tomatoes, an onion, some fruit—to larger grocery stores and markets. If a Nigerian says they are going to the market, they are likely referring to one of many open-air, wet markets—think farmers' markets but larger—where you can buy everything from fresh produce to dried goods. Vibrant, colorful, loud, the market can be an assault on your senses. Smoked fish aromas mingle with the citrus scents of peeled oranges, which will have you thinking about orange and almond cake when really, all you are there to buy are fresh red tomatoes, a selection of peppers, and some red onions.

Nigerian open markets are a vibe—bright and busy. Some markets, like Balogun Market in Lagos, stock everything from clothing to food. Some, like Oyingbo Market, also in Lagos, sell fruits, vegetables, herbs, spices, meat, and seafood—though mostly frozen, dried, or smoked. Other markets are known for specific ingredients or specialize in wholesale or bulk buying, like Mile 12 International Market in Lagos. There are markets known for specific produce, like Zaki Biam Yam Market in Benue state. Onitsha Main Market in the east of Nigeria, one of the largest markets in West Africa, is known for a variety of foodstuffs, and in the late 1940s through the 1960s was associated with a unique brand of literature— Onitsha Market Literature, pamphlets authored mostly by men in pidgin English. These books were for the people, by the people—everyday stories and primers on love, life, language, local history, folktales, and more,

Two things are interesting and standard in Nigerian markets: the use of the word "customer," and the practice of bargaining, which Nigerians call "pricing." In the market, both buyer and seller are "customer." I have my customer who sells me spices, greens, and all my other needs; and I, in turn, am their customer. Pricing is part of relationship-building and banter.

Most fresh produce—including tomatoes, onions, peppers—is "shaded," or measured out by volume, in little pyramids or in bowls, tins, tubs, buckets, and baskets. Some other things, though, like carrots, green beans, cabbage, peas, spring onions (scallions), and items we consider to be salad or fried rice ingredients, may be sold by weight in open markets or by volume from street sellers' mobile carts.

It is the same for dried ingredients as it is for fresh: You can buy dried beans and cowpeas, rice, millet, cracked corn, and grits, in various volume measures, mostly mounded, rarely leveled. Like punnets and dry pints, there are several unique Nigerian measures, by name and by size; they are generally loose estimates and approximate amounts and used only in the open markets. In stores, you'll find the same ingredients measured out and commonly

Fresh produce in the market under the bridge, Apongbon, Lagos

weighed. You'll find fresh produce—roots, tubers, rhizomes, fruits, and vegetables in the markets—and dry ingredients, from seafood to spices, meat, grains, cereals, and legumes, much of it local, but some of it imported—apples, grapes, plums, to name a few, from South Africa and the Netherlands. Some markets are perfect for shopping for small quantities, and others are specialists in wholesale and bulk-buying. It is not uncommon to see friends and family members plan and make pilgrimages, combining their purchasing power so they reap the benefits of buying large quantities, which they split among themselves.

When I was growing up in Nigeria, the deep freezer was key to preserving seasonal produce, like tomatoes and peppers, and for meat and fish. Now, in late summer in Canada, I freeze red Roma (plum) tomatoes, red shepherd peppers, and green bell peppers when there's a glut. The freezer is also a great place for storing high-fat nuts and seeds like ẹ̀gúsí and ògbònò, irú, and spice blends like yaji and nutty yajin kuli so they stay fresh and last longer.

When I find fresh Nigerian herbs like scent leaf, bitterleaf, and uziza leaves, I get large batches and freeze them in bags. I also freeze mọ́ínmọ́ín and banana (or plantain) leaves for when I'm homesick and want that leafy taste. Frozen greens like spinach and kale from the grocery store are a must. I have them on hand for Ẹ̀fọ́ Rírò (page 250), Ẹ̀gúsí Soup (page 253), and other dishes.

I buy dried black-eyed peas and rice from the grocery store. Growing up in Nigeria, we added whole dried chiles, cloves, and bay leaves (Indian and Mediterranean) to containers of dry ingredients like beans and grains to keep them bug-free.

I buy red, yellow, and white onions by the bag and store them in vegetable baskets; I do the same with potatoes, garlic, and ginger.

Whenever I go to a meat shop or an Asian grocer, I stock up on stewing beef, stewing hen, beef bones, and chicken carcasses for stock (see page 27).

COOK LIKE A NIGERIAN

◇◇◇◇◇◇◇◇◇

My earliest memories of cooking at home in Nigeria didn't feature recipes per se, or cookbooks. As a teenager, I watched both my mum and my dad ladle spoonfuls of pureed tomatoes, onions, and peppers, and I knew that for pepper sauces, Daddy always added twice as much onion as tomato, tasting his way to perfectly balanced stews. Making good Classic Stew (page 193)—sweet, dark red, thinly veiled with oil, the texture underneath dimpled and desiccated—is a rite of passage, and with experience, you learn the sensory qualities that make for well-fried stew.

Loose estimation—"just add small, or a little," as we say in Nigeria—guided a lot of our cooking, with measurements from the heart and spoonfuls instead of measuring cups. My siblings and I learned to cook by watching and experimenting, guided by oral instruction. We mastered peeling, slicing, and drying unripe plantains to make plantain flour for àmàlà (page 224); how to keep a sack of onions fresh (lay them out to "sun" on breathable mats or jute bags); and how to make and cook with spice blends. We learned to season meat, and how to understand spices and tastes so we could make flavorful stocks: Green bell pepper is a must for Curry Stock (page 333), and traditional Nigerian stock should have onions, pepper, and sometimes crayfish or dry fish powder—both stocks are typically salted.

We learned the habits of Nigerian cooks: hitting the spoon against the top of the uncovered pot after a round of stirring to make sure every drop or grain goes back into the pot; how to taste food—stirring and lifting a tiny amount of rice, stew, soup, whatever, blowing on it gently to cool before dropping it into the palm of one's hand to be tasted, after which adjustments are made, if required.

This approach gave me confidence in the kitchen, and I learned where loose estimation worked, and where it didn't. I developed a habit of documentation, for reference's sake. I now find this a good balance between creativity and consistency, knowing when either or both are required.

Some dishes are more about the concept than strict proportions, so exercise creative freedom as you explore them. Fancy serving your Nigerian Salad (page 97) with a chopped-up omelet instead of the traditional boiled eggs? Go for it. Many of the recipes are easy to modify and moderate according to your preferences. You can adjust the amount of chiles in a recipe, or modify cooking times for firmer or softer textures. Ingredients in some recipes, though, like Àkàrà (page 64) and mọ́ínmọ́ín (page 69), require correct proportions for success. There are no rewards for getting the ratios wrong.

Here are some prep tips that may help you succeed:

Store red palm oil in jars instead of bottles. Because some red palm oil "sleeps," meaning it solidifies at cooler temperatures, it's easier to scoop from a jar than pour from a bottle.

Thanks to its mild and nontoxic antibacterial properties, salt is a popular ingredient for cleaning fruits, vegetables, and dried seafood, on its own or in the form of a brine. Fill a large container with 2½ quarts (2.4 L) water and stir in 1 cup (290 g) table salt until dissolved. Soak fruits or vegetables in this brine for up to 20 minutes, then rinse before using or storing. To clean dried seafood, rinse it under cold running water, then gently rub with salt to release grit or sand and rinse thoroughly. For smaller shellfish like periwinkles, oysters, clams, and whelks, rinse under running water, rub with salt to remove grit or sand, then rinse again. Soak in hot water to cover and leave until softened, about an hour. Gently massage, swish around, and lift out into a strainer. Rinse one more time, then drain.

Prep your essentials—spices, spice blends, ground seafood like crayfish or dry fish powder, stocks, and stew bases ahead of time so you have them on hand for your classic Nigerian dishes.

NOTES ON MEASUREMENTS AND INGREDIENTS

- Measurements have been rounded to the nearest round number or decimal point. For instance, ¼ cup of whole wheat flour is about 1 ounce, or 28 grams. In the ingredient list, that quantity has been rounded up to 1 ounce (30 g).

- Sugar is regular granulated (white) sugar unless otherwise stated.

- Salt is fine sea salt.

- All-purpose flour is always sifted after measuring.

- With dried beans, cooking times will vary depending on the age and source (and also processing) of the beans.

Periwinkles, out of the shell and soaked

A PARTY IN YOUR MOUTH

SMALL CHOPS

SMALL CHOPS ARE OFTEN APPETIZERS OR AFTER-PARTY
bites, eaten before or after Item 7, the main refreshments
(the name comes from historical programs of events, where
"Refreshments" was the seventh item on the list.)

Prior to the 1960s, "small chops" were chips, dips, crackers,
fritters, and more, for cocktail parties. In the 1970s and '80s,
the meaning of the phrase changed to describe bites served
between meals, as well as street snacks. They are essential
celebration fare (as opposed to everyday snacks), enjoyed at
events and owambes or parties.

The classic small chops is a group of five, combining
Nigerian gastronomy—puff puff, mọsa, and grilled, peppered,
or fried protein, like stick meat and yòyò—with Nigerianized
versions of "imported" meals: Chinese spring rolls and Indian
samosas.

They come in packs, so are portable, with elements small
enough to finish in a few bites but substantial enough to hold
your stomach for a couple of hours. Puff puff and mọsa are
usually the most plentiful, with anywhere from three to six
balls served (Nigerians aren't into numerology in this way, so
there isn't a lucky number), while the other elements tend to
be single pieces.

Today, you can find small chops sold in ready-made
packs in grocery stores or order them from vendors, but
the recipes are simple enough that you can rustle up this
collective of chewy, crunchy, deep-fried, meaty, and flavor-
packed deliciousness for yourself at home. Best of all, there is
something for everyone.

CLOCKWISE FROM LEFT: *Small chops; artisans' baskets; pepper sauce for awara;*
dry pepper

FEATURED IN THESE RECIPES

1. **Curry powder.** Nigerian-style curry powder is turmeric-heavy and aromatic. It is a fairly recent feature in Nigerian cuisine, appearing in records after the 1960s. Though it is commonly store-bought, I've included a recipe for making it at home on page 25.

2. **Curry stock.** A seasoned stock flavored with curry powder and used in many Nigerian dishes; see the recipe on page 333.

3. **Dry pepper.** This consists of dried hot red peppers ground into fine or coarse blends. Substitute cayenne pepper, *not* chili powder.

4. **Ginger.** Nigeria is one of the leading producers of ginger in the world, growing several varieties, including a yellow rhizome, Tafin Giwa, and a dull-gray rhizome, Yatsun Biri. Ginger is available in several forms: fresh, dried in slices, and ground.

5. **Nutmeg.** Whole seeds of nutmeg (*Myristica fragrans*) are grated fresh as needed.

6. **Overripe plantains.** These super-ripe plantains with blackened skins are soft and sweet, and form the basis for Mọsa (page 41) and other delights.

7. **Salt.** Lake salt from the North Central regions in Nasarawa state. This moist, fine-grained salt has a pleasant fleur de sel quality.

8. **Yams.** Also known as West African yam (white fleshed), Guinea yam (white and yellow fleshed), and true yams, to differentiate them from orange sweet potatoes, which are known in North America as yams. These tubers of the genus *Dioscorea* grow vertically belowground to produce brown, cylindrical roots of varying lengths, up to 3 or 4 feet (0.9 to 1.2 m) long. The skin is barklike and can be smooth or rough and hairy. On the inside, the flesh may be white, yellow, reddish, or spotted like cocoyam (taro).

PUFF PUFF

Puff puff are sweet golden balls of deep-fried yeasted dough, similar to no-knead drop doughnuts. Like doughnut holes in appearance, they have a crisp exterior and a chewy, spongy interior.

2 cups (8.5 ounces/240 g) all-purpose flour, sifted

½ cup (3.5 ounces/100 g) sugar

3 tablespoons full-fat powdered milk

2 teaspoons instant yeast

1 teaspoon baking powder

¼ teaspoon freshly grated nutmeg

½ teaspoon fine sea salt

Neutral oil, for frying

NOTE: *If you're using non-instant yeast, bloom the yeast for up to 10 minutes by stirring into a mixture of 1 teaspoon sugar and 1 cup (240 ml) warm water*

This beloved snack probably gets its name from the way it puffs up when fried and takes on its signature golden brown color. Many Nigerian dishes have reduplicated names, pronounced with a singsong quality—puff puff, mọ́ínmọ́ín (page 69), Garau Garau (page 157), Chin Chin (page 269)—perhaps a way of emphasizing deliciousness.

In Nigeria, home cooks make puff puff about an inch (2.5 cm) in diameter, while street food vendors make them twice as large. For even browning, it's best to add as many portions of dough to the hot oil as will fit into your pot; with little room to move, the puff puff tend to stay in place once turned over.

Serve plain, with Yòyò (page 54), Ata Dindin (page 332), or even with sweet sauces.

In a large transparent bowl (it makes it easier to see how much the dough has risen), whisk together the flour, sugar, powdered milk, yeast, baking powder, and nutmeg. Make a well in the center of the flour mixture and pour in 1⅓ cups (320 ml) lukewarm water. With clean hands or a wooden spoon, mix gradually in one direction. The mixture will resemble lumpy oatmeal at first and then smoothen out to form a cohesive, sticky dough.

Sprinkle the dough with the salt and mix until it becomes smooth and thick, 2 to 3 minutes. Cover the bowl loosely with a large, damp kitchen towel and let sit at room temperature (75°F/24°C) until doubled in size, 45 to 60 minutes. The top might remain smooth, but if you tear it open, you should see a network of bubbles.

Gently deflate the dough, knocking out the air bubbles. Stir the dough to even out the texture and let sit to allow the gluten to relax, about 30 minutes. Fill a wok or large Dutch oven with 1½ to 2 inches (3.8 to 5 cm) of oil; it should come no more than halfway up the vessel. Heat the oil over medium-high heat to 330°F (165°C). Line a rimmed baking sheet with a wire rack or paper towels.

Dip a 2-teaspoon cookie scoop into the hot oil, then scoop up a portion of dough and carefully drop it into the oil. (Alternatively, dip two spoons into the hot oil, then use one of them to scoop the dough

PUFF PUFF PARTY

Serve a variety of sweet and savory puff puff. You can fry the puff puff an hour or two before guests arrive. Place it in a food warmer (or cooler) with the lid slightly ajar so it doesn't sweat.

Serve with lots of sides and dips, including:

- Ata Dindin (page 332)
- Dambun Nama (page 172)
- Beef Sūya (page 173)
- Sweet fruit sauces or jams
- Basic Yaji (page 26— stir in some sugar)

and the other to shape the portion into a round before dropping it into the oil.) Working quickly, repeat the process to add more dough until the surface of the oil is full. Fry, using a fork or skewer to turn the puff puff as needed, until puffed and golden brown on all sides, 5 to 6 minutes. Use a spider or slotted spoon to transfer the puff puff to the prepared baking sheet. Repeat with the remaining dough, allowing the oil to return to temperature between batches.

Serve hot or warm. Leftover puff puff can be cooled and then frozen in freezer bags or containers for up to 1 month and reheated in the microwave.

DOUGH-PIPING TECHNIQUES

Here are a couple of additional techniques for forming the puff puff.

- **Shaping by hand:** Some Nigerian cooks who are comfortable with deep-frying use a hand-shaping and -piping technique to drop the puff puff dough into the oil. With clean hands, sometimes moistened with water or lightly greased with oil, mix the dough. Using your fingers, pull some dough into the palm of your dominant hand and gently close it to make a loose fist. Hold your hand above the oil as though you were pouring a drink from a bottle. To "pipe" the dough, open a ring between your thumb and index finger to release the dough, then press the sides of your thumb and index finger together to "cut" the portion of dough into the oil.

- **Piping bag or large zip-top bag:** Put a piping bag or large zip-top bag in a tall, wide glass or jug. Scoop in the dough, being sure to leave 3 to 4 inches (7.5 to 10 cm) unfilled at the top of the bag so you can wrap and seal the bag, as well as to give you something to hold on to as you pipe the dough. With a pair of scissors, snip off the pointed end of the bag (or one corner of the zip-top bag) to make a ½-inch-wide (1.25 cm) hole. Dip the scissors into the hot oil, then pipe the dough into the oil, using the oiled scissors to cut off ½-inch (1.25 cm) segments as you pipe. Move around the pan to ensure the dough balls are evenly distributed in the oil.

MỌSA
PLANTAIN FRITTERS

2 or more (about
1 pound/450 g) soft, super-
ripe plantains, peeled and
diced

1 teaspoon fine sea salt

1 Scotch bonnet or habanero
pepper, minced

½ teaspoon dry pepper
(see page 22)

1 cup (4.25 ounces/120 g) all-
purpose flour, sifted

1 teaspoon baking powder

½ teaspoon freshly grated
nutmeg

2 tablespoons granulated or
brown sugar

¼ cup (60 ml) hot water

Neutral oil, for frying

Made with super-ripe and sweet plantains, Yorùbá bananas (similar to Mexican and Southeast Asian burro bananas), or a combination, these soft brown bites are puff puff's fruity cousin with less chew. Leavened with baking powder, mọsa tend to shrink a tad once fried.

For the classic mọsa texture, mash the plantains or bananas by hand. Avoid using wooden utensils, as they absorb moisture and change the texture of the mọsa. Leftover mọsa can be frozen and reheated in the microwave.

In a large bowl, combine the plantains, salt, Scotch bonnet, and dry pepper. Mash until lumpy and sticky. You should have about 1½ cups (350 g).

In a separate bowl, whisk together the flour, baking powder, and nutmeg. Add half the flour mixture to the mashed plantains, stirring to form a sticky batter. Add the remaining flour mixture and stir until smoothish.

In a liquid measuring cup, whisk together the sugar and the hot water until the sugar has dissolved, then pour the water into the plantain mixture and stir to form a thick batter with a few bubbles. Cover and let rest for at least 30 minutes and up to 5 days in the fridge. (If refrigerating, let sit at room temperature for 30 minutes, then stir well before frying.)

Fill a wok or large Dutch oven with 1½ to 2 inches (3.8 to 5 cm) of oil; it should come no more than halfway up the vessel. Heat the oil over medium-high heat to 330°F (165°C). Line a rimmed baking sheet with a wire rack or paper towels.

Dip a 1-teaspoon cookie scoop into the hot oil, then scoop a portion of batter and carefully drop it into the oil. Working quickly, repeat the process until the surface of the oil is full. Fry, using a fork or skewer to turn the mọsa as they cook, until golden brown on all sides, about 6 minutes. Use a spider or slotted spoon to transfer the mọsa to the prepared baking sheet. Repeat with the remaining batter, allowing the oil to return to temperature between batches.

Serve hot or warm.

YAM BALLS

About 1 pound (450 g) West African yams, peeled and cut into 1- to 2-inch (2.5 to 5 cm) chunks

2½ teaspoons fine sea salt

2 tablespoons unsalted butter, melted (optional)

2 tablespoons diced red onion

2 tablespoons diced green bell pepper

2 tablespoons diced red, yellow, or orange bell pepper

2 tablespoons thinly sliced scallion greens

4 large eggs (see Variations)

1 teaspoon dry pepper (see page 22)

¾ cup (3.2 ounces/90 g) all-purpose flour, sifted

2 cups (8 ounces/225 g) dried bread crumbs (see Variations)

Neutral oil, for frying

This recipe creates a delicious snack that is crunchy on the outside and tender, colorful, and flavorful on the inside, like a croquette. Use freshly boiled yam or reheat leftovers—just mash them, add some vegetables and meat if you like, then deep-fry to perfection. Yam balls are great on their own, with a dip or sauce like Ata Dindin (page 332), or with Classic Stew (page 193), beans, and more.

For best results, mash the yam while still warm, until just broken down. Be careful not to overmash; you want it soft and crumbly, not smooth and stretchy like Pounded Yam (page 226).

Rinse the yams and place them in a large pot. Add cold water to cover them by 2 inches (5 cm) and season with 2 teaspoons of the salt and stir. Dip a piece of paper towel in the oil and grease the top 2 inches (5 cm) of the inside of the pot, from the rim down; this helps prevent the water from boiling over. Bring to a boil over high heat, cover the pot with the lid ajar, and cook for about 10 minutes; some foam will form on the surface. Reduce the heat to medium and cook until the yams are fork-tender, 12 to 15 minutes. Drain the yams and let them dry out a bit in the pot, about 10 minutes.

Transfer the yams to a large bowl and mash with a potato masher just until broken down and crumbly (alternatively, pass them through a potato ricer into the bowl or mash with a large mortar and pestle). Drizzle in the melted butter (if using), stir to combine, and then spread the mashed yam in the bowl and let cool for about 15 minutes.

In a small bowl, combine the onion, both bell peppers, and the scallions. Season with the remaining ½ teaspoon salt, stir well, and let stand for a few minutes.

In a separate small bowl, lightly beat 2 of the eggs with the dry pepper.

Add the onion mixture, the beaten eggs, and ¼ cup (30 g) of the flour to the bowl with the yam and mix to form a cohesive dough.

Line a rimmed baking sheet with parchment paper. With a 1-tablespoon cookie scoop, place 30 portions of the yam mixture on the baking sheet. Roll each portion into a ball. Cover and refrigerate for at least 1 hour and up to 12 hours.

Place the remaining ½ cup (60 g) flour in a wide, shallow bowl. Lightly beat the remaining 2 eggs in a second wide, shallow bowl and place the bread crumbs in a third wide, shallow bowl.

Working with a few at a time, roll the balls in the flour, then the eggs, then the bread crumbs, ensuring that they are completely coated at each stage and returning them to the baking sheet after coating. Cover and refrigerate until firm, about 1 hour.

Fill a wok or large Dutch oven with 1½ to 2 inches (3.8 to 5 cm) of oil; it should come no more than halfway up the vessel. Heat the oil over medium-high heat to 340°F (170°C). Line a rimmed baking sheet with a wire rack or paper towels.

Working in batches, use a spider or slotted spoon to add some yam balls to the hot oil, being careful not to overcrowd them. Fry, turning often, until browned, about 4 minutes. Transfer the yam balls to the prepared baking sheet. Repeat with the remaining yam balls, allowing the oil to return to temperature between batches.

Serve hot or cold. Store leftovers in an airtight container in the refrigerator for up to 1 week.

VARIATIONS

To make this recipe without eggs, add an extra 2 tablespoons all-purpose flour plus 1 tablespoon hot water to the mix, and use milk instead when breading.

You can use panko breadcrumbs for a different crunch. For a great, though far from traditional, gluten-free replacement for the breadcrumbs, use dry garri (see page 139) or cornmeal.

SPRING ROLLS

Neutral oil, for frying

1 tablespoon toasted sesame oil

1 small red onion, thinly sliced

1 tablespoon grated fresh ginger

1 teaspoon minced garlic

½ teaspoon fine sea salt, plus more as needed

8 ounces (225 g) ground beef, 20% fat or less

3 cups (300 g) shredded white or green cabbage

3 cups (300 g) shredded carrots

1 small red bell pepper, thinly sliced

1 small green bell pepper, thinly sliced

2 tablespoons light soy sauce

1 scallion, chopped

1 Scotch bonnet or habanero pepper, minced

½ teaspoon freshly ground white pepper, plus more as needed

½ teaspoon sugar

24 (8-inch/20 cm) square frozen spring roll wrappers, defrosted (see Note)

Ata Dindin (page 332) or your favorite dip, for serving (optional)

NOTE: *Spring roll wrappers are found in the frozen section of the grocery store. Let them defrost, ideally in the refrigerator overnight, before using.*

Spring rolls came to Nigeria via the Chinese who first arrived in the 1930s. By the 1960s, post–Nigerian independence, they had set up thriving hospitality businesses, perhaps the reason Chinese cuisine is one of the most popular international cuisines in the country. Everything you know and love about spring rolls—crisp shells and well-seasoned shredded vegetables—can be found here. Spring rolls are adaptable and freezer-friendly, too. Be sure to drain the cooked ground beef so its liquid doesn't turn the spring rolls soggy, or omit the beef altogether, if you like. Use a (super fresh) bagged coleslaw mix in place of the shredded vegetables to save some time.

In a wok or large skillet, heat ¼ cup (60 ml) neutral oil and the sesame oil over medium heat. When the oils are shimmering, add the onion, ginger, garlic, and salt. Cook until softened and aromatic, then add the ground beef and cook, stirring to break up any large clumps, until browned and somewhat dry, 10 to 12 minutes.

Stir in the cabbage and carrots and cook until slightly softened. Add both bell peppers, the soy sauce, scallion, Scotch bonnet, white pepper, and sugar. Cook until softened, about 5 minutes. Taste for salt and white pepper and add more, if needed. Remove from the heat and transfer the mixture to a large fine-mesh strainer set in the sink. Spread the mixture into an even layer and let cool completely, about 30 minutes.

Set a bowl of water and a couple of rimmed baking sheets next to your cutting board. Separate the individual spring roll wrappers and cover them with a damp kitchen towel to keep them from drying out. Working with one at a time, set a wrapper in front of you, oriented like a diamond, with a pointed end closest to you. Spoon 1 heaping tablespoon of the cooled beef mixture about a quarter of the way up the wrapper. Spread the filling across, about 3 inches (7.5 cm), leaving at least 2 inches (5 cm) of wrapper exposed on each side. Lift the pointed end over the filling to the midline (so it aligns with the left and right points on the diamond), then tuck it underneath to secure. Tightly roll up the wrapper to enclose the filling up to the midline, creating a triangle of sorts. Press the filling in on both sides to make it compact. Fold in the left and right sides to resemble an open envelope.

With your fingers or a brush, dab water along the exposed part of the wrapper, to the pointed top, and roll up to the tip to seal. Place the spring roll seam-side down on a baking sheet and cover with a damp kitchen towel. Repeat with the remaining wrappers and filling. (At this point, the rolls can be placed on a smaller rimmed baking sheet in a single layer and frozen until firm, then transferred to a zip-top freezer bag, sealed with the air pressed out, and frozen for up to 3 months. To fry from frozen, add an extra minute to the cooking time.)

Fill a wok or large Dutch oven with 1½ to 2 inches (3.8 to 5 cm) of oil; it should come no more than halfway up the vessel. Heat the oil over medium-high heat to 350°F (175°C). Line a rimmed baking sheet with a wire rack or paper towels.

With a spider or slotted spoon, add a few spring rolls at a time to the hot oil, being careful not to overcrowd them. Fry until golden brown, about 4 minutes. Transfer to the prepared baking sheet and repeat with the remaining spring rolls, allowing the oil to return to temperature between batches.

Enjoy hot or cold, on their own or with ata dindin.

SAMOSAS

Neutral oil, for frying

8 ounces (225 g) ground
beef, at least 20% fat

1 red Scotch bonnet or
habanero pepper, minced

1 teaspoon grated fresh
ginger

1 teaspoon minced garlic

1 teaspoon fine sea salt

1 teaspoon Curry Powder
(page 25)

1 teaspoon dried thyme

1 small red onion (170 g),
finely diced (¾ cup)

1 small carrot (100 g), cut
into ¼-inch (6 mm) dice

¼ cup (40 g) frozen green
peas

¼ cup (50 g) sweet corn
kernels

1 scallion, chopped

1 small green bell pepper
(75 g), diced (½ cup)

½ teaspoon freshly ground
white pepper

¼ cup (1 ounce/30 g) all-
purpose flour

2 tablespoons cornstarch

12 (8-inch/20 cm) square
frozen spring roll wrappers,
defrosted (see Note, page 44)

Ata Dindin (page 332) or
your favorite dip, for serving
(optional)

Nigerian samosas are tetrahedral parcels with crispy-crunchy shells and beautifully spiced minced meat and vegetable filling. Their origins are likely Persian, but their journey to Nigeria was via India. Nigeria's strong historical connections to India stretch back to the 1800s, first through trade and mercantile relations, then shared colonial history and military connections, and in the 1970s Nigeria was a place of refuge for Indians leaving East Africa.

In a wok or large skillet, heat 1 tablespoon oil over medium heat. When the oil is shimmering, add the ground beef, Scotch bonnet, ginger, garlic, salt, curry powder, and thyme. Cook, stirring to break up any large clumps, until browned and somewhat dry, 10 to 12 minutes.

Add the onion, carrot, peas, and corn. Stir well and cook until slightly softened, about 5 minutes. Add the scallion, bell pepper, and white pepper and cook for 2 minutes. Remove from the heat.

Drain the beef filling in a fine-mesh strainer set over a bowl so your samosas won't get soggy. Spread the mixture into an even layer and let cool completely, about 30 minutes.

In a small bowl, combine the flour and cornstarch. Mix well to combine. Drizzle in ⅔ cup (160 ml) water, mixing with a fork or spoon until you get a pasty, gluelike consistency (this is your pastry glue). Set the pastry glue, a pastry brush, and a couple of rimmed baking sheets next to your cutting board.

With a sharp knife and, if you like, a clean metal ruler (as a guide to ensure even halves), cut the stack of spring roll wrappers in half on the diagonal to create 2 triangles per wrapper. Separate the wrappers and keep them covered with a damp kitchen towel while you assemble the samosas.

To make each samosa, you'll fold the wrapper over itself five times, alternating the corner you're working with—up, down, up, down, up, down; making sure the edges align, maintaining a triangle and gluing with the cornstarch mixture as you progress.

RECIPE CONTINUES →

Lay one triangle down, with the long edge facing you, parallel to the long side of the cutting board. Pull the point at the top down toward you so it touches the center of the long edge. You'll have two 1-layer triangles on either side, and a larger two-layer central section between them. Starting on the right, pick up the bottom right corner and pull up to align the top and right edges. Spread a ½-inch (1.3 cm) portion of the bottom wrapper with pastry glue, from the right edge to the center. Pull the top right corner of the wrapper down so the sides align, then press it into the glued section to create a pocket. Fill the pocket with 1 tablespoon of the filling, pressing it in to fill.

Spread pastry glue over the rest of the wrapper and continue folding: Pull up the bottom right corner over to the top, forming another compact triangle. Repeat one more time to use up most or all of the wrapper. Fold and press any loose pastry over. Set the samosa on the baking sheet, seam-side down, and cover with a damp kitchen towel. Repeat with the remaining triangles and filling. (At this point, the rolls can be placed on the baking sheet in a single layer and frozen until firm, then transferred to a zip-top freezer bag, sealed with the air pressed out, and frozen for up to 3 months. To fry from frozen, add an extra minute or two to the cooking time.)

Fill a wok or large Dutch oven with 1½ to 2 inches (3.8 to 5 cm) of oil; it should come no more than halfway up the vessel. Heat the oil over medium-high heat to 350°F (175°C). Line a rimmed baking sheet with a wire rack or paper towels.

Working in batches, use a spider or slotted spoon to add the samosas to the hot oil, being careful not to overcrowd them. Fry, turning often, until golden brown, about 4 minutes. Transfer to the prepared baking sheet. Repeat with the remaining samosas, allowing the oil to return to temperature between batches.

Enjoy hot or cold, on their own or with ata dindin or your favorite dip.

MEAT PIES

FOR THE DOUGH

1¼ cups (5.3 ounces/150 g) all-purpose flour, sifted, plus more for dusting

¼ cup (1 ounce/30 g) whole wheat flour

1 teaspoon fine sea salt

½ teaspoon baking powder

6 tablespoons (3 ounces/ 85 g) cold unsalted butter

1 large egg, lightly beaten

¼ cup (60 ml) ice-cold water, plus more as needed

FOR THE FILLING

1 tablespoon cornstarch

3 tablespoons neutral oil

8 ounces (225 g) ground beef, 20% fat or less (see Variation)

½ teaspoon fine sea salt, plus more as needed

½ small yellow onion, finely diced

1 medium white or yellow potato, peeled and cut into ½-inch (1.3 cm) dice

1 small carrot, cut into ¼-inch (6 mm) dice

1 teaspoon Curry Powder (page 25)

1 teaspoon dried thyme

1 cup (240 ml) Curry Stock (page 333) or water

½ small green bell pepper, finely chopped

Freshly ground black pepper

1 large egg yolk

These hand pies feature tender pastry wrapped around an aromatic, curry-spiced mixture of ground beef, onions, potatoes, and carrots. Enjoy them with cold drinks, including Zōbò (page 317) and sodas. Introduced to Nigeria during British colonial rule, meat pies resemble Cornish pasties and Jamaican beef patties in some ways.

There are two parts to this recipe: the short crust pastry and the filling, both of which can be made ahead and refrigerated or frozen. You can also use store-bought short crust or puff pastry.

Other filling options include chopped, shredded, or ground chicken or a plant-forward filling with beans (popular in Warri), potatoes, and mushrooms. The final egg wash can be replaced with milk. Whatever you do, don't skip the green bell pepper; it adds a fresh, vegetal flavor and aroma to the finished pies.

Make the dough: In a large bowl, whisk together the all-purpose flour, whole wheat flour, salt, and baking powder.

Using the large holes of a box grater, grate the butter into the flour mixture and use clean hands to combine until the butter is evenly distributed.

Make a 4-inch-wide (10 cm) well in the center of the flour mixture. In a liquid measuring cup, whisk together the beaten egg and the water, then pour it into the well. Use a flexible spatula to gradually stir the flour mixture into the egg mixture until a cohesive dough with visible bits of butter forms. If the dough is too dry, add more water 1 tablespoon at a time until it comes together. Shape the dough into a flat disc, wrap tightly in plastic wrap, and refrigerate for at least 30 minutes and up to 2 days.

Make the filling: In a small bowl, whisk together the cornstarch and ½ cup (120 ml) water until well combined.

In a 10-inch (25 cm) cast-iron or stainless-steel skillet, heat 1 tablespoon of the oil over medium heat. When the oil is shimmering, add the ground beef, season with the salt, and cook, stirring and breaking up any large clumps, until the meat loses its raw look, about 5 minutes. Transfer to a heatproof bowl to cool.

RECIPE CONTINUES →

Add the remaining 2 tablespoons oil to the skillet and heat over medium heat. When the oil is shimmering, add the onion, potato, and carrot and season lightly with salt. Cook, stirring occasionally, until the vegetables are just beginning to soften, about 4 minutes. Add the curry powder and thyme and cook, stirring frequently, until fragrant and evenly distributed, about 2 minutes.

Return the cooked beef to the pot and add the curry stock. Cover and bring to a boil. Reduce the heat so the liquid is barely bubbling and cook, stirring once or twice, until the vegetables have softened, 12 to 15 minutes. Stir in half the bell pepper, cover, and cook until it has just softened, 15 minutes.

Stir the cornstarch slurry and pour it into the beef mixture. Bring to a simmer and cook, uncovered, stirring occasionally, until the beef and vegetables are coated in a thickened sauce, about 5 minutes.

Stir in the remaining bell pepper and season with salt and black pepper to taste. Transfer the filling to a separate heatproof bowl to cool for about 30 minutes. (At this point, the filling can be refrigerated in an airtight container for up to 3 days or frozen for 1 month).

When ready to assemble, generously flour a work surface and rolling pin and lightly flour a rimmed baking sheet. Unwrap the chilled dough and portion it into 6 equal balls (2⅓ ounces/65 g each). Roll out each ball into a 6-inch (15 cm) round that's about ⅛ inch (3 mm) thick, lightly reflouring the work surface as needed to prevent sticking. Transfer the rounds to the prepared baking sheet and cover loosely with plastic wrap.

Line a rimmed baking sheet with parchment paper. Place one dough round on your work surface and add ½ cup (3 ½ ounces/98 g) of the filling to the bottom half of the round, leaving a ½-inch (1.3 cm) border. Fold the top half down over the filling to form a half-moon shape, then press gently around the edges to seal. Use the tines of a fork to crimp the edges, pressing down firmly, then transfer to the parchment-lined baking sheet. Repeat with the remaining dough rounds and filling. Cover the baking sheet loosely with plastic wrap and refrigerate for at least 30 minutes and up to 2 hours.

Twenty minutes before baking, position a rack in the center of the oven and preheat the oven to 400°F (205°C).

Uncover the meat pies. Whisk together the egg yolk and 1 tablespoon ice-cold water in a small bowl and brush each meat pie with the egg

wash. Use a fork to prick the pies all over, five or six times. Bake on the middle rack for about 25 minutes, rotating the pan from front to back halfway through, until golden brown.

Let cool for 10 minutes before serving, or serve at room temperature.

VARIATION

Substitute canned corned beef for 1 to 2 ounces (30 to 60 g) of the ground beef. Hold back on salting until you've added the corned beef, as it is salty. Add the corned beef after the cornstarch slurry, when the beef and vegetables are coated in the thickened sauce.

STICK MEAT

2 medium red onions:
1 coarsely chopped, 1 cut
into 1-inch (2.5 cm) dice

2 small green bell peppers:
1 coarsely chopped, 1 cut
into 1-inch (2.5 cm) dice

1 to 2 thumb-size pieces
fresh ginger, peeled

2 medium garlic cloves,
peeled

1 pound (450 g) stewing
beef, cut into 1-inch (2.5 cm)
pieces (about 26 pieces)

1 Scotch bonnet or habanero
pepper, stemmed and
left whole or seeded and
chopped (optional)

1 tablespoon Curry Powder
(page 25)

1 teaspoon dried thyme

1 teaspoon fine sea salt, plus
more as needed

½ teaspoon freshly ground
black pepper, plus more as
needed

2 dried bay leaves

Neutral oil, for frying

1 small red, yellow, or orange
bell pepper, cut into 1-inch
(2.5 cm) dice

SWITCH UP
THE COLORS

Explore other
combinations of fresh,
grilled, or even pickled
fruits or vegetables.
Squash, cucumbers,
tomatoes are a few
ideas.

These cute mini kebabs on toothpicks or small skewers are a colorful combination of fried, sometimes sauced or peppered meat and vegetables. They are popular as street food and home party food.

Each skewer should have two or three pieces of meat alternated with colorful vegetables cut the same size as the meat. If you aren't a fan of raw onion and pepper, lightly sauté the vegetables for a minute or two, until they soften but still retain their vibrant colors, then let cool before threading them onto the sticks.

In a food processor or blender, combine the chopped onion, chopped green bell pepper, ginger, and garlic. Pulse to create a uniform, coarse mixture. Transfer to a large stockpot and add the beef, Scotch bonnet (if using), curry powder, thyme, salt, and black pepper. Cover and cook over medium-high heat, stirring now and again, until the beef loses its raw color and sweats out its juices, and the liquid begins to boil, about 10 minutes.

Uncover and stir in the bay leaves and 1 cup (240 ml) water. Increase the heat to bring the mixture to a boil; cook for 3 to 4 minutes, then reduce the heat to low and cook until the stock is aromatic and the beef is tender but retains some resistance, 20 to 30 minutes. Taste and add more salt or black pepper, if needed.

Set a strainer over a large bowl. Use tongs to transfer the beef to the strainer to drain and cool for about 15 minutes; reserve the stock for another use.

Fill a wok or large Dutch oven with 1½ to 2 inches (3.8 to 5 cm) of oil; it should come no more than halfway up the vessel. Heat the oil over medium-high heat to 350°F (175°C). Line a strainer with paper towels.

Working in batches if need be, add the drained beef, being careful not to crowd the pan. Fry on one side until golden around the edges, about 4 minutes. Carefully turn the pieces over and cook until brown, 3 to 4 minutes more. Transfer the fried meat to the strainer, shaking off any excess oil. Repeat with the remaining beef, allowing the oil to return to temperature between batches.

Thread the beef onto skewers, alternating with pieces of the diced onion and diced bell peppers. Serve warm or at room temperature.

YÒYÒ

FRIED WHITEBAIT

Neutral oil, for frying

1 cup (4.25 ounces/120 g) all-purpose flour, sifted (see Note)

2 teaspoons fine sea salt

1 teaspoon dry pepper (see page 22)

1 pound (450 g) whole fresh whitebait, rinsed, drained, and dried (see headnote)

NOTE: *Use fine garri or cornmeal for coating instead of flour, if you like.*

OTHER WAYS TO ENJOY YÒYÒ

- With Puff Puff (page 39)
- With soft Agege bread (see page 75)
- With Soaked Garri (page 72)
- With Stewed Beans (page 153)

Also called ẹja yòyò or ẹja Èkọ ("Èkọ fish"), named after Èkọ (Lagos), these small silver fish collectively known as whitebait of herring, smelt, and sprats are abundant during the rainy season and are tossed in seasoned flour and deep-fried until crisp.

Smaller whitebait (under 3 inches/7.5 cm) do not require cleaning, as the soft bones and fins are edible, but examine them before use, as you would with any seafood purchase, and discard any that don't look fresh or are torn or broken. Larger whitebait with their heads and guts removed also work well.

Enjoy yòyò with Ata Dindin (page 332).

Fill a wok or large Dutch oven with 1½ to 2 inches (3.8 to 5 cm) of oil; it should come no more than halfway up the vessel. Heat the oil over medium-high heat to 350°F (175°C). Line a rimmed baking sheet with a wire rack or paper towels.

In a large bowl, whisk together the flour, salt, and dry pepper. Working in batches, coat the fish well in the seasoned flour. Shake off any excess and place the fish on another rimmed baking sheet.

Use a spider or slotted spoon to add a few of the coated fish to the hot oil, being careful not to overcrowd the pot. Fry, stirring as needed to keep them separate as they cook, until golden brown and crisped all over, 4 to 5 minutes. Transfer to the rack to drain and repeat with the remaining fish, allowing the oil to return to temperature between batches.

Serve hot, warm, or cold. Store leftovers in an airtight container in the refrigerator for up to 2 days.

VARIATION

To bake the fish, preheat the oven to 350°F (175°C). Line a rimmed baking sheet with parchment paper and brush the parchment with oil. Spread the coated fish in a single layer over the prepared baking sheet and drizzle with oil. Bake on the middle rack until golden and crisp, 40 to 45 minutes, turning halfway through.

PLANTAINS AND POSSIBILITY

Plantain is to Nigerians what potatoes are to North Americans: a beloved, versatile staple. The starchy fruit, cousin to the banana but eaten cooked, is enjoyed at all stages of ripeness, from unripe, green-skinned, and firm to super-ripe, black-skinned, sweet, and soft. While you can eat them raw, most people don't, except when they are ripe or overripe, and only as a light snack, often as one cuts them in preparation for cooking—Nigerians have a standing joke about how hard it is to resist (salted) raw ripe plantains just before they are fried! Across the plantain's color gradients and ripening, the sweetness and textures change once cooked—unripe plantains are firm, starchy, and less sweet than soft, ripe ones.

In Nigerian cuisine, most traditional applications and preparation of plantains are savory, such as appetizers like Mọsa (page 41), mains like pottages (see page 117), and sides like Dòdò (page 120). Even when sweet, ripe plantains are cooked, they aren't meant for dessert.

Plantains are as important as yams in Nigerian cuisine. While there isn't a historic plantain festival associated with the fruit, there is a contemporary one, World Plantain Day, launched in 2017 and celebrated on the fifth of June each year. Created by entrepreneur Dimeji Eyiowuawi, who wanted an annual gathering to unite plantain lovers all over the world and commemorate plantain, the festival explores classic and creative plantain recipes.

Some of the sweetest plantains come from the southern region of Ogoni, where plantains have been cultivated since before colonial times, when they played an important role in trade, just as they do today.

When they are unripe and still green, they are peeled, sometimes cut, and sun-dried until firm. They are then ground and milled into plantain flour (àmàlà ògèdè) and used to make chews and swallows. Super-ripe plantains can also be fermented into drinks, from beers to wine. Agadagidi is a locally brewed wine, like banana wine, made from overripe plantains and enjoyed at home, in local bars, and at celebrations.

Bunches of plantain on enamel trays; Oniru New Market, Lagos

WHEN YOU WAKE UP IS YOUR MORNING

BREAKFAST

Mgbe onye ji tete ụra bụ ụtụtụ ya.

—AN IGBO SAYING FROM THE SOUTH EAST: "WHENEVER YOU
WAKE UP IS YOUR OWN MORNING," MEANING YOUR LIFE'S
JOURNEY BEGINS WHEN YOU'RE READY, LIKE YOUR DAY.

NIGERIAN BREAKFASTS ARE A MIX OF SWEET AND
savory. You can get sliced bread from a bakery, or unsliced
loaves from sellers singing "Buy your fresh Agege bread,"
"Sweet butter bread," or some other sales pitch. Your purchase
of an unsliced loaf could be cut open like a book, sliced from
the side (leaving the spine intact), before it is spread thick with
butter, margarine, or Bama, a brand name that's become the
generic descriptor for all mayonnaise.

Eggs—bright with sweet and hot peppers, tomatoes, and
purple onions—range from curds to omelets. Instant cereal
and porridges of corn, millet, fonio, and oats are common,
especially on weekdays when quick-and-easy is required.
Weekend and festive breakfasts are more involved affairs.

Out and about, you might head to the tea maker
extraordinaire, a mai shayi (from the Arabic *shay*, meaning tea),
a Nigerian man from the north who owns the neighborhood
open-air café where tea (every hot drink is called tea), bread,
eggs, and instant noodles are enjoyed.

The mai shayi keeps a large, lidded pot of water going all
day. You place your order and then sit on a bench at a table
with plastic tablecloths until it is ready. You might end up
with a smorgasbord of delights, as the mai shayi attracts others
whose offerings pair well with his, from sellers of boiled yam,
beans, and stew to vendors a few feet away with display boxes
of golden brown àkàrà.

After feasting on these delights, you will wake up to
embrace the morning and conquer your day, or, in some cases,
head back to bed or the couch for a little post-enjoyment nap.

CLOCKWISE FROM LEFT: *A seller of Agege bread; eggs and ground fresh pepper; a mai
shayi at work; his pot of boiling water*

1. **Àkàmù.** Also known as kamu, ògì, koko, or pap. This fermented corn mix, commonly made from white or yellow dried corn, or a mix of corn, millet, or Guinea corn (sorghum), is loved by both old and young, and is one of the first weaning foods for babies. It is available in cakes, as a paste stored in water, or as a powder.

2. **Black-eyed peas.** A common bean in the Nigerian kitchen.

3. **Canned corned beef.** Sold in trapezoidal cans (and different from the sliced corned beef sold in delis), it is as popular in Nigeria and West Africa as Spam is in South Korea.

4. **Condensed and evaporated milk.** Popular for drinks and porridges.

5. **Pearl millet.** Whole-grain and ground millet can be made into pottage. Ground millet flour is used for porridges like Ibyer (page 78).

6. **Shinkafan tūwō or shinkafa.** A barely polished rice, similar to Thai jasmine rice. It is popular across the North East and North West for making Māsǎ (page 85), Tūwōn Shinkafa (page 214), drinks, paps, and more.

ÀKÀRÀ

FRIED BEAN FRITTERS

Neutral oil, for frying

1 small red onion, coarsely chopped, plus ½ small red onion, finely chopped (optional)

⅓ Scotch bonnet or habanero pepper, plus 1 Scotch bonnet or habanero, minced (optional)

½ teaspoon fine sea salt

2 cups (9.7 ounces/275 g) washed (see page 67) black-eyed peas or cowpeas

NOTE: *If you want smaller àkàrà, scoop and fry the batter by the teaspoonful. Once cooked, you can sandwich the hot fritters between slices of bread, pressing the bread together so it flattens and the fritters burst to make a spread that's equal parts crunchy and creamy.*

With crunchy bits on the outside and a creamy inside, these versatile fritters are everyday eats, and the quintessential Saturday breakfast.

They are commonly made with dried black-eyed peas or other cowpeas—soaked, skinned, and then blended with onions and peppers. You can use skin-on beans or bean flour, but these will result in fritters with a denser texture. And while you *can* make fritters with pureed canned beans, they wouldn't be àkàrà.

Serve with slices of soft Agege bread (see page 75)—or better still, chunks torn off, uncorrupted by the silver of a knife—and Basic Yaji (page 26). You can also enjoy àkàrà with hot Àkàmù (page 76), Mọ́ínmọ́ín Elewe (page 69), Soaked Garri (page 72), or oatmeal.

Fill a wok or large Dutch oven with 2 inches (5 cm) of oil; it should come no more than halfway up the vessel. Heat the oil over medium-high heat to 350°F (175°C). Line a rimmed baking sheet with a wire rack or paper towels.

In a blender or food processor, combine the coarsely chopped onion, ⅓ Scotch bonnet, salt, and ½ cup (120 ml) water. Puree until smooth. Add the beans and puree to form a thick paste, 1 to 2 minutes, stopping a few times to scrape down the sides of the blender. The mixture shouldn't be super-smooth—when you rub a bit between your fingers, it should look and feel grainy.

Transfer the batter to a large bowl. With a whisk or a handheld mixer, beat until light and fluffy, 1 to 2 minutes. If desired, sprinkle the finely chopped onion and minced Scotch bonnet over the batter and fold them in.

Dip a large heatproof spoon into the hot oil, then use it to scoop up about 1 tablespoon of the batter. Partially dip the spoon into the oil to help the batter slide off. Repeat to add about 7 more portions of batter, until the pan is full but not overcrowded. Fry, turning the fritters as needed, until golden brown all over, about 6 minutes. Use a slotted spoon to transfer the fritters to the baking sheet to drain. Repeat with the remaining batter, allowing the oil to return to temperature between batches.

Serve warm, although some people like their fritters very hot.

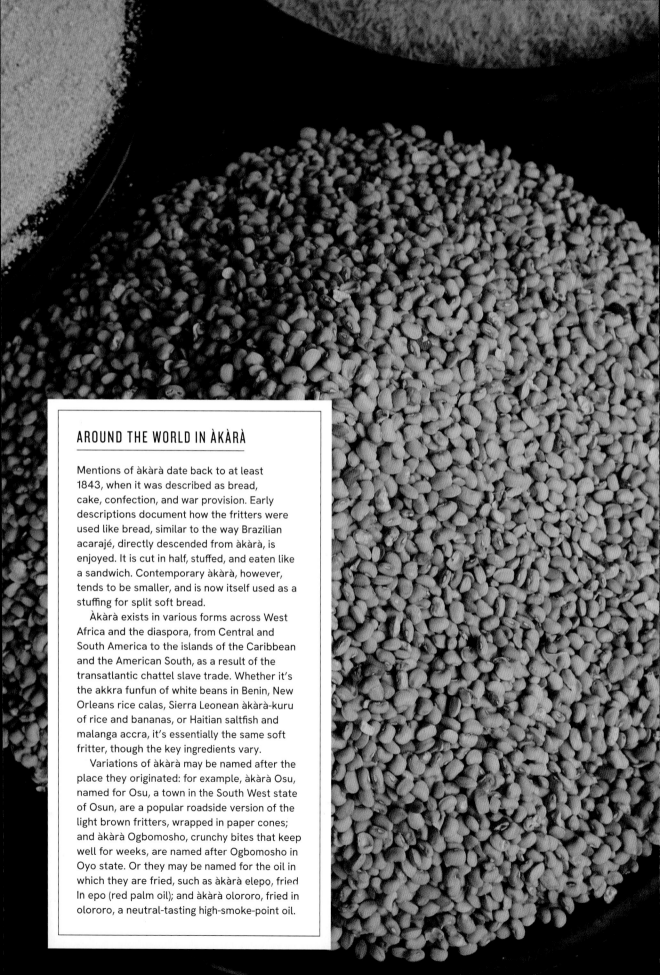

AROUND THE WORLD IN ÀKÀRÀ

Mentions of àkàrà date back to at least
1843, when it was described as bread,
cake, confection, and war provision. Early
descriptions document how the fritters were
used like bread, similar to the way Brazilian
acarajé, directly descended from àkàrà, is
enjoyed. It is cut in half, stuffed, and eaten like
a sandwich. Contemporary àkàrà, however,
tends to be smaller, and is now itself used as a
stuffing for split soft bread.

Àkàrà exists in various forms across West
Africa and the diaspora, from Central and
South America to the islands of the Caribbean
and the American South, as a result of the
transatlantic chattel slave trade. Whether it's
the akkra funfun of white beans in Benin, New
Orleans rice calas, Sierra Leonean àkàrà-kuru
of rice and bananas, or Haitian saltfish and
malanga accra, it's essentially the same soft
fritter, though the key ingredients vary.

Variations of àkàrà may be named after the
place they originated: for example, àkàrà Osu,
named for Osu, a town in the South West state
of Osun, are a popular roadside version of the
light brown fritters, wrapped in paper cones;
and àkàrà Ogbomosho, crunchy bites that keep
well for weeks, are named after Ogbomosho in
Oyo state. Or they may be named for the oil in
which they are fried, such as àkàrà elepo, fried
In epo (red palm oil); and àkàrà olororo, fried in
olororo, a neutral-tasting high-smoke-point oil.

Washing Dried Beans

In Nigeria, we describe removing the skins or hulls from a variety of cowpeas, including black-eyed peas, for Àkàrà (page 64), Mọ́ínmọ́ín Elewe (page 69), Gbẹ̀gìrì (page 243), and a host of other recipes as "washing" the beans. Washed beans freeze well, so it is a good idea to double or triple the quantity you need so you can explore other recipes. That way, you have them on hand for future use.

To make 2 cups (9.7 ounces/275 g) washed beans, pick over 1 cup (6¾ ounces/190 g) dried black-eyed peas for any debris, then rinse them and place in a medium bowl. Add water to cover by 2 inches (5 cm). Set aside to soak at room temperature, uncovered, for at least 15 minutes and up to 1 hour. (This short soaking time loosens the skins without overly softening the beans.)

Have a small trash bag ready to put the skins in. They begin to stink if left for too long, so you may want to remove them from the kitchen when you're done washing the beans.

Drain the beans, then transfer to a blender or food processor (work in batches, if needed). Add 4 cups (about 1 L) water. Pulse to slightly break up the beans, twenty to thirty 1-second pulses, then pour the beans and water back into the bowl. Gently rub to loosen more of the skins, then let stand at room temperature for up to 30 minutes—as the skins separate from the beans, they will float to the top. With a fine-mesh sieve, scoop out the skins and discard them in the trash bag.

Set a colander in the sink. Slowly pour the soaking water into the colander while using your free hand to keep the beans in the soaking bowl; the goal is to pour off as many of the floating skins as possible while leaving the beans behind. Pick out any beans that sneak into the colander and return them to the bowl, then discard the skins. Cover the beans with fresh water and repeat until the beans are nearly free of skins—you may need to gently massage them with your hands to separate any stubborn skins.

Transfer the beans to a tray and pick off any remaining skins. Give the beans one final rinse, then portion into freezer-safe containers and freeze for up to 3 months. Thaw the skinned beans overnight in the fridge or place in a bowl of cold water to quickly defrost before using.

MÓÍNMÓÍN ELEWE
STEAMED BEAN PUDDING

14 to 16 móínmóín leaves, rinsed and dried

2 cups (9.7 ounces/275 g) washed (see page 67) black-eyed peas or cowpeas

¼ large red onion, coarsely chopped

1 red tatashe pepper or ½ red shepherd pepper, coarsely chopped

1 cup (240 ml) Curry Stock (page 333)

1 teaspoon fine sea salt

½ teaspoon freshly grated nutmeg

½ to 1 Scotch bonnet or habanero pepper, stemmed (optional)

¼ cup (60 ml) neutral oil, warmed

2 hard-boiled large eggs, peeled and quartered lengthwise

Boiling water as needed

MÓÍNMÓÍN MYTH

Some people believe that if more than one person wraps the móínmóín batter in leaves, the móínmóín won't set, regardless of how long it cooks, unless each person ties a three-leaf knot and places the knot on top of the pile of wrapped móínmóín before it cooks.

A contraction of moyin-moyin, *móínmóín* translates from Yorùbá as "that which sticks to the teeth." Originally known as ọ̀lẹ̀lẹ̀ or ọ̀lẹ̀, it is a steamed cake made with the same soft, creamy pureed bean base as Àkàrà (page 64), with additions like stock, oil, and protein. It reminds me of pâté and pudding—some people describe the cooked texture as buttery.

Móínmóín elewe, or móínmóín wrapped in ewe eran leaves (also known as broad leaves, from the *Thaumatococcus daniellii* plant) or in banana or plantain leaves, is arguably the tastiest version. Fishing out the slivers of mix that have firmed up between the creases and folds of the leaf and been imbued with its earthy fragrance is pure joy. It can also be steamed in corn husks, ramekins, or in containers like empty milk tins.

Móínmóín leaves are available fresh and frozen at African markets and online. You can use 8 by 12-inch (20 by 30 cm) rectangular cuts of cleaned banana or plantain leaves instead—be sure to heat the leaves first to prevent them from splitting across the ribs.

Enjoy móínmóín—on its own, or with Ata Dindin (page 332), or, my personal favorite, with Soaked Garri (page 72). You can also pair it with Àkàmù (page 76), smear it on toast, sandwich it in soft bread to eat as a Móíburger, or serve it with rice, oatmeal, Nigerian Salad (page 97), and more.

Móínmóín leaves have central ribs that need to be trimmed and partly removed so they don't puncture and tear the leaves. Hold a leaf matte-side (back) up in your nondominant hand. The ribs are thickest about two-thirds of the way down the length of the spine from the tip. Gently fold the leaf at this two-thirds mark and the protruding portion of the rib should detach. Pull downward to the base, where it meets the stalk. Trim the rib and the excess stalk at the base of the leaf. Reserve the stalks to make a platform for the wraps, or discard them. Repeat with the remaining leaves.

In a blender or food processor, combine the beans, onion, tatashe, stock, salt, nutmeg, and habanero (if using). Blend on high, stopping to scrape down the sides occasionally, until smooth, 1 to 2 minutes. Transfer to a large bowl, add the oil, and whisk until well combined.

RECIPE CONTINUES →

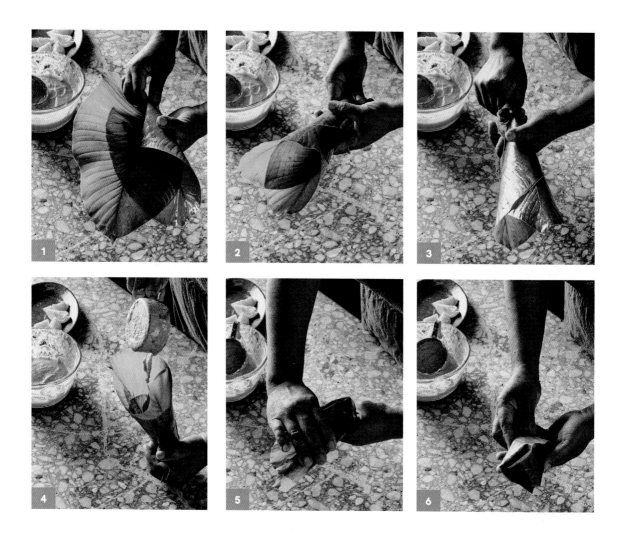

Fill a stockpot with 2 to 3 inches (5 to 7.5 cm) of water. Place a steamer basket in the pot, making sure the water does not touch the bottom of the basket. Cover and bring to a boil over high heat.

In your nondominant hand, hold a móínmóín leaf vertically with the shiny side up. Set a second leaf on top of the first so that the bottoms of their midribs meet and the second leaf is angled a little less than 45 degrees from the first leaf (it should look like the leaves are the hands of a clock, joined at the bottom, with the first leaf pointing to 12 o'clock and the second leaf pointing to just past 1 o'clock).

Using both hands and starting from the first leaf, roll the leaves to form a cone, with the bottoms of the midribs at the bottom point and open at the top. Fold the bottom 2 inches (5 cm) of the cone back and up to seal.

There is regular
mọ́ínmọ́ín—whether
elewe, or in
containers—and then
there's mọ́ínmọ́ín elemi
meje, or mọ́ínmọ́ín with
seven lives or souls
(i.e., ingredients), each
one an addition to the
mixture. These may be
cooked vegetables like
carrots, bell peppers,
and corn; and/or
protein, such as hard-
boiled eggs, canned
corned beef, minced
meat, sardines or tuna
in oil, boiled or smoked
mackerel, prawns,
liver, kidney, fried
meat, and more. For
this recipe, about 1 cup
total (by volume) of a
combination of added
ingredients works well.

Holding the cone with its open top facing up (and securing the folded bottom with one hand), spoon ⅓ cup (80 g) of the mọ́ínmọ́ín puree into the cone. Place one of the egg quarters at the center of the puree, then cover with another ⅓ cup (80 g) puree.

To close the cone, use your fingers to push a section at the top of the leaf cone in so it lays flat against the surface of the puree, then fold a second adjacent leaf section in over the first one. Fold the remaining excess leaf back and down so it meets the folded-up point at the bottom (they may not touch, or they may overlap, depending on the size of the leaves). Set the sealed cone in the steamer basket. Repeat with the remaining leaves, puree, and egg quarters; you should have 6 filled mọ́ínmọ́ín. You may need to stack them on top of one another.

Place the remaining mọ́ínmọ́ín leaves on top of the wrapped mọ́ínmọ́ín, cover the pot, and return to a boil. Reduce the heat to medium and steam until the leaves go from bright to dull green and the mọ́ínmọ́ín is aromatic, about 45 minutes; a cake tester or skewer inserted into the thickest part of the mọ́ínmọ́ín should come out clean. Be sure to maintain the water level as they cook, checking every 10 to 15 minutes and pouring in more boiling water at the sides as needed.

Transfer the cooked mọ́ínmọ́ín to a wire rack and let stand for 10 minutes to firm up before serving.

VARIATION

To make mọ́ínmọ́ín in ramekins: Lightly grease eight 4-ounce ramekins with warmed neutral oil. Fill each ramekin halfway with some of the puree. Place an egg quarter, cut-side up, at the center of each one, then cover with the remaining puree until the ramekins are about three-quarters full (the puree will rise as it cooks).

Fill a large pot with 4 inches (10 cm) of water. Place a steamer rack inside, set the ramekins on the rack, cover, and bring to a boil over high heat. Reduce the heat to medium and cook until the mọ́ínmọ́ín form a domed top, are firm to the touch, and spring back when gently pressed, about 30 minutes. Be sure to check the water level every 10 to 15 minutes and pour in more boiling water as needed.

Transfer the ramekins to a wire rack and let the mọ́ínmọ́ín stand for 10 minutes to firm up. If you prefer to unmold the mọ́ínmọ́ín, run a butter knife around the edges to loosen them from the ramekins, then turn them out onto serving dishes.

SOAKED GARRI

½ cup (70 g) Ijebu garri

Ice cubes, whole or crushed

FOR SERVING (OPTIONAL)

1 tablespoon sugar, or to taste

Pinch of salt

Roasted skinned groundnuts (peanuts)

Fresh coconut pieces

Powdered or evaporated milk

Sweetened chocolate drink, such as Milo

FOUR WAYS TO EAT SOAKED GARRI

1. With Àkàrà (page 64), Mọ́ínmọ́ín Elewe (page 69), or Stewed Beans (page 153)
2. With Fried Meat (page 330) or Beef Sūya (page 173)
3. With fried seafood like Yòyò (page 54) or Fried Fish (page 167), or smoked or dry seafood
4. With chopped and salted red Scotch bonnets

Or any combination of the above

Soaked garri or drinking garri is similar to breakfast cereal in how it's prepared and enjoyed. Essentially, you put some dry garri (toasted cassava granules) into a bowl or cup—filling it only a third or half of the way, because the garri swells when you add cold or room-temperature water (never hot, which will cause the garri to gelatinize, and you'll be on your way to making Ẹba, page 216)—then customize it as you like.

You can add the water to the bowl without much ado, or you can "wash" your garri: adding enough to cover it by an inch or two (2.5 to 5 cm) and stirring so any fibers rise to the top, then pouring off the liquid and replacing it with fresh water (do this by the sink so you manage your time). From there, customize your bowl at will. Sometimes I make a drink of garri water, a really light version of soaked garri, with only a couple of spoonfuls of the ground cassava, sweetened with sugar, and topped with crushed ice.

Place the garri in a medium bowl. Pour 1 cup (240 ml) or more cold water into the bowl and stir with a spoon. Carefully decant and discard the water and any fibrous bits.

Add the ice and fresh water to cover the garri by 1 or 2 inches (2.5 to 5 cm, or about 1 cup/240 ml water). Add the sugar, if desired—some people add a pinch of salt as well or replace the sugar entirely with salt—and stir well. Add any of the other optional ingredients at this point, and more water if desired.

Enjoy immediately, on its own or with any of the suggestions on the left.

AGEGE BREAD

Agege bread is a soft, white, slightly sweet four-cornered loaf, baked in lidded tins and named after the Lagos suburb where bakeries were established in the late 1980s. *Succulent* and *thick* are also descriptions for this bread, a favorite across the country. Sold in transparent bags without nutritional labels, it comes in a range of sizes and is one of the most delicious breads you'll ever eat.

Agege bread is similar to many breads across the world in texture and flavor—Ghanaian sweet and tea bread, French pain de mie, Chinese milk bread, and Japanese shokupan among them. And if Agege bread reminds you of Jamaican hardo bread, you'll be pleased to know there's a connection. In 1915, a Jamaican-born railway worker, Amos Shackleford (1887–1954), started a commercial bakery in Lagos with his wife, Catherine. Shackleford introduced a unique kneading machine known as a dough brake, which resembles a giant pasta dough roller. Today, Shackleford is known as the Bread King of Nigeria, and dough brakes are found in Nigeria, Jamaica, Cuba, and Haiti. They are essential for the proper kneading of dough for Agege bread, creating the unique fine-grained texture that makes it perfect for tearing and dunking in tea or stew without crumbling or disintegrating.

Find it in your nearest Nigerian or African store, or grab some milk bread instead.

TEN WAYS TO ENJOY AGEGE BREAD

1. With butter, butter substitute, mayonnaise, or avocado
2. With eggs—boiled, or in a Nigerian Omelet (page 81)
3. With sardine or corned beef butter (page 329)
4. With Àkàrà (page 64) or Beef Sūya (page 173)
5. With stew or Corned Beef Sauce (page 82)
6. With Stewed Beans (page 153)
7. With Móínmóín Elewe (page 69—this is known as a Móíburger)
8. With Nigerian Salad (page 97)
9. With Roasted Groundnuts (page 200)
10. Dipped in milky tea or chocolate drinks, or enjoyed with soft drinks

ÀKÀMỤ

FERMENTED CORN PUDDING

1 cup (250 g) àkàmù paste (page 328) or semisolid block, at room temperature, or 1 cup (125 g) àkàmù powder

Evaporated milk or milk of your choice, for serving

Sugar or other sweetener, for serving

Across West Africa, you'll find this fermented corn mix—part starch, part flour—cooked into a smooth pudding with a pourable consistency. It is enjoyed hot, and either drunk or served in bowls and eaten by the spoonful.

The starch-flour mix is sold as a paste, a semisolid block, or a powder and is combined with water or milk and cooked until smooth and translucent. It is best served with milk and, if you like, sugar. Some people top their àkàmù with fresh lime, lemon, or tamarind juice. Regardless of how you serve it, make sure everyone is at the table when the àkàmù is ready to be eaten, because once it's cooked, a skin quickly forms on the surface, which can detract from the àkàmù's smooth, silky texture.

Serve with Àkàrà (page 64), Mọ́ínmọ́ín Elewe (page 69), or Dòdò (page 120).

In a medium bowl, combine the àkàmù and 1 cup (240 ml) room-temperature water, stirring to form a smooth slurry with the consistency of crepe batter.

Fill a medium pot with 3 cups (720 ml) water and bring to a boil over high heat, then reduce the heat to low. Restir the àkàmù slurry and while whisking, gradually pour it into the water, then continue to whisk as the mixture thickens and becomes translucent and smooth, 5 to 6 minutes more. If the àkàmù becomes too thick, whisk in some hot water in a steady stream until you achieve your desired consistency.

Cook for 2 to 3 minutes more to ensure the àkàmù is evenly hot and cooked through, then whisk well and serve immediately, with milk and sweetener at the table. If not serving immediately, sprinkle some room-temperature water over the surface of the àkàmù to prevent a skin from forming; just before serving, stir the àkàmù to incorporate the water.

IBYER
WHOLE-GRAIN MILLET PORRIDGE

1 cup (125 g) millet flour

1 teaspoon ground ginger, or more as needed

¼ teaspoon dry pepper (see page 22)

¼ teaspoon ground cloves

¼ cup (60 ml) evaporated milk or milk of your choice, plus more for serving

2 tablespoons sugar or other sweetener, plus more for serving

This comforting, nourishing Tiv porridge of millet flour and spices is the perfect start to your day: earthy, nutty, and simple to rustle up. You can also make it ahead and reheat it as you like. Similar whole-grain porridges are made with acha (fonio), Guinea corn (sorghum), or a combination. Serve it thick in a bowl to scoop with a spoon or thin in a mug to sip, finished with your favorite milk and sweetener. Ibyer is enjoyed on its own, or with akpukpa (the Tiv name for mọ́ínmọ́ín, page 69) or bread.

In a medium bowl, whisk together the millet, ginger, dry pepper, and cloves. Add 2 cups (480 ml) room-temperature water, whisk to incorporate, then set aside for a few minutes to hydrate.

Fill a medium pot with 3 cups (720 ml) water and bring to a boil over high heat, then reduce the heat to medium-high. Stir the millet mixture (it may have settled). While whisking, gradually add the millet mixture to the hot water, then continue to whisk until the mixture thickens and becomes translucent, 2 to 3 minutes more.

Add the milk and sugar and cook until heated through. Taste and adjust with more ginger, if you like.

Whisk well and serve immediately, with additional milk and sugar at the table, if desired.

NIGERIAN PANCAKES

1 cup (240 ml) evaporated milk

2 large eggs

3 cups (12.75 ounces/360 g) all-purpose flour, sifted

¼ cup (50 g) sugar

4 tablespoons (2 ounces/ 60 g) unsalted butter, melted

1 teaspoon vanilla extract

1 teaspoon baking powder

½ teaspoon freshly grated nutmeg

½ teaspoon fine sea salt

⅓ cup (80 ml) neutral oil

Honey, pancake syrup, or jam, for serving

NOTE: *To make wainar fulawa (also called yar lallaba), from the north, replace the milk with water and skip the eggs. Stir 1 small diced onion and 1 finely diced red habanero pepper into the batter. Fry in red palm oil or neutral oil and serve with Basic Yaji (page 26).*

These pancakes are known as diet, probably after "balanced diet," because they have the major food groups: carbs, protein, and fat. Nigerian pancakes are thinner and chewier than fluffy American-style pancakes but slightly thicker than crepes.

Though this recipe uses evaporated milk, which adds some creaminess and a slight caramelized flavor, feel free to use whole milk or a plant-based milk of your choice. The batter can be refrigerated in an airtight container for up to 3 days, so feel free to mix up a batch to have on hand so you can make fresh pancakes as desired.

Place an ovenproof dish in the oven and preheat the oven to 250°F (121°C).

In a blender, combine the milk, 2 cups (480 ml) water, eggs, 2 cups (240 g) of the flour, sugar, butter, vanilla, baking powder, nutmeg, and salt. Blend on high until a smooth batter forms. Add the remaining 1 cup (120 g) flour and blend until smooth and combined. Pour the batter into a large bowl.

Heat a 9-inch (23 cm) nonstick skillet over medium heat. Brush the surface of the hot skillet with a teaspoon of the oil. When the oil is shimmering, add ⅓ cup (80 ml) of the batter to the skillet and immediately swirl to fully coat the bottom in an even layer. Cook until the surface of the pancake is dry and small bubbles have appeared, the bottom is golden, and the edges begin to brown, 2 to 3 minutes. Carefully turn the pancake over and cook until the underside is golden, another minute or two. Transfer the pancake to the dish in the oven to keep warm and repeat with the remaining batter, adding more oil to the skillet between batches.

Serve warm, with honey, pancake syrup, or jam.

VARIATION

For a savory option, combine 1 cup (240 ml) pancake batter with ½ teaspoon dry pepper (see page 22), ½ teaspoon fine sea salt, and about 1 tablespoon each of finely diced red onion, two or three different colors of bell peppers, and carrots (about 5 tablespoons vegetables total).

WHEN EGGS BECAME POPULAR IN NIGERIA

Today, eggs are beloved in Nigeria, but that wasn't always the case. They became popular in the interwar period between the 1920s and '30s, under British colonial rule, when colonial teachers wrote egg recipes into cooking textbooks as part of domestic science curricula.

Global malnutrition was a major concern at this time. Rather than address the root causes of these concerns—poverty resulting from changes in agricultural practices from polycultures to monocultures, conversion of farming resources to produce cash crops instead of food crops, and high import taxes on food—the British government focused instead on education as the solution, positioning eggs as valuable food and inexpensive protein alternatives to meat.

We enjoy eggs many ways: Hard-boiled eggs are added to dishes like Mọ́ínmọ́ín Elewe (page 69). Eggs are used in soups, stews, and snacks like egg rolls and Scotch eggs. Fried eggs accompany bread in many forms, including shayi burgers—egg sandwiches ("risky burgers"), sometimes with sūya ("super shayi burgers"), pressed and toasted in a pan until golden—rice, yam, and plantain. And raw eggs are mixed into batters to enrich them.

NIGERIAN OMELET

3 large eggs

½ teaspoon fine sea salt

½ teaspoon dry pepper (see page 22), or 1 Scotch bonnet or habanero pepper, minced

2 tablespoons neutral oil

1 small onion, thinly sliced

1 Roma (plum) tomato, chopped

½ small green bell pepper, chopped

Golden brown, soft, and studded—not stuffed—with vegetables, Nigerian omelets are easy to rustle up for one or as part of a spread for family and friends. Don't be worried about making the perfect-looking omelet—focus more on its flavor. If you want to make the omelet more substantial, mash tinned sardines, canned corned beef, or flaked smoked mackerel into the eggs when you whisk them or sauté with the vegetables.

In a medium bowl, whisk the eggs lightly with the salt and dry pepper until frothy, 1 to 2 minutes.

In a large skillet or wok, heat the oil over medium-low to medium heat. When the oil is hot, add the onion and cook until just softened, 3 to 4 minutes. Add the tomato and bell pepper and cook until they soften, 2 to 3 minutes more.

Gently pour the whisked eggs evenly over the vegetables. Reduce the heat to low and cook until the eggs have set on the bottom, 2 to 3 minutes.

With a fish spatula, lift up the cooked egg and tilt the pan so the runny uncooked egg flows onto the surface of the pan. Cook until the underside is set, 1 to 2 minutes, then flip the omelet (if it breaks, don't worry). Cook until set on the second side, 1 to 2 minutes more.

Slide the omelet onto a plate and serve.

CORNED BEEF SAUCE

¼ cup (60 ml) neutral oil

1 large red onion, diced

2 dried bay leaves

1 teaspoon fine sea salt

½ large green bell pepper, diced

1½ teaspoons Curry Powder (page 25)

1½ teaspoons dried thyme

½ to 1 teaspoon freshly ground black or white pepper

3 cups (720 ml) Tomato Stew Base (page 335)

1 (12-ounce/340 g) can corned beef

½ medium red tatashe pepper or red bell pepper, diced

NOTE: *Instead of using canned corned beef, substitute crumbled tofu, mashed canned sardines, sausages (cut up and sautéed, then incorporated), or smoked mackerel (deboned and flaked before being added).*

This sauce is part of the quintessential Nigerian weekend breakfast. It reminds me of Bolognese, but made with canned corned beef crumbled into the tomato sauce.

Hold back on salting, as canned corned beef tends to be a touch salty. Serve with Boiled Yam (page 124), boiled or fried plantains, spaghetti, white rice, Agege bread (see page 75), or a host of other options.

In a medium sauté pan or wok, heat the oil over medium heat. When the oil is shimmering, stir in the onion, bay leaves, and ½ teaspoon of the salt and cook until the onion begins to caramelize, about 8 minutes.

Add half the bell pepper, the curry powder, thyme, and black pepper (to taste) and cook until aromatic, 1 to 2 minutes. Stir in the stew base, reduce the heat to low, cover, and cook until the flavors come together, 4 to 5 minutes.

Uncover and add the corned beef, mashing it with a fork or potato masher so it crumbles into the sauce. Stir well, cover with the lid ajar, and cook until the corned beef absorbs some sauce and the mixture resembles Bolognese, about 10 minutes.

Add the remaining bell pepper and the tatashe pepper. Stir until well incorporated and cook just until the pepper softens, 1 to 2 minutes. Taste and add some or all of the remaining salt as needed. Discard the bay leaves before serving.

EGG SAUCE

FOR THE SAUCE BASE

1 medium onion, cut into chunks

2 Roma (plum) tomatoes, cut into chunks

1 Scotch bonnet or habanero pepper, stemmed

FOR THE EGGS

½ cup (120 ml) neutral oil

1 medium onion, thinly sliced

2 dried bay leaves

2 teaspoons Curry Powder (page 25)

1 teaspoon sea salt

1 teaspoon dried thyme

2 Roma (plum) tomatoes, chopped

1 Scotch bonnet or habanero pepper, minced

½ medium green bell pepper, chopped

6 large eggs, lightly beaten

Boiled Yam (page 124), for serving

Think of this as eggs cooked in the classic Nigerian stew base of tomato, onion, and pepper (see page 335). The resulting dish has the consistency of soft curds, like scrambled eggs. Don't skip the green bell peppers. If you have leftover Classic Stew (page 193) on hand, use 1 cup (240 ml) of that instead of the sauce base.

Make the sauce base: In a blender, combine the onion, tomatoes, and Scotch bonnet and blend on high speed until just broken down.

Make the eggs: In a large sauté pan or skillet, heat the oil over medium heat. When the oil is shimmering, add the onion, bay leaves, curry powder, ½ teaspoon salt, and the thyme and cook, stirring to avoid scorching, until the onion softens, 3 to 4 minutes. Add the tomatoes, Scotch bonnet, and half the bell pepper and cook until they soften, 2 to 3 minutes.

Stir in the sauce base and the remaining ½ teaspoon salt. Bring to a boil, then reduce the heat to low, cover with the lid ajar, and cook, stirring every few minutes, until the sauce thickens and some oil comes up around the sides and surface, 8 to 10 minutes.

Gently stir in the eggs. Cover and cook, stirring every few minutes, until the eggs are cooked through and oil bubbles up around the sides and on top, 6 to 8 minutes. Stir in the remaining bell pepper, cover, and cook until the bell pepper brightens and softens a touch, 1 to 2 minutes. Remove from the heat and let stand for 2 to 3 minutes. Discard the bay leaves.

Serve with boiled yam.

VARIATION

Aji a kesen is a Tiv version made with red palm oil and a light stew base, then seasoned with fresh ginger, locust beans, and uziza peppercorns (see page 95). Add leafy vegetables like amaranth greens (see page 20) in the last few minutes of cooking.

1 cup (200 g) uncooked
shinkafan tūwō or Thai
jasmine rice

½ cup (120 ml) plus
2 tablespoons room-
temperature filtered water,
plus more for soaking

¼ cup (45 g) cooked white
rice

2 tablespoons plain full-fat
yogurt

3 tablespoons sugar

1½ teaspoons (0.15 ounce,
4.5 g) instant dry yeast

½ teaspoon fine sea salt

½ teaspoon baking powder

Neutral oil, for greasing

NOTE: *Cut leftover māsà
into 1-inch (2.5 cm) pieces
to make a hash. (This is my
preferred approach and
is not traditional.) I like to
add sūya bits (page 173),
with chopped fresh tomato,
onion, peppers, and lettuce,
finished with a sprinkling
of Yajin Kuli (page 26) and
a light groundnut (peanut)
butter sauce.*

MĀSÀ
SWEET FERMENTED RICE CAKES

I love these sweet and sometimes sour pancakes, commonly made
from fermented yeasted rice batter (but sometimes from millet,
wheat, or corn flour, a gift to us from the North East). Somewhat
crusty on the outside, soft and chewy (spongy) on the inside, they
are popular at home and as street food, served with yaji, soups, and
stews.

To make the batter, you'll need a high-powered blender. To cook
the rice cakes, you'll need a pan with divots or wells—a traditional
māsà pan called a kasko—or a clay, cast-iron, nonstick, or even
electric pan, similar to those used for East African vitumbua, Dutch
poffertjes, and Danish aebleskivers. The yield will vary depending on
the pan you use. The divots on most pans are 1 inch (2.5 cm) deep in
the center, but the diameter can vary, from 3 to 4 inches (7.5 to 10 cm)
wide for kaskos to about 2 inches (5 cm) wide for aebleskivers.

If you can't find Nigerian shinkafan tūwō, use Thai jasmine rice
or any short- or medium-grain rice, like idli, sushi, paella, or risotto
rice. To enjoy māsà for breakfast, start the recipe the evening before
so the rice has sufficient time to soak and soften—I've provided a
suggested timeline.

Enjoy māsà with Basic Yaji (page 26) and Beef Sūya (page 173) or
Mīyan Taushe (page 255) for savory takes, or drizzle with honey and
serve with fresh fruit for a sweet version.

Day 1, 10 p.m.—Soak the rice overnight.

Place the uncooked rice in a medium bowl and cover it with room-
temperature water. Use your hands to vigorously swish the rice
around for about 30 seconds, until the water turns cloudy. Drain in a
fine-mesh strainer set in the sink.

Return the drained rice to the bowl and add the filtered water to
cover by at least 2 inches (5 cm). Cover the bowl with a damp tea
towel and let it sit at room temperature for 6 to 12 hours. The rice
will whiten, grow in volume, and soften (it should break or crumble
when rubbed between your fingers), and may have a light, sweet
aroma.

RECIPE CONTINUES →

Day 2, 8 a.m.—Blend the mixture, then let it rise.

Drain the rice in a fine-mesh strainer set in the sink, shaking out as much water as possible, then transfer to a high-powered blender. Add the cooked rice, yogurt, 1 tablespoon of the sugar, yeast, and ½ cup (120 ml) of the filtered water. Blend on medium-high speed until you have a thick, smooth, and creamy batter. You may need to take breaks so you don't wear down the motor of the blender. Add the salt and blend again.

Pour the batter into a large bowl and cover with a damp tea towel. Let stand at warm room temperature (about 75°F/24°C), until domed or bubbling on top and sweetly aromatic, 1 to 2 hours. For a more sour māsà, ferment for longer.

Add the baking powder and the remaining 2 tablespoons sugar and whisk to fully incorporate and aerate the batter, 2 to 3 minutes. Add the remaining 2 tablespoons filtered water and whisk until well blended.

Heat a kasko or aebleskiver pan over medium-low heat. Use a pastry brush to grease each well of the pan with oil—let a little oil pool in each one. When the oil is shimmering, fill each well with batter to ⅛ inch (3 mm) from the rim (leaving some space unfilled ensures the batter won't spill over when you turn the māsà).

Reduce the heat to low, cover with a lid or heatproof bowl, and cook until the edges begin to dry—the center might still be liquid, 1 to 2 minutes. Run a spoon round the edge of each māsà to loosen it, then, using a chopstick, skewer, or tablespoon, turn each māsà over— use a scooping motion as though you were going to remove the māsà but then flip it over. Cook, turning the māsà three or four times, until light golden brown all over, 4 to 5 minutes total. Transfer the māsà to a heatproof bowl and cover with a tea towel so they stay soft. Repeat with the remaining batter, brushing the wells with more oil between batches.

Serve warm.

VARIATION

Sinasir, made from a thinned version of māsà batter (add ½ cup/ 120 ml water to the mix before cooking), is the perfect option for cooking in a frying pan or skillet, like pancakes. It is often cooked on one side only so you have a somewhat crunchy golden bottom with a

soft, white top with lots of bubbles, a bit like a crumpet. Heat a 9-inch (23 cm) nonstick skillet over low heat and grease it lightly with oil. Pour ⅓ cup (80 ml) of the māsà batter into the pan and swirl the pan gently to coat the bottom. Cover and cook until the surface is full of bubbles and dry to the touch, 3 to 4 minutes. Loosen the edges of the pancake with a small spatula and remove it from the pan. Place it on the counter and cover with a tea towel so it stays soft while you cook the remaining batter, greasing the pan between batches.

BEANS AND REMEMBRANCE

Beans are important in Nigerian daily life, and are essential in dishes during festivals and celebrations, particularly among the Yorùbá in the South West. When ìbejì (twins) are born to a family in Yorùbá, it is considered a special sign, full of blessings, and a celebratory dish of boiled ẹ̀wà ìbejì (a variety of black beans) is typically offered.

Popular varieties include Bambara beans, lima (butter) beans, red kidney beans, and pigeon peas. Cowpeas are the most common, with black-eyed peas at the top of the list. In Nigeria, the largest producer in the world (generating more than 90 percent of the world's production), they are simply called beans. In addition to several kinds of creamy white black-eyed peas, there are brown varieties that include the tan ẹ̀wà oloyin (which translates to "honey beans," because they have some sweetness) and darker brown drum and olo varieties.

In ancient times, àkàrà was an essential provision during wars, when the bean fritters were not only eaten and enjoyed as part of the victory feast after a battle but also used as ammunition. Today, it features during rites of passage: When an elder over seventy passes away, àkàrà is on the menu because "Àkàrà ni ounje oku"— àkàrà is the meal for the dead.

Across the South West and at various times of the year, àkàrà, mọ́ínmọ́ín, and a selection of bean dishes are prominent during festivals, many of which are steeped in history and mythology. In Uromi, in the south of Nigeria, the Iduamukpe festival is held annually in August to celebrate the oncoming harvest and arrival of new yams with ikpakpa, a variety of red kidney bean. The beans are gifted from younger to older siblings and from older to younger farmers.

Brown cowpeas/honey beans (top left), drum beans
(bottom right), and rice (top right)

KNEE CHOP

SALADS

Nor was dinner to be confused with knee chop which in terms of intake of calories closely approximated that of the dinner party with cold meats, salads, homemade crisps, and other relatively substantial fare available at a buffet table. A knee chop gathering was a highly informal affair where guests might be invited to remove their jackets and ties and were seated sometimes in the most unusual ways like sitting on a pouffe made in traditional Oyo leatherwork based on traditional prayer mat designs of the kind on which it was customary for the faithful to kneel upon when bowing in prayer in the direction of Mecca.

—IAN MCCALL, SWEET PASS KEROSENE

SALADS IN NIGERIA GENERALLY FALL INTO TWO GROUPS. One is based on indigenous ingredients, and the other, found across the country, is a variation on coleslaw, a vestige of British colonialism. The indigenous salads come from the east, dressed in emulsions of red palm oil, and from the north, tossed in nutty spice blends.

Many of the salads are served at room temperature, or warm, except for Nigerian salad, which is best served cold. This is the most popular salad to accompany jollof rice (page 143), Nigerian Fried Rice (page 149), and Mọ́ínmọ́ín Elewe (page 69), and is served at parties, in restaurants, and as street food. Salad cream, another remnant of British colonialism, is the dressing of choice. Like mayonnaise, it is a mix of acid, oil, and eggs, but it is made with hard-boiled-egg yolks instead of raw eggs and is runnier and more acidic thanks to the inclusion of mustard and vinegar. When it comes to flavor and texture, various salts and seasonings, from akaun (see page 95) to derivatives from it like Alkaline Water (page 334, sometimes made with food-grade ashes) feature in the salads and dressings, and fermented seasonings like ogiri (fermented seed pastes, page 25), dàddawā (fermented locust beans, page 24), and seasoning cubes (beef stock cubes) are common today.

CLOCKWISE FROM LEFT: *A vendor and his lettuce; red onions; "salad" and fried rice ingredients; kola nuts and bitter kola*

FEATURED IN THESE RECIPES

1. **Àbàchà.** An ingredient made from whole cassava roots that are peeled, cooked, shredded, soaked, and dried; also a dish.

2. **Akaun.** Gray rock salt also known as kaun, kanwa, or potash. Ground to a powder before use or made into Alkaline Water (page 334).

3. **Dry catfish.** Sold in rounds or chunks.

4. **Ehuru.** Has spicy notes with hints of lemon. Grind, grate, or pound before use.

5. **Garden eggs.** Roughly the size of hens' eggs, after which they are named, they are related to eggplant but are edible out of hand. Substitute Thai eggplant for raw dishes such as Àbàchà Ǹcha (page 103).

6. **Kola nuts.** The caffeine-rich edible seeds extracted from the pods of the kola tree.

7. **Kulīkulī.** Crackers, sticks, and cookies made from roasted groundnut (peanut) meal. See the recipe on page 277.

8. **Okana leaves.** Also known as afang (Efik, Ibibio) or ọkazī (Igbo). These leaves are used in Yedem'blong (page 110).

9. **Pea eggplants.** Also known as turkey berry. These small, bitter eggplants are crunchy, with a fresh, grassy, okro-like flavor.

10. **Red palm oil.** A staple, used in a variety of sauces like ǹcha (page 103).

11. **Scent leaves.** Fresh leaves with a delicate flavor somewhere between mint and holy basil, and a lemony brightness.

12. **Stock cubes.** Used to season sauces, and in some cases as a tableside condiment.

13. **Ugba.** Nutty and earthy, these chewy-crunchy fermented slices of African oil bean (*Pentaclethra macrophylla*) are sold fresh and dried.

14. **Uziza leaves.** Spicy, peppery leaves used fresh, frozen, dried, or ground.

15. **Uziza peppercorns.** Grown on the vine and sold fresh or dried. The peppercorns have curved tails and fruity, piney, and floral flavors; substitute black or cubeb pepper.

NIGERIAN SALAD

1 cup (100 g) shredded white or green cabbage

1 cup (100 g) shredded carrots

1 cup (75 g) shredded romaine or iceberg lettuce

½ cup (90 g) chopped firm Roma (plum) tomatoes (seeded, if you like), plus 1 firm tomato, cut into ¼-inch-thick (6 mm) slices

½ cup (65 g) chopped peeled cucumber (seeded if you like), plus ½ medium cucumber, cut into ¼-inch-thick (6 mm) slices (peeled and seeded, if you like)

¼ cup (30 g) diced green bell pepper

¼ cup (25 g) chopped scallions

Up to 3 tablespoons Homemade Salad Cream (recipe follows), plus more for serving

½ cup (125 g) canned vegetarian baked beans, preferably Heinz Original brand

2 hard-boiled eggs, peeled and cut into quarters, wedges, or slices

Simply known as "salad," this colorful, coleslaw-like mix is present at almost every Nigerian event, dressed with sweet, tangy, pale yellow salad cream.

In its simplest form, the salad is vegetarian, and combines cabbage, carrot (raw and grated, or chopped and cooked), lettuce, tomato, cucumber, green bell pepper, and boiled eggs. Add-ins might include cooked elements like baked beans, boiled potatoes, cooked green beans, fresh or blanched white or red onions, sweet corn, green peas (commonly marrowfat peas), kidney beans, and pasta (elbow macaroni and fusilli are common). Non-vegetarian versions might feature canned corned beef, sardines in oil, or flaked panfried tilapia.

Whichever way you choose to make it, this salad is best served cold. Make it up to a day ahead and store in an airtight container in the refrigerator until ready to serve. Leftovers can be refrigerated for up to 3 days.

In a shallow dish or platter, combine the cabbage, carrots, lettuce, chopped tomatoes, chopped cucumber, bell pepper, and scallions. Drizzle 2 to 3 tablespoons of the salad cream over the top. With a spoon, combine the vegetables gently but thoroughly.

Spread the coated vegetables into an even layer over the dish and spoon the baked beans over the top. Garnish with small piles of the tomato slices, cucumber slices, and hard-boiled eggs. Cover and refrigerate until cold, about 1 hour.

Serve with extra salad cream.

RECIPE CONTINUES →

Homemade Salad Cream

MAKES 1 CUP (240 ML)

1 tablespoon white wine vinegar

1 tablespoon confectioners' sugar

1 teaspoon yellow or Dijon mustard

1 cup (230 g) store-bought mayonnaise

Fine sea salt (optional)

Evaporated milk (optional)

Salad cream, like mayonnaise, is a mix of acid, oil, and eggs. It is runner than mayo, thanks to mustard and vinegar, and made with boiled egg yolks rather than raw. Heinz is the most popular brand of store-bought salad cream in Nigeria. You can make a version with mayonnaise that's runny, slightly sweet, and tangy—this no-cook recipe is ready in a few minutes. Feel free to adjust the amounts of vinegar (or lemon juice), sugar, and/or mustard to suit your palate. A splash of evaporated milk works well to loosen the consistency and bring a touch of sweet creaminess to the mix.

In a small bowl, whisk together the vinegar, confectioners' sugar, and mustard until well combined. Add the mayonnaise and whisk until well blended. Taste and add salt and/or evaporated milk, if desired. Use immediately or refrigerate in an airtight container for up to 1 week.

KA NANNAḌE
STEAMED TOESHOOT BEANS SALAD

2½ teaspoons fine sea salt, plus more as needed

½ pound (230 g) young toeshoot beans or trimmed fresh green beans or haricots verts

3 tablespoons neutral oil

1 small red onion, thinly sliced

4 scallions, white and light green parts separated and thinly sliced, plus more for garnish

½ Scotch bonnet or habanero pepper, minced

1 teaspoon Basic Yaji (page 26), plus more as needed

½ cup (70 g) toasted white or brown sesame seeds, coarsely ground

2 hard-boiled eggs, peeled and quartered, or garden eggs (see page 95), quartered, for serving

1 to 2 medium red tomatoes, quartered in wedges

2 tablespoons toasted white or brown sesame seeds (optional)

White rice and stew, for serving

NOTE: *Substitute roasted groundnuts (peanuts), cashews, or almonds for the sesame seeds, if need be.*

This bean salad dressed in a sesame seed mix is a gift from Celina Amanta Dabo (JP), my friend Linda's mum. It's popular with the Goemai and Ankwei people of the Plateau state in the North Central, and uses young, coiled toeshoot beans, similar to ram's horn or pretzel beans. The beans resemble fiddleheads, but they aren't ferns. When they are young, the mostly green pods, sometimes with streaks and tips of pink or purple, house small, soft, tender beans, much like green beans. And, like green beans, they only need to be cooked for a short time.

This salad is perfect for all your green bean needs, every day and for celebrations.

In a large bowl, prepare an ice bath by combining 1 cup (220 g) of ice with 4 cups (about 1 L) cold water.

Fill a saucepan with 4 cups (about 1 L) water and 2 teaspoons of the salt. Stir well and bring to a boil over high heat. Add the beans and blanch until they just begin to soften and brighten, about 2 minutes.

With a spider or slotted spoon, move the beans into the ice bath, stirring to cool, for about 20 seconds. Drain in a colander and set aside.

In a medium saucepan, warm the oil over medium heat for 1 to 2 minutes, then add the onion, scallion whites, and Scotch bonnet. Season with the remaining ½ teaspoon salt and the yaji and cook until a touch softened, 2 to 3 minutes. Remove half the mixture and reserve.

Add the cooked beans to the pan with the remaining onion mixture, stirring to combine. Top evenly with half the ground sesame seeds, and continue to cook, 3 to 4 minutes. Taste and adjust the seasoning with more yaji and/or salt as needed.

Transfer the bean mixture to a serving dish. Top with the reserved onion mixture, scallion greens, eggs, and tomatoes. Sprinkle on the toasted whole sesame seeds, if using.

Serve with the remaining ground sesame seeds, with rice and stew or on its own.

KWAɗÒN ZŌGALE

MORINGA SALAD

6 cups (250 g) fresh moringa leaves (see Notes and page 20)

1 teaspoon fine sea salt, or more as needed

1 large Roma (plum) tomato, diced

½ red onion, thinly sliced

½ medium cucumber, diced (seeded and peeled, if you like)

½ small green bell pepper, diced

¼ cup (60 ml) groundnut (peanut oil) or other neutral oil

About 1 cup (110 g) Kulīkulī Dressing (recipe follows)

4 to 8 beef seasoning cubes, for serving (see Notes; optional)

NOTES: *You'll find fresh moringa leaves in African, Indian, and even South American markets. For 6 cups (½ pound/250 g), you'll need just under 1 pound (about 400 g) of greens. You can substitute lacinato kale leaves for the moringa; remove the ribs and chop the leaves before cooking, then reduce the steaming time to 10 to 12 minutes and skip the bitterness test and adjustment, too.*

In the north of Nigeria, it is common not only to use stock cubes in cooking but to serve them at the table alongside meals as a condiment instead of salt.

Spicy, nutty, and earthy with some bitter notes, this salad of moringa leaves has its origins in the North West. The flavor of the leaves reminds me of the fermented tea leaves used in the classic Burmese salad laphet thoke. I steam and rinse the moringa leaves—steaming brings a silkiness to them but deepens their bitterness, hence the hot water rinse at the end. To finish? A sweet, salty, and nutty dressing.

Pluck the moringa leaves off their stalks and discard the stalks. Rinse the leaves in a colander, then drain.

Fill a stockpot with 2 to 3 inches (5 to 7.5 cm) of water. Place a steamer basket in the pot, cover, and bring to a boil over high heat. Place the moringa leaves in the steamer basket and season with the salt. Cover the pot tightly and steam until the leaves soften, wilt, and turn dark green, 35 to 40 minutes. Taste a leaf; if you find it too bitter, remove the leaves from the steamer and dunk them in freshly boiled water for about 1 minute to rinse off some of the bitterness.

Spread the leaves on a large plate to cool for about 10 minutes, then transfer them to a large bowl. Add the tomato, onion, cucumber, and bell pepper and stir to incorporate. Drizzle the oil over the greens and vegetables. Sprinkle two-thirds of the kulīkulī dressing over the greens and vegetables. Gently massage the leaves until everything is coated and evenly distributed.

Serve the salad at room temperature or chilled, with the remaining kulīkulī dressing alongside salt and 1 or 2 seasoning cubes per person, if using.

RECIPE CONTINUES →

Kulīkulī Dressing

**MAKES 1 HEAPING CUP
(110 G)**

1 cup (100 g) Kulīkulī
(page 277)

1 teaspoon Basic Yaji
(page 26), plus more as
needed

½ teaspoon sugar, plus
more as needed

½ teaspoon fine sea salt,
plus more as needed

1 or 2 beef seasoning cubes
(optional)

This dressing is made with kulīkulī, groundnut (peanut) crackers that are crushed to make a crumble of sorts. It gets sprinkled and mixed into the salad base, and you can serve an extra bowlful on the side.

In a food mill or food processor, or using a mortar and pestle, break down the kulīkulī until it becomes uniformly coarse and resembles almond meal. Transfer to a medium bowl or jar. Add the yaji, sugar, and salt. Crumble in 1 seasoning cube, if desired. Cover tightly or seal and shake until well blended. Taste and adjust the seasoning with more yaji, sugar, and/or salt, if needed, and crumble in some or all of the remaining seasoning cube.

Use right away, or cover and store at room temperature for up to 1 week or in the refrigerator for up to 1 month.

KWADO, MANY WAYS

Kwado, the collective name for salads in Hausa (a language in the north of Nigeria), features a main ingredient tossed in a sweet and nutty dressing made with neutral oil, Kulīkulī (page 277), and Basic Yaji (page 26), sweetened with sugar. The name reflects the main ingredient, so a version with kabeji (cabbage) becomes kwaɗòn kabeji.

There are many directions to take this salad, from fresh vegetables—cucumbers; garden cress, also known as labsur, lausur, and (erroneously) lansir; lettuce—to steamed ones with alayyahu (amaranth greens); cooked ingredients—like rice, couscous, and pasta; or root vegetables, or a combination. Though the main ingredient can be prepared from scratch, it is also a great way to transform leftovers.

Some examples: Kwaɗon Māsà features cut-up Māsà (page 85), similar to Lebanese fattoush or Italian panzanella. Boiled root vegetables like yam (page 124) and sweet potatoes work well, like potato salads. Want some protein? Add sūya (page 173) or Fried Awara (page 181). Kanzo, aka bottom pot (see page 145), the toasty, crunchy layer of rice or starch at the bottom of the pot (similar to Spanish socarrat), goes into kwaɗòn kanzo, broken up, softened in water, drained, then dressed. Regardless of the kwado you choose, the goal is a mix of textures and flavors—soft, crunchy, sweet, slightly salty, nutty, and more. Include other vegetables you enjoy, such as carrots, sweet peppers, pea eggplants, or garden eggs.

ÀBÀCHÀ ǸCHA

SHREDDED CASSAVA SALAD WITH PALM OIL DRESSING

2 cups packed (3½ ounces/ about 100 g) dried àbàchà

Boiling water, as needed

1 teaspoon fine sea salt, plus more as needed

1 cup (3.2 ounces/90 g) ugba, rinsed and drained

¼ cup (60 ml) red palm oil

2 tablespoons ground crayfish (see page 23)

1 teaspoon ground ehuru (see page 25)

½ teaspoon dry pepper (see page 22), plus more as needed

½ teaspoon ogiri (see page 25; optional)

1 beef seasoning cube (optional)

½ cup (65 to 75 g) deboned and flaked dry fish, smoked fish, or cooked stockfish (1-inch/2.5 cm pieces; see page 24; optional)

2 tablespoons Alkaline Water (page 334), plus more as needed

FOR SERVING

1 small red onion, sliced into rings

1 cayenne or other long red pepper, sliced

Handful of pea eggplants, and/or 4 garden eggs, sliced

2 or 3 utazi or uziza leaves (see page 95), shredded

4 (3-ounce/85 g) pieces Fried Fish (page 167) or grilled fish

Àbàchà is a combination of softened rehydrated shredded cassava and chewy-crunchy sliced ugba, or oil bean seeds, dressed in ǹcha, a sauce made by combining alkaline water with palm oil. My method of preparing ǹcha is not traditional, but I find it easier to make this way. Also known as African salad, this Igbo delicacy from the east of Nigeria is a popular appetizer at parties, but is also a popular street food, and can be served with a host of things, from smoked fish and stockfish to garden eggs, red onions, hot peppers, and herbs like uziza, utazi, and scent leaves. The sweetness of the cassava, the umami-earthiness of the ugba, and the chewy-crunchy textures make a delightful combination.

NOTES: *If you can't find precooked and fermented ugba, rinse and rehydrate ¾ cup (75 g) dried ugba in hot water until it softens, about 20 minutes, then use as you would cooked.*

If using fish with bones, be sure to remove and discard them before incorporating the fish into the dish.

Place the àbàchà in a large bowl and add boiling water to cover. Let it sit for a minute, then drain, rinse with cold water, and drain again.

Transfer the àbàchà to a large bowl and add the salt and cold water to cover the àbàchà by 2 to 3 inches (5 to 7.5 cm). Stir well to distribute the salt, cover, and let stand at room temperature for about 1 hour to soften and rehydrate. Drain and set aside.

Steep the ugba in a medium bowl filled with hot water for a minute or two, then rinse and drain; set aside.

In a medium pot off the heat, combine the palm oil, ground crayfish, ehuru, dry pepper, and ogiri (if using). Stir until well mixed. Add the ugba and àbàchà to the pot and stir well so the shreds are somewhat coated in the sauce.

Stir in the fish (if using) and cook over low heat, stirring until the mixture is warmed all the way through and well combined, 7 to 8 minutes. Remove from the heat, allow to cool for 4 to 5 minutes,

then stir in the alkaline water; the sauce will lighten in color, turning yellow-orange, and thicken.

Taste and season the mixture with more salt, dry pepper, and/or the seasoning cube, if needed.

Serve warm (it is also great at room temperature), topped with onion, cayenne pepper, pea eggplant, garden eggs, utazi, and fried fish. Leftovers can be refrigerated in an airtight container for up to 2 days. Gently reheat before serving.

VARIATIONS

To make stir-fried àbàchà, cook some red palm oil with onions and hot peppers, season with ground crayfish, ground ehuru, dry pepper, ogiri (optional), salt, and seasoning cube (optional), then stir in the rehydrated àbàchà, ugba, and fish. The result is orange-tinged àbàchà but without the creamy coating that ǹcha provides. If stir-fried àbàchà is the lean version, àbàchà ǹcha is the luxe one.

To make àbàchà akïdï, add ½ cup (85 g) cooked akïdï, small black beans that are popular in the South East of Nigeria.

ÌMÓYÒ ẸLẸ̀JA
FISH ESCABECHE WITH SALSA

1 small green bell pepper, finely chopped

½ to 1 Scotch bonnet or habanero pepper, minced

2 garlic cloves, finely chopped

1 teaspoon whole uziza peppercorns (see page 95), plus ground uziza pepper as needed

2 teaspoons fine sea salt, plus more as needed

⅓ cup (80 ml) white wine vinegar or fresh lime or lemon juice

⅓ cup (80 ml) extra-virgin olive oil

1 pound (450 g) fresh tilapia fillets

2 dried bay leaves

1 heaping teaspoon tomato paste

Dry pepper (see page 22; optional)

1 large red tomato, such as Roma (plum), finely chopped

1 small red onion, finely chopped

This delicious árá Ẹ̀kọ (traditional Lagos) dish is a vinegar- or lime juice–marinated fish prepared in the manner of ìmóyò dishes, which combine West African, Brazilian, and Portuguese culinary traditions and typically feature green peppers, olive oil, vinegar, lime or lemon juice, and garlic in the manner of escabeche. Tilapia, snapper, croaker and mackerel are popular choices for the fish, which is cooked and flaked. This recipe combines elements of Portuguese molho escabeche with Brazilian molho à campanha, a salsa of sorts.

The cooking stock is used for both the marinade in this dish and for Ìmóyò Ẹba (page 220). You can use whole fish or fillets, add shrimp or prawns, even explore other kinds of seafood. Though not traditional, cilantro or parsley makes a great finish to the mix.

Enjoy on its own, or with white rice or ìmóyò ẹba.

In a small mortar, combine half the bell pepper, half the Scotch bonnet, 1 garlic clove, the uziza peppercorns, and 1½ teaspoons of the salt. Pound with the pestle until the ingredients come together to form a paste. Stir in 2 tablespoons of the vinegar and 2 tablespoons of the olive oil. Taste and adjust the salt as needed.

Rub the paste all over the fish fillets. Cover and set in the refrigerator to marinate for at least 10 minutes and up to 1 hour.

In a large sauté pan, combine 4 cups (about 1 L) water, the bay leaves, the remaining ½ teaspoon salt, the remaining garlic clove, and half the tomato paste. Cover and bring to a boil over medium heat. Reduce the heat to low and add the seasoned fish. Cover and poach until the fish is just cooked through, 7 to 8 minutes. Do a flake test: With the blunt side of a table knife, gently pull apart the flesh of the fish at the thickest part—it should flake easily. Remove from the heat and transfer the fish to a heatproof bowl (leave the liquid in the pan). Gently break up the fish into 1- to 2-inch (2.5 to 5 cm) chunks. Cover and set aside.

Whisk the remaining tomato paste, 2 tablespoons of the vinegar, and 2 tablespoons of the olive oil into the poaching liquid. Bring to a gentle simmer over medium heat. Taste the stock and adjust the seasoning, if needed, with salt and hot or dry pepper. Cook, uncovered, stirring gently, until the flavors meld, 4 to 5 minutes.

RECIPE CONTINUES →

Remove from the heat. Spoon ¼ cup (60 ml) of the stock over the fish and gently fold. Taste and season the fish with additional salt and ground uziza pepper, if needed. Reserve the rest of the seafood stock for serving and for Ìmóyò Ẹba (page 220; you'll need about 2 cups/480 ml).

Put the chopped tomato in a medium bowl. Season with salt and the remaining olive oil. Gently toss, then cover and set aside until the tomato releases its juices, 10 to 15 minutes. Add the remaining vinegar, bell pepper, Scotch bonnet, and the onion. Taste and season with more salt, lemon or vinegar, and/or dry pepper (if using). Discard the bay leaves and fold in the fish and stock.

Serve, or cover and refrigerate for at least 1 hour and up to 2 days before serving cold or at room temperature.

ABOUT ÌMÓYÒ

The fifteenth-century transatlantic trade in enslaved Africans began with the Portuguese, who forcibly took West Africans to Madeira, the Canary Islands, and then Brazil, where West African culinary traditions took root. In the nineteenth century, when chattel slavery was abolished, formerly enslaved West African people returned home. In Nigeria, they settled on the coast and brought with them new ingredients and flavors such as green bell peppers, olive oil, vinegar, and garlic.

Ìmóyò, from the Portuguese *molho*, meaning sauce or gravy, shows up in Nigerian dishes in two key ways: ọbẹ̀ ìmóyò, a light stew with a blend of tomatoes, onions, and peppers; and ìmóyò dishes like this one that are more salad than sauce, made with seafood like fish, crab, and prawns and with chicken. There is also Ìmóyò Ẹba (page 220), in which a seasoned ìmóyò stock is used as the base for a dough.

Fish sellers at Makoko Market, Lagos

YEDEM'BLONG
LEAF WRAPS WITH FISH AND KOLA NUT

3 Scotch bonnet or habanero peppers, coarsely chopped

⅓ cup (80 ml) red palm oil

1 medium red onion, grated or finely chopped

2 teaspoons ground eheru (see page 25)

1 teaspoon fine sea salt, plus more as needed

¼ cup (37.5 g) Roasted Groundnuts (page 200), skinned

4 cups (200 g) fresh young okana leaves (see Note), washed

2 kola nuts, cut in half, then into roughly ¼-inch-thick (6 mm) wedges

2 garden eggs, cut into eighths

1 whole smoked or dry catfish, broken into 1-inch (2.5 cm) pieces

1 cup (200 g) chopped cooked pomo (cowskin; see page 21; 1-inch/2.5 cm pieces)

NOTE: *If you can't find okana leaves, use soft, leafy lettuce.*

My friend Carol introduced me to this feast of okana leaf wraps, perfect for gatherings and beloved in her hometown of Ugep, in southern Nigeria. The name yedem'blong combines *yedem*, "that which is of men," and *blong*, "things," in the Yakurr language. It is the first traditional Nigerian recipe I know of that incorporates kola nuts—the original source of cola essence for the popular soft drink—as part of a dish.

Rinse and drain the peppers. In a mortar, pound the peppers with a pestle until they are broken down.

In a small pot, warm the oil over medium-high heat. Add the onion, ground eheru, and salt. Stir and cook, until the onion reduces, 7 to 8 minutes. Add the pounded peppers, stir, reduce the heat, and cook until the peppers no longer look raw, 4 to 5 minutes. Remove from the heat and gently stir in ¼ cup (60 ml) water so the mixture becomes saucy.

Just before serving, stir the groundnuts into the sauce. Set up a platter with the okana leaves, kola nuts, catfish, pomo, garden eggs, and pepper sauce.

To serve, make leaf wraps by laying 2 or 3 okana leaves over each other. Put a piece of kola nut in the leaves, then fold or roll the leaves to enclose it. Dip the roll into the pepper sauce and enjoy, with garden eggs, fish, and pomo alongside. Repeat until you've had enough.

THE SIGNIFICANCE OF KOLA NUTS IN NIGERIA

Nigerians believe that "He who brings kola brings life." The caffeine-rich kola nut plays a huge role in Nigerian culture and hospitality, featuring in religious ceremonies and rites, events, and celebrations where elders "break kola" into tiny pieces, which are placed in bowls or trays and passed around for guests.

An orange seller's cart
filled with Nigerian oranges,
which are green-yellow in color

FRUITS

If you want to know what's in season in Nigeria, look to the streets, where wooden tables and stalls, roadside baskets, and wheelbarrows are brimming with fresh and colorful fruits and vegetables—whole, peeled, cut, or prepared to order.

Some, like June plums with their spiky cores, herald harmattan, the peak of the dry season in December. Others, like agbalumo, cashew apples, cucumbers, mangoes, passion fruit, velvet tamarind, rose apples, pitanga (Surinam cherries), soursop, and guavas, traverse seasons, from dry to rainy. When the rains come in March, the fruits fall hard, leaving petrichor and lush green in their wake. Save for a few weeks in August when it's dry, it rains until October. With overcast skies, gray and thunderous, you might find ackee on trees, monkey kola (*Cola lepidota, C. millenii*), fresh dates, and groundnuts (peanuts; see page 267).

Fruits are mostly eaten fresh and out of hand throughout the day, or sometimes as side dishes; only a few fruits, such as tamarind (page 309) and baobab, are dried or preserved, or processed into syrups, like amoriri (black plums).

For many Nigerians, there's a strong association with fruit in childhood, from the trays of fruit for sale outside school at break time and at the end of the day. Growing up, eating fruit from our backyards and gardens was common. My siblings, friends, and I would play suwe, a game like hopscotch and ten ten—like rock paper scissors but with rhythmic clapping and chanting, and using legs instead of hands. These games stirred up hunger and thirst, which we assuaged with fruits like ebelebo (sea almond or Malabar almond, known simply as "fruit"

in some parts), pitanga, guavas, mangoes, and lots more.

Watching as orange sellers peel the fruits is mesmerizing. Once you're done selecting yours from tables stacked high or wheelbarrows or basins filled with them, you can choose to have your oranges peeled. The clean fruit begins in the peeler's nondominant hand, and a peeling tool—a sharp knife or razor blade—in the other, and then the dance begins between the orange, gently rotated, and the peeler, cutting in and removing slivers or ribbons of skin, all without slicing too deep into the pith and bruising it. The skin is added to a pile of peels, scented with a delightful combination of sweet, citrusy, and refreshing notes, and the peeled orange is cut—at the top, or across its equator, ready to squeeze.

Temperate fruits, like strawberries and mulberries, grow in parts of the north, particularly in Jos, a region that sits about 4,000 feet (1,200 m) above sea level. From November to January, temperatures in Jos can dip below 70°F (21°C), perfect for the most delicious "winter" berries.

There's ube, the African pear (*Dacryodes edulis*), worthy of mention because it has a similar deep purple color to Filipino ube, though that's where the resemblance ends. Nigerian ube is a drupe, not a yam, 2 to 3 inches (5 to 7.5 cm) long, and an inch (2.5 cm) or so wide. The skin is pink to deep purple and dark blue, covering flesh that's yellow to various shades of bright green.

Whatever season you find yourself in, in Nigeria, you're bound to find a variety of fruits to enjoy. In fact, Nigerians in diaspora have been known to plan trips home around seasonal produce.

ALL DAY, EVERY DAY

MAINS AND SIDE DISHES

YAMS, SWEET POTATOES, POTATOES, CASSAVA, AND

cocoyam (taro), even fruits treated as vegetables like plantain and breadfruit, are an essential part of Nigerian meals, eaten any time of day and year-round because they are abundant, accessible, easy to grow, and affordable.

On the streets, vendors prepare vegetables round the clock and sell them in various combinations. In Lagos, a quartet of fried foods—Àkàrà (page 64), fried yam, fried sweet potato, and Dòdò, served with Ata Dindin (page 332)—is popular in the morning and evenings, though in some parts of the city you will find them throughout the day. They're bought by everyone and anyone, including schoolchildren and office workers.

Roots, tubers, and vegetables are often salted before—not after—frying. The salt is for seasoning, not for drawing out moisture. The result is salted foods without the sharp saltiness and layer of grit that salting after frying might bring.

You won't find many cooks checking oil temperatures with thermometers. For shallow- or deep-frying, Nigerians will test the readiness of the oil by putting in a piece of onion—a ring, a quarter, or a piece of the vegetable to be fried—much in the same way as people test with bread; when the oil bubbles around the onion, it's ready. There is caution and respect for hot oil, without a lot of fear. Typically, food is fried as needed, removed from the oil, transferred to a strainer to drain, and served as desired. Use your oven to keep the fried food warm if preparing large batches, though this isn't a classic approach in the Nigerian kitchen.

Pottages, sometimes called porridges, are one-pot dishes made from cereals, grains, or starchy vegetables, in chunks or grated. Sometimes, one vegetable stars, and other times, they are combined, as in yam and plantain pottage.

CLOCKWISE FROM LEFT: *A roadside stall, with green bananas on display; oven-roasted yam; dry fish and stockfish with ose nsukka, a hot aromatic pepper; tubers of yam*

FEATURED IN THESE RECIPES

1. **Scotch bonnet and habanero peppers.** These peppers are interchangeable, and are the most common.

2. **Green plantains.** These are unripe plantains, with pale, firm flesh and mild, slightly tangy flavors. They are the starchiest plantains (compared with ripe and overripe ones), and hold their shape during cooking.

3. **Yellow plantains**. Medium-ripe to ripe plantains; softer, sweeter, and not as starchy as green (unripe) plantains. Unlike bananas, plantains can be refrigerated, so if you find some at a stage of ripening you like, pop them in the fridge until you're ready to cook them.

4. **Trinidad pimento peppers.** These peppers, also known as Caribbean seasoning peppers, though not traditional to Nigerian cuisine, deliver a lot of flavor without heat and are perfect for cooking.

5. **Red onions.** The most common onion used in Nigerian cooking.

6. **Sweet potatoes.** White- and yellow-fleshed sweet potatoes are the most common in Nigeria. Dry-textured, like yams, with a sweet, earthy, nutty flavor, there are two main varieties: a purpled-red-skinned variety similar to Cuban boniato and Japanese satsumaimo, and a tan-skinned variety similar to the Hannah variety.

7. **Yams.** Brown skinned, and much larger than sweet potatoes.

DÒDÒ

(SWEET) FRIED RIPE PLANTAIN

4 ripe plantains, yellow
with black spots (about
2 pounds/900 g total), rinsed

1½ teaspoons fine sea salt

Neutral oil, for frying

**THREE WAYS TO CUT
PLANTAINS**

You can cut plantains
different ways,
depending on how you
are eating them or
pairing them:

- On the bias when
  they make up the
  main meal or are
  paired with white
  rice
- Diced for jollof
  rice (page 143) and
  Gizdòdò (page 169)
- In rounds, especially
  for super-sweet,
  soft, overripe
  plantains, with beans
  or white rice

Cooking times will vary
depending on the size
of the plantain pieces.

Dòdò is made with sweet ripe plantains, yellow with black streaks
and spots, deep-fried until caramelized. You can serve dòdò with
savory dishes at any time of day. Some people prefer their plantains
unsalted, while others—like me—know the best plantains are salted
before frying to bring out the perfect swalty (sweet-salty) flavor.

Fried plantains are best enjoyed immediately with Nigerian
Omelet (page 81), beans, jollof rice (page 143), stew, or Ata Dindin
(page 332).

On a cutting board, use a sharp knife to cut off the pointed ends of
the plantains. With the tip of the knife, slice into the skin along the
length of the plantain without cutting into the flesh. Pry the skin
apart and discard it, along with any fibrous strings.

Cut the plantains as you like: ½-inch (1.3 cm) dice, ⅓-inch-thick
(8.5 mm) rounds, or slices on the bias, about 2 inches (5 cm) long and
⅓ to ½ inch (8.5 mm to 1.3 cm) thick. Place the pieces in a large bowl,
sprinkle with the salt, toss, and gently rub so each piece is salted.

Preheat the oven to 200°F (95°C). Line a rimmed baking sheet with
a wire rack or paper towels.

Fill a wok or large Dutch oven with 1½ to 2 inches (3.8 to 5 cm) oil;
it should come no more than halfway up the vessel. Heat the oil over
medium-high heat to 350°F (175°C).

Carefully add some plantain pieces to the hot oil without
overcrowding the pan. Ensure the pieces stay separate; otherwise,
they will not cook properly. Cook, stirring occasionally until the
plantain edges caramelize and begin to brown, then flip the pieces
over and cook until golden brown and caramelized all over, 8 to
10 minutes. With a spider or slotted spoon, transfer the dòdò to
the prepared baking sheet and keep warm in the oven. Repeat with
the remaining plantains, allowing the oil to return to temperature
between batches.

Serve warm. Leftovers can be refrigerated in an airtight container
overnight. Reheat in the microwave, refry, or warm in a moderate
(350°F/175°C) oven.

BỌLẸ
ROASTED PLANTAIN

4 large plantains (about
2 pounds/900 g total), rinsed

Fine sea salt

Dry pepper (see page 22)

Red palm oil

This street snack goes by many names, and is eaten in different ways. In Warri, bọlẹ is enjoyed with groundnuts (peanuts) or palm oil; in Lagos, boli is accompanied by groundnuts or groundnut oil; and in Port Harcourt, bọlẹ is paired with a red pepper sauce and grilled fish like mackerel or croaker. Some sellers, like Mama Chika, my favorite bọlẹ vendor, who has a stall off Old Aba Road in Port Harcourt, include a number of sides like ugba (see page 95), utazi (see page 20), and red onions.

Just-ripe plantains have the perfect texture and flavor for bọlẹ—firm enough to withstand turning on the grill, with the right amount of sweetness. Super-ripe plantains can be grilled, too, but become very sweet and sticky. If you don't have a grill, an oven or air fryer would work well for this recipe, albeit without the smoky flavor.

On a cutting board, use a sharp knife to remove the pointed ends of the plantains. With the tip of the knife, slice into the skin along the length of the plantains without cutting into the flesh. Pry the skin apart and discard it, along with any fibrous strings. Leave the plantains whole or cut them in half on a bias along the length.

Cook using one of the following methods:

Outdoor grill: Grill the plantains over direct heat, turning every few minutes, until they're cooked somewhat evenly with dark patches, about 20 minutes.

Oven: Preheat the oven to 425°F (218°C). Line a rimmed baking sheet with parchment paper and set the plantain on it. Roast for 20 minutes, flipping several times, until golden brown.

Broiler: Preheat the broiler to high. Place the plantains on a clean wire rack or sturdy baking sheet and position them 6 to 8 inches (15 to 20 cm) from the broiler heat source. Broil for about 20 minutes, flipping the plantains three or four times, until browned all over.

Air fryer: Arrange the plantains on the air fryer tray in a single layer. Air-fry at 350°F (175°C) for about 10 minutes, then flip them and cook until golden brown in parts, 5 to 6 minutes more.

Serve with salt, dry pepper, and red palm oil alongside.

BOILED YAM

1 pound (450 g) West African yams

1½ teaspoons fine sea salt

Peanut oil or other neutral oil

EIGHT WAYS TO ENJOY BOILED YAM

1. With Nigerian Omelet (page 81) or Egg Sauce (page 84)
2. With spiced oil (see page 157)
3. With Chicken Pepper Soup (page 239)
4. With Corned Beef Sauce (page 82)
5. With Classic Stew (page 193)
6. With Èfọ́ Rírò (page 250)
7. With salted palm oil or butter
8. With Garden Egg Sauce (page 204)

I was a student in the United Kingdom in the late 1990s the first time I bought yam abroad. I was stunned—you didn't have to buy a whole tuber, you could buy sections. Whole tubers were so expensive, I joked that I could get a barn full of yams back home in Nigeria for the same price! These days, it's much easier to find West African yams across the world, and whole tubers are more affordable than they used to be.

Unlike potato skins, boiled yam skins are not edible. Like potatoes, however, the yams can be boiled skin-on or peeled. Some people experience an itch when they come in contact with raw yam skins, so for them, cooking skin-on is a good alternative. You can also oil your hands or wear food-safe gloves when handling the yams. When boiling skin-on yams, scrub them well with a piece of steel wool to remove any debris or dirt before cooking, and remove the skin before serving.

Boiled yam can be served whole or roughly mashed.

On a cutting board, cut the yams crosswise in half and stand them cut-side down. With a vegetable peeler or sharp knife, peel the yams. Rinse the yams under cold running water and rinse the cutting board, too. Cut the peeled yams crosswise into 1-inch-thick (2.5 cm) rounds, or cut them into 2-inch (5 cm) rounds and then quarter the rounds to make smaller pieces. If you're not cooking them immediately, place the yams in a bowl and cover with cold water to prevent them from discoloring. Drain and rinse before cooking.

Put the yams in a large pot and add cold water to cover by at least 2 inches (5 cm). Add the salt and stir. Dip a piece of paper towel in the oil and grease the top 2 inches (5 cm) of the inside of the pot, from the rim down; this helps prevent the water from boiling over.

Cover and bring to a boil over high heat, about 10 minutes. Reduce the heat to medium and cook until the yams are fork-tender, 10 to 15 minutes. Drain the yams and return them to the pot for 3 to 5 minutes so they can dry out a bit.

Serve warm. Store leftovers in an airtight container in the refrigerator for up to 5 days. Leftovers can also be used for Yam Balls (page 42) or Doya (page 127). Reheat by putting the yams in a medium pot with some water and warming over low heat until hot all the way through.

VARIATIONS

To make candied yams (not the same as North American candied yams made with sweet potatoes), add 2 to 4 tablespoons (25 to 50 g) sugar to the water when you add the salt. Some people also use less water to cook the yams so that at the end, there's a creamy caramel sauce at the bottom of the pot.

Plantains can be boiled like yams, and just-ripe plantains are perfect for this. Firm, with yellow skin sometimes streaked with green, they offer the right balance of starch and natural sugars, bringing a measured sweetness that isn't overwhelming. Cook them peeled or with the skin on—boiling the plantains in their skins deepens the flavor. The cook time will vary depending on how ripe your plantains are and the size of the cut pieces. Just-ripe plantains cut into 2- or 3-inch (5 to 7.5 cm) pieces will cook in 12 to 15 minutes.

Cooked plantains will soften and should be fork-tender—unripe plantains will be firm. They are opaque, and light yellow, orange, peach, or a mix of colors when raw. Once cooked, they become translucent, with colors varying from light to sunny yellow.

DOYA

FRIED YAM

2 pounds (900 g) West African yams

2 teaspoons fine sea salt

Neutral oil, for frying

Fried yam is to Nigerians what french fries and chips are to North Americans and Europeans. Many years ago, when I worked on Lagos Island, my colleagues and I would treat ourselves to a special quartet of street foods for breakfast—Àkàrà (page 64), fried yam, fried sweet potatoes, and Agege bread (see page 75) from the Iya oni Dundu, the mama (market vendor) who sells fried yam. On the side, we would have pomo (cowhide) in Ata Dindin (page 332).

Serve with Nigerian Omelet (page 81), Classic Stew (page 193), beans, èfó (page 250), or anything else you like.

On a cutting board, cut the yams in half crosswise and stand them cut-side down. With a vegetable peeler or sharp knife, peel the yams. Rinse the peeled yams under cold running water and rinse the cutting board, too. Cut the peeled yams crosswise into 1-inch-thick (2.5 cm) rounds, then cut the rounds into smaller pieces. Options:

Rounds: Cut into thinner rounds, about ⅓ inch (8.5 mm) thick.

Quarters: Cut each round into 4 parts.

Crescents: These are like potato wedges but larger. Cut each round in half to make half-moons, then cut each half-moon in half diagonally to form wedges.

Chips: Cut ½- to ¾-inch-thick (1.3 to 2 cm) batons.

Fill a large bowl with cold water, add 1 teaspoon of the salt, and stir well to dissolve. Add the yams to the salted water. For best results, set the yams aside to soak for 1 to 2 hours on the counter or in the refrigerator overnight (you can, however, drain and fry them immediately).

Preheat the oven to 200°F (95°C). Line a rimmed baking sheet with a wire rack or paper towels.

Fill a wok or large Dutch oven with 1½ to 2 inches (3.8 to 5 cm) of oil; it should come no more than halfway up the vessel. Heat the oil over medium-high heat to 350°F (175°C).

RECIPE CONTINUES →

Drain the yams and transfer to a large bowl. Sprinkle with the remaining 1 teaspoon salt and toss to coat. Working in batches, add the yams to the hot oil and fry, stirring occasionally, until light yellow on both sides, crispy and crunchy on the outside, and soft and fluffy on the inside, 5 to 10 minutes. With a spider or slotted spoon, transfer the yams to the prepared baking sheet and keep warm in the oven for no more than 15 to 20 minutes while you fry the remaining yams. Allow the oil to return to temperature between batches.

Allow the yam to rest for a couple of minutes before serving—the insides tend to become even fluffier. Leftovers can be refrigerated in an airtight container overnight and refried to reheat before serving.

VARIATIONS

Air-fried yam: Lightly grease the yams with neutral oil. Arrange the yams on the air fryer tray in a single layer. Air-fry at 350°F (175°C) for about 10 minutes, then flip them and cook until golden brown in parts, 5 to 6 minutes more.

Fried cocoyam: Known as dundu koko in Yorùbá. Replace the yam with cocoyam (taro); soak and cook as directed.

YAM POTTAGE
YAM COOKED IN A SAUCE

1½ pounds (680 g) West African yams

¼ cup (60 ml) red palm oil

1 medium red onion, thinly sliced

1 teaspoon fine sea salt, plus more as needed

1 teaspoon dry pepper (see page 22), plus more as needed

2 tablespoons ground crayfish (see page 23) or fish powder

1 cup (240 ml) Pepper Stew Base (page 335)

About 8 ounces (250 g) dry fish, deboned and broken into pieces (optional)

1 cup (30 g) shredded ugu (optional)

2 tablespoons shredded scent leaves (optional)

1 small red tatashe pepper, cut into short strips

This is a dish of yam chunks cooked in a stew base—either tomato or pepper, historically called Palm Oil Chop. You can add meat, shellfish, or fish (fresh, dried, or smoked) and finish with leafy greens like ugu or herbs like scent leaves. There are versions made with only yam and those like ji na u̱gbò̱gù̱rù̱ (Igbo, eastern Nigeria) that feature a combination of yam, orange muskmelons or pumpkin, and cooked beans.

This plant-forward dish is quick to the table and can be easily made without meat or seafood—mushrooms, garden eggs, or Fried Awara (page 181) can be added. Red palm oil is often used, but there are versions made with peanut oil or other neutral oils, and even palm nut cream (page 235).

Serve on its own, or with Classic Stew (page 193), Fried Meat (page 330), Fried Fish (page 167), or Dòdò (page 120).

On a cutting board, cut the yams crosswise in half and stand them cut-side down. With a vegetable peeler or sharp knife, peel the yams. Rinse the yams under cold running water and rinse the cutting board, too. Cut the peeled yams crosswise into 1-inch-thick (2.5 cm) rounds, or cut them into 2-inch-thick (5 cm) rounds, then quarter them to make smaller pieces. Place the yams in a large bowl and add cold water to cover to prevent discoloring.

In a medium saucepan, warm the palm oil over medium heat. When the oil is shimmering, add the onion and salt. Stir well and cook until somewhat softened, translucent, and orange-tinged, about 5 minutes. Add the dry pepper and ground crayfish and stir for a minute, until aromatic. Add the pepper stew base and cook until the sauce thickens a bit and oil floats to the top, about 15 minutes. Add 6 cups (about 1.5 L) water and the dry fish (if using). Stir well. Reduce the heat to the lowest setting, cover, and cook for 5 to 10 minutes, until hot.

Drain the yams, then add them to the pepper mixture. Stir well, cover, and cook, stirring occasionally, until the yam is fork-tender and the sauce has thickened, about 30 minutes. Mash some of the yams to thicken the mixture until the sauce is like light porridge—it will thicken further as it stands. Taste and add salt and dry pepper, if needed.

RECIPE CONTINUES →

Remove from the heat. Add the ugu and/or scent leaves (if using), along with the tatashe pepper. Sprinkle some salt over the top. Cover and let steam in the residual heat of the pottage for 5 minutes, then serve.

VARIATIONS

Yam and plantain pottage. Just-ripe or ripe plantains work well here and bring a touch of sweetness to the pottage. Add one just-ripe plantain, cut into 1- or 2-inch (2.5 to 5 cm) pieces, when you add the yam.

Unripe plantain pottage, also known as kekefia (Ijaw land, South South). Replace the yam with 4 unripe plantains, cut into 1- or 2-inch (2.5 to 5 cm) pieces. Season with 1 to 2 teaspoons each of ground ehuru and uziza seeds, adding them along with the plantain.

Cocoyam pottage. Replace the yam with the same weight of cocoyam (taro), cut into chunks. Cook as directed.

Sweet potato pottage. Also known as aketoh or akutor (Tiv). Replace the yam with the same weight of white sweet potatoes, cut into chunks. Cook as directed. Grind ¾ cup (105 g) toasted white or brown sesame seeds, then stir them into the pottage once cooked. Top with ¼ cup (35 g) toasted sesame seeds before serving.

THE ANATOMY OF YAMS

Yams are described anatomically as having a head, middle, and tail. The head is a 3- to 4-inch (7.5 to 10 cm) section closest to the root and surface, sometimes with bumps and remnants of the root. It is typically harder and drier than the rest of the yam. The tail is a 3- to 4-inch (7.5 to 10 cm) section on the opposite end, deepest in the ground, and the rest is the middle.

Because yams are large, a tuber might last a few weeks, with portions cut off as needed. Start cutting (and eating) your yam from the head and make your way to the tail. People typically trim 1 to 2 inches (2.5 to 5 cm) of the topmost head section to plant, or to discard. The cut yam can be stored at room temperature; dip the exposed cut side of the yam in distilled white vinegar, lemon juice, or lime juice to slow down oxidation. Alternatively (and preferably), peel, rinse, and cut the yam into the desired size pieces for boiling, frying, or roasting. Add to boiling water and cook for 3 to 4 minutes. Remove, drain, and cool. On rimmed baking sheets, freeze them in a single layer until rock hard, then transfer to freezer-safe containers and freeze until needed. Use from frozen.

YAMS, SWEET POTATOES, AND CELEBRATION

Yams, of the genus *Dioscorea*, family Dioscoreaceae, are highly revered and considered the king of crops in Nigeria. Nigeria is the largest producer of yams in the world, responsible for about 70 percent of global production.

This tropical vine, related to lilies and grasses, is planted in mounds and is part of a quartet of companions—yams, corn, beans, and melons—that support each other in the growing cycle, like the Indigenous Three Sisters planting method in North America.

Yams are described in many ways, by their provenance and where they are from, like the Onitsha yam from the eastern trading center and city of Onitsha, and Benue yam, from the North Central; and by age, relative to when they are harvested, typically at the end of the rainy season so there are new and old yams. New yams are harvested from June to September, depending on the species and other factors, and old yams are new yams that have aged. New yams have higher moisture content and are lighter in flavor compared with older yams, which are a touch drier and more flavorful.

The arrival of new yams marks the end of one season of harvest and the start of planting widely celebrated in New Yam feasts and festivals around the country, from Iwa Ji in Igboland to Leboku in the South South and Orureshi in the North Central. Like harvest celebrations all over the world, the festivities involve prayers of gratitude and thanksgiving, blessings from the elders, folk dances, masquerade displays, processions, and parades. In my hometown, Igarra, where being woken up with steaming mounds of creamy, chewy pounded yam with ẹ̀gúsí soup is normal, the Enu festival is a slate of events—the planting of Guinea corn (sorghum; see page 324), the celebration of the first new yams in June, setting a date for the larger festival based on seeing the full moon, and finally the larger harvest of yams in August.

Sweet potatoes (*Ipomoea batatas*) are from a different family—the morning glory. These tuberous roots are sometimes labeled as yams outside of the African continent, but yams and sweet potatoes are distinctly different in size, appearance, texture, and taste. Sweet potatoes likely became a stand-in for true yams during the transatlantic trade in enslaved African people; and more recently in the 1930s when growers in Louisiana wanted to distinguish their soft, orange-fleshed sweet potatoes from firm varieties of sweet potatoes and so marketed them as yams.

THE MAIN, THE MAIN

RICE AND BEANS

"THERE'S RICE AT HOME" IS A SIMPLE AND SHORT

statement familiar to most Nigerians across the world, a refrain from parents, aunties, uncles, and elders. Ask for fast food while out and about with your family and the answer will likely be "There's rice at home." Rice—raw or cooked—is ever-present.

Nigerians love rice and beans. They are often the main attraction, and feature in meals both freshly cooked (mostly on the stovetop) and as leftovers. They are eaten throughout the day, at home, on the street, and in dining establishments from bukas (a contraction of *bukateria*, from the Hausa word for hut, *bukkà*, and *cafeteria*) to restaurants.

There are only two species of cultivated rice in the world—*Oryza glaberrima*, or African rice, and *Oryza sativa*, or Asian rice—and you'll find both in the fields and on the Nigerian table. Long-grain rice is the most common, including red-streaked local varieties, both regular and fermented (like Ofada). Parboiled (also known as converted) long-grain rice is quite common. This golden rice, cooked in its husk during processing, is considered more nutritious than regular white rice. The processing changes the way the starches gelatinize; the grains stay firm, hold their shape better, and don't quickly turn to mush when cooked, which is perfect for making jollof rice, fried rice, and other dishes. In the north, shinkafan tūwō is also popular. Cooked for swallows (including Tūwōn Shinkafa, page 214), made into drinks, paps, and more, it is a long-grain rice similar to Thai jasmine rice.

Beans are beloved in various forms, for their flavor and for their ability to fill you up. Beans are eaten both as a main dish—on their own, as pottage, and combined with rice—and as a side.

CLOCKWISE FROM LEFT: *A variety of rice and beans; green habaneros and Scotch bonnets; a bag of rice; Freezinhot Bucket coolers, popular up until the 1980s for transporting jollof rice*

FEATURED IN THESE RECIPES

1. **Black-eyed peas.** Used across regional cuisines in a variety of ways. There is a diversity of black-eyed peas, varying in size from ¼ to ½ inch (6 mm to 1.3 cm).

2. **Converted rice.** Parboiled processed rice with golden grains.

3. **Garri.** A granular cassava flour; the cassava is milled, fermented, then roasted, so it is edible out of hand. This gluten-free flour comes in a variety of textures, from fine to coarse, and in a range of colors, from cream to sunny yellow like cornmeal.

4. **Indian Golden Sella basmati rice.** Parboiled processed basmati rice with long, golden grains.

5. **Nigerian rice.** One of several varieties of long-grain rice with red streaks and a sweet flavor and aroma.

6. **Oloyin beans.** Also known as honey beans, these brown cowpeas have a sweetness that makes them treasured. They also cook a bit quicker than regular black-eyed peas.

7. **Red cayenne peppers.** Also known in Nigeria as sombo (shombo) peppers, these are long, slim (about ½-inch-wide/1.3 cm) chiles with moderate heat. Red Thai chiles make a good substitute.

8. **Red Fresno peppers.** These resemble Nigerian tatashe peppers, but are hotter.

9. **Red shepherd peppers.** These also resemble Nigerian tatashe peppers, but are pointed, thin-skinned, and sweet, with only a whiff of spice. They come in a range of sizes, from 4 to 10 inches (10 to 25 cm) long and about 3 inches (7.5 cm) wide, and are generally two or three times longer than tatashe.

10. **Sugar cubes.** St. Louis, with its blue packet, is the most famous brand of sugar cubes in Nigeria.

11. **Tomato paste.** Also known in Nigeria as tomato puree (though that is a different product). Thick and concentrated, it lends color and flavor to red dishes like jollof rice (page 143).

12. **White and black peppercorns.** Some Nigerian cooks put white peppercorns on their list of essential jollof rice ingredients.

GROUNDNUT CHOP
WHITE RICE, GROUNDNUT STEW, AND LOTS OF SIDES

FOR THE CHOP

6 cups cooked white rice

1 recipe hot Groundnut Stew
(page 198)

TOPPINGS

2 hard-boiled eggs, peeled
and sliced

½ avocado, sliced

2 tablespoons Dòdò
(page 120)

2 tablespoons chopped
fresh cilantro

1 tablespoon Roasted
Groundnuts (page 200)

1 tablespoon chopped fresh
tomatoes

1 tablespoon minced green
bell pepper

1 tablespoon ripe papaya
chunks

1 tablespoon pickled onion

This platter is excellent party food, perfect for a crowd, and you need only three elements: cooked white rice, stew, and toppings. The beauty is that you can prepare them all ahead of time.

When I was growing up, Sunday lunch was often rice and stew with lots of sides, including ripe papaya, bananas, Sharwood's mango chutney, and dòdò.

The toppings play a critical role, so create a balance of sweet, spicy, soft, crunchy, salty, herby, and creamy. Some say three or four toppings is fine, others say sixteen is the minimum; I have heard tales of a chop with 103 toppings!

Make the chop: Spoon the rice onto a large platter, spreading it so it is 2 inches (5 cm) high. Gently make a shallow well at the center.

Fill the center with 2 or 3 spoonfuls of stew, leaving a 2- to 3-inch (5 to 7.5 cm) margin of rice around it. Spoon or scatter some of the toppings over the rice and stew—just enough to add color and texture.

Serve with a cake slicer or fish spatula, spooning some onto each plate and letting your guests add more toppings.

CREATING BALANCE WITH YOUR CHOP TOPPINGS

Think about a selection of colors, textures, and flavors. Here are some ideas to get you started:

- **Sweet and fruity:** apples, bananas, mangoes, pineapple
- **Fresh fruits and vegetables:** avocado, tomatoes, cucumber, cabbage, lettuce, okro, carrots, garden eggs, sautéed greens
- **Beans and peas:** boiled beans, chickpeas
- **Dried fruit, nuts, and seeds:** raisins, sultanas, coconut shreds, sesame seeds, toasted ègúsí seeds
- **Protein:** hard-boiled or fried eggs, meat floss, sūya
- **Sauces and condiments:** yogurt, Ata Dindin (page 332), mango chutney
- **Herbs:** scent leaves, cilantro, mint, basil
- **Bread:** naan, pita, tortilla

CLASSIC NIGERIAN JOLLOF RICE

⅓ cup (80 ml) neutral oil

1 medium red onion, thinly sliced

3 dried bay leaves

2 teaspoons Curry Powder (page 25), plus more as needed

2 teaspoons dried thyme

1½ teaspoons fine sea salt, plus more as needed

1 teaspoon freshly ground black or white pepper, plus more as needed

¼ cup (60 g) tomato paste (see Notes)

3 teaspoons unsalted butter

3 cups (720 ml) Tomato Stew Base (page 335)

3½ cups (840 ml) Curry Stock (page 333)

3 cups (570 g) converted long-grain rice, rinsed and drained (see Notes)

1 Roma (plum) tomato, halved lengthwise, then thinly sliced crosswise into half-moons

NOTES: *If you like slim-grained rice, use Indian Golden Sella basmati, which is also parboiled. Start off with less liquid and adjust accordingly.*

When selecting tomato paste, choose a product that is made with just tomatoes and salt—some tomato pastes are super acidic and will change the balance of the dish.

Historically, jollof rice was a one-pot dish made with protein and carrots, peppers, and leafy vegetables. Today, it's all about the rice; the vegetables tend to show up as a side, à la Nigerian Salad (page 97). A seasoned tomato base spiced with curry powder gives this rice its orange-red color. For great jollof, the tomato mix for the stew base is cooked twice—first to soften and round out the raw, tart flavors, and a second time to fry and season it, concentrating the flavors.

To get grains that are "one-one" (fluffy) and well seasoned to the core of each grain, start with parboiled (not parcooked) or converted rice (husk-on rice that is partly cooked before dehusking). The result is golden grains of raw rice that are sturdy and capable of absorbing stews without turning to mush. Cook the rice over low heat so it absorbs the sauce properly and doesn't scorch on the bottom. Stirring occasionally ensures evenly cooked rice.

Serve with Dòdò (page 120), Mọ́ínmọ́ín Elewe (page 69), an assortment of meat (page 330) or fish (page 167), and Nigerian Salad.

In a 4- or 5-quart (4 or 5 L) pot or Dutch oven, heat the oil over medium heat. When the oil is shimmering, add half the onion, the bay leaves, curry powder, thyme, ½ teaspoon of the salt, and ½ teaspoon of the pepper. Cook, stirring, until the mixture is fragrant and the onion softens slightly, about 3 minutes.

Reduce the heat to low and stir in the tomato paste and 2 teaspoons of the butter. Cook for 10 minutes, stirring continuously, until the tomato paste darkens and splits in the oil. Stir in the stew base. Increase the heat to medium, cover the pot with the lid ajar, and cook for about 15 minutes, stirring frequently and carefully—it will splatter—until the mixture thickens and oil pools on top.

Stir in 3 cups (720 ml) of the curry stock and bring to a boil over high heat. Season with the remaining 1 teaspoon salt and ½ teaspoon pepper.

Add the rice and stir until evenly coated in the sauce. Cover the pot with a double layer of aluminum foil or parchment paper, crimp down around the edges to seal, then top with the lid (this will trap steam to lock in the flavor and aid in even cooking). Reduce the heat to the lowest setting possible and cook for 20 minutes, then uncover the pot and gently but thoroughly stir, from top to bottom, to combine the top layer of sauce and the rice underneath. Cover and cook until the rice is just tender and most of the liquid has been absorbed, about 15 minutes more. If it still has a firm bite and needs to soften, add the remaining ½ cup (120 ml) curry stock, cover, and cook for 10 minutes more, or until the rice is tender and cooked through.

Add the tomato, remaining onion, and remaining 1 teaspoon butter and cook, stirring, until the butter has melted. Remove from the heat, cover, and let stand for 10 minutes. Discard the bay leaves. Taste the rice and adjust with salt and pepper, if needed, before serving.

THE HISTORY OF JOLLOF RICE

Sometimes just called jollof (which means "enjoyment"), this dish is named for the historic Jolof state (present-day Senegal and Gambia) of the Wolof empire, which ruled from the mid-fourteenth to mid-sixteenth century. The region was known as the Grain or Rice Coast due to the high concentration of rice, millet, and other grain cultivation on the banks of the Senegal River. Jollof is believed to have traveled across the coast of West Africa with the Dyula, merchants who traversed both the trans-Saharan trade routes and established routes south of the Sahara. Other related versions of the dish—red rice in the Lowcountry of the American South, jambalaya in New Orleans, and Mexican arroz rojo—are descendants of jollof via the transatlantic trade in enslaved African people.

PARTY JOLLOF

1 recipe Classic Nigerian
Jollof Rice (page 143)

Party jollof and celebrations are linked. This rice dish with smoky flavors is associated with owambes and festive cooking, where women (aunties, cousins, neighbors) set up large pots of bubbling sauce and rice over woodfires, stirring with wooden paddles.

To me, these aunties are full of superpowers, wielding utensils in the face of smoke and fire to cook the rice. As it simmers, the rice takes on layers of sweet, smoke, and spice, and the Maillard reaction is pushed to the very edge, creating bottom pot—the caramelized rice that forms at the bottom of the pan, similar to socarrat in paella and Persian tahdig. Some don't tamper with this crust, letting its flavors rise through the rice, while others stir the burnt bits in with the rest of the rice.

The crunch of bottom pot is what turns jollof into party jollof. Though the dish is traditionally cooked outdoors, you can coax out similar smoky flavors on the stovetop.

Follow the directions for cooking the jollof rice. After stirring in the tomatoes, onion, and butter, increase the heat to high, leaving the pot covered. Cook for 3 to 5 minutes; the rice will snap, pop, crackle, and smell smoky. Remove from the heat and let stand, covered, for 10 minutes. Discard the bay leaves.

Serve as you would jollof rice.

BOTTOM POT BY ANOTHER NAME

Bottom pot has compatriots around the world, and you may know it by another name: kanzo in the north of Nigeria and Ghana, xoon in Senegal, kose in Guinea, and intshela in South Africa; socarrat in Spain, tahdig in Persia, bay kdaing in Cambodia, and tutong in the Philippines. Guoba in China, kazmag in Uzbekistan and Azerbaijan, pegao in Colombia and Puerto Rico, cocolón in Ecuador, concón in the Dominican Republic, and nurungji in Korea. Okoge in Japan, intip in Indonesia, cơm cháy in Vietnam, khao taen in Thailand, hikakeh in Iraq, graten in Haiti, and bunbun in Jamaica.

PALM OIL JOLLOF

½ cup (120 ml) red palm oil

1 large red or white onion, thinly sliced

2 tablespoons ground crayfish (see page 23)

2 tablespoons fresh or dried irú (see page 25; optional)

1 teaspoon fine sea salt, plus more as needed

3 cups (720 ml) Pepper Stew Base (page 335)

1 dry catfish (about 4 ounces/120 g), rinsed, softened, and broken into bits

2 ounces (60 g) dried prawns or other dried seafood (optional)

2 cups (380 g) converted long-grain rice, rinsed and drained

Dry pepper (see page 22)

1 cup (30 g) thinly sliced amaranth greens

⅓ cup (40 g) diced red bell pepper

¼ cup (7.5 g) thinly sliced scent leaves

NOTE: *If you aren't a fan of the fish head, blitz it into powder and use some of it to season the stew base.*

This native jollof shares many of the same characteristics as classic jollof, including the bright orange-red tinge of the rice. The differences? Palm oil jollof is cooked with red palm oil, which adds an earthy, vegetal flavor, and seasoned with ground crayfish and sometimes irú, upping the umami levels. Dried and smoked seafood are common additions, but you can also use fresh.

Serve with Dòdò (page 120) and a lager.

In a medium pot, warm the palm oil over medium heat. When the oil is shimmering, add half the sliced onion, the ground crayfish, irú (if using), and salt. Stir well and cook until the onion has somewhat softened and turned translucent and orange-tinged and the irú is aromatic, about 5 minutes.

Add the stew base and 1 cup (240 ml) water and stir. Cover, reduce the heat to low, and cook until the sauce thickens a bit and oil floats to the top, about 15 minutes.

Add the catfish and dried prawns (if using) and stir well. Cover, reduce the heat to the lowest setting, and cook until the fish softens a touch, about 5 minutes.

Add the rice and stir well. Cover with aluminum foil or parchment paper, then the lid. Cook until the rice is al dente, 15 to 20 minutes more. Add water by the ½ cup (120 ml) if the rice needs to soften more. Carefully remove the lid (it'll be hot and steamy) and stir the rice gently but well. Taste and adjust the seasoning with salt and dry pepper, if needed.

In a medium bowl, combine the remaining onion, the amaranth, bell pepper, and scent leaves. Reserve ¼ cup of the vegetable mixture for serving; scatter the rest over the rice in the pot. Cover and steam until the greens wilt and the onion and bell pepper just soften, 2 minutes. Remove from the heat and gently fold the steamed onion mixture into the pot with the rice. Let stand for a few minutes before serving.

Garnish with the reserved vegetable mixture and serve.

NIGERIAN FRIED RICE

CHINESE FRIED RICE MEETS INDIAN PILAU MASALA

4 cups (about 1 L) Curry Stock (page 333), plus more if needed

2 cups (380 g) Indian Golden Sella basmati rice, rinsed and drained

2 tablespoons neutral oil

1 medium carrot, cut into ¼-inch (6 mm) dice

1 small red or white onion, cut into ¼-inch (6 mm) dice

1½ ounces green beans, trimmed and cut into ¼-inch-thick (6 mm) rounds on an angle

1 teaspoon fine sea salt, plus more as needed

2 scallions, white and green parts separated and thinly sliced crosswise

½ large red bell pepper, cut into ¼-inch (6 mm) dice

½ medium green bell pepper, cut into ¼-inch (6 mm) dice

¼ cup (60 g) drained canned sweet corn kernels

2 teaspoons Curry Powder (page 25)

1 teaspoon dried thyme

¼ teaspoon freshly ground black pepper, plus more as needed

2 dried bay leaves

½ cup (65 g) small-diced cooked beef liver (see page 150; optional)

14 ounces (113 g) cooked peeled tiny shrimp (100–200 count; optional)

Nigerian fried rice combines the technique of Chinese fried rice with the seasoning and turmeric of Indian pilau masala. This confluence of Nigerian-Chinese-Indian elements can also be found in small chops (see page 35), where Nigerian Puff Puff (page 39), Chinese spring rolls (page 44), and Indian samosas (page 47) come together. Converted (or parboiled) rice is the rice of choice; in this case, opt for the slimmer grains of Indian Golden Sella basmati rice.

Classic Nigerian fried rice sports cubes of cooked beef liver and small fried shrimp, which are like treasures of deliciousness in the rice. Some tips: Don't skip or skimp on the green bell pepper, which adds flavor and aroma. And as always, use a flavorful stock.

Serve with Dòdò (page 120), Móínmóín Elewe (page 69), an assortment of meat or fish (page 330), and Nigerian Salad (page 97).

NOTE: *This recipe calls for tiny shrimp, often sold already cleaned and cooked. Thaw them before use. To prepare, season them lightly with salt, dry pepper, curry powder, and dried thyme, then sauté to seal in the spices, 2 to 3 minutes.*

In a medium pot, bring 2½ cups (600 ml) of the stock to a boil over high heat. Stir in the rice, return the stock to a boil, and reduce the heat to low. Cover and cook until the stock has been absorbed and the rice grains have softened but are still hard in the center, about 10 minutes. Transfer the rice to a rimmed baking sheet, spread it out into an even layer, and let cool for 10 to 15 minutes. Using a fork, fluff the rice to separate the grains and set aside.

In a large sauté pan, heat the oil over medium heat. When the oil is shimmering, add the carrot, onion, and green beans. Season with ½ teaspoon of the salt and cook until the vegetables are coated in oil and shiny, about 2 minutes.

RECIPE CONTINUES →

Add the scallion whites, red bell pepper, half the green bell pepper, and the corn. Cook the vegetables until slightly softened, about 2 minutes. Stir in the curry powder, thyme, black pepper, and bay leaves and cook until aromatic, about 1 minute.

Add the half-cooked rice and stir gently to combine. Add the remaining 1½ cups (360 ml) stock and bring to a boil, then reduce the heat to low. Cover and cook until the rice is soft and cooked through, about 12 minutes. Season with the remaining ½ teaspoon salt and black pepper to taste. If the rice is too dry and the grains are not soft or cooked through, add more stock in ¼-cup (60 ml) increments and cook, covered, until the rice is soft and cooked through.

Stir in the scallion greens, remaining green bell pepper, liver (if using), and shrimp (if using). Cover and cook just until the bell pepper brightens and softens slightly, about 2 minutes. Discard the bay leaves and serve. Store leftovers in an airtight container in the refrigerator for up to 5 days or freeze for up to 2 weeks.

HOW TO PREPARE AND COOK LIVER

Often sold in large pieces, fresh beef liver should be medium to dark reddish-brown and moist, with no dry patches. It might come with a smooth outer membrane similar to silverskin. Before cooking, separate the membrane from the liver with a small knife, then peel it off.

Rinse the liver, then set it on a cutting board and pat dry with paper towels. With a sharp knife, trim and discard any visible fat, connective tissue, membrane, etc. Cut the liver into 1- to 2-inch (2.5 to 5 cm) pieces.

To blanch the liver, fill a pot with lightly salted cold water and bring to a boil over medium heat, stirring to dissolve the salt, about 8 minutes. Add the liver to the boiling water, reduce the heat to low, and cook until it firms up and loses its rawness, about 4 minutes. Drain and rinse with cold water, then place in a bowl with fresh water to cover and set aside to soak for about 10 minutes. Drain and let cool completely, then use as directed. It can be refrigerated in an airtight container for up to 2 days or frozen for up to 3 months.

STEWED BEANS

2 cups (13.4 ounces/380 g) dried black-eyed peas or brown beans, picked over and rinsed

1½ teaspoons fine sea salt, plus more as needed

½ cup (120 g) red palm oil

1 small red onion, diced

3 or 4 uda pods (see page 164), smashed (optional)

3 tablespoons whole crayfish, rinsed (see page 23; optional)

2 cups (480 ml) Pepper Stew Base (page 335)

3 tablespoons ground crayfish (see page 23; optional)

1 teaspoon dry pepper (see page 22), plus more as needed

NOTE: *You can cook the beans in a pressure cooker following the manufacturer's directions.*

This is a saucy dish of whole dried black-eyed peas, brown beans, or other cowpeas cooked in a red sauce with a slick of palm oil. Popular on its own and in pottages with vegetables like yams, plantains, and sweet potatoes, it can be enjoyed in a variety of ways. The grains of Selim (uda pods) lend the beans hints of smoke and musk, a tip that comes from a dear friend, Timi Yeseibo, a Nigerian writer and storyteller.

Serve with fried yam (page 127) and Ata Dindin (page 332).

Place the beans in a large bowl and cover with about 4 inches (10 cm) of water. Soak for 4 to 8 hours. Drain, rinse, and transfer the beans to a medium pot.

Add 4 cups (about 1 L) water and ½ teaspoon of the salt to the pot with the beans. Cover with the lid ajar and bring to a boil over medium-high heat. Cook for about 10 minutes, then reduce the heat to medium-low and cook until the beans are tender but still holding their shape, 25 to 30 minutes.

In a medium pan, warm the palm oil over medium heat. When the oil is shimmering, add the onion, 1 teaspoon of the salt, and the uda (if using) and cook until the onion softens, 4 to 5 minutes.

Add the whole crayfish (if using) and cook for 1 to 2 minutes to fry them slightly. Add the stew base, ground crayfish (if using), and dry pepper. Reduce the heat to low, cover with the lid ajar, and cook until just reduced and thick, about 12 minutes.

Drain the beans, reserving the cooking liquid; set the cooking liquid aside. Add the beans to the pot with the stew base and stir well to combine. Cover and cook, stirring every 10 minutes and making sure to stir from the bottom to keep the beans from scorching, for about 20 minutes, until the flavors meld. Taste and adjust the seasoning with more salt and dry pepper, if needed. Cook, stirring now and again, until the beans are saucy and tender, 10 minutes more. Taste and check the salt again, adjusting accordingly.

Cover and cook, stirring and scraping the bottom once or twice to prevent scorching, until the stew thickens some more and begins to dry at the bottom, about 20 minutes. If you want the stew to be thicker, mash some of the beans against the side of the pot with a wooden spoon or puree with an immersion blender. If you prefer the stew looser, don't cook the beans for as long, or stir in some of the reserved cooking liquid in ¼-cup (60 ml) increments until you reach your desired consistency.

Remove from the heat and let stand to allow the flavors to develop, about 10 minutes, then serve.

VARIATION

You can make a version of stewed beans with "washed beans," which are dried beans with the skins removed (see page 67); it's called domboro.

SEVEN WAYS TO ENJOY STEWED BEANS

1. With Agege bread (see page 75) or any soft white bread
2. With dry garri sprinkled over the top
3. With Soaked Garri (page 72)
4. With plantain—boiled (page 125), Dòdò (page 120), or in a pottage (page 130)
5. With yam—boiled (page 124), fried (page 127), or in a pottage (page 129)
6. With Fried Fish (page 167)
7. With white rice

FREJON
CREAMY BEANS IN COCONUT MILK

2 cups (13.4 ounces/380 g) èwà dúdu or èwà ìbejì, picked over and rinsed

1 teaspoon fine sea salt, plus more as needed

2 cups (480 ml) full-fat coconut milk, or more as needed

¼ teaspoon ground cloves, plus more as needed

1 tablespoon sugar, plus more as needed

½ teaspoon ground cinnamon, plus more as needed

Frejon is a smooth and creamy dish of beans and coconut milk. Like Brazilian feijão com leite de coco, it is typically enjoyed on Good Friday.

It's traditionally made with dried èwà dúdu or èwà ìbejì, special dark brown or black beans; you can substitute dried brown cowpeas or black-eyed peas.

You can also use canned black-eyed peas or black beans, drained and rinsed—1 cup (190 g) dried beans is about 2 to 3 cups (370 to 560 g) cooked, equivalent to two 15-ounce (425 g) cans.

Serve frejon hot as a savory dish with dry garri and fish stew.

Place the beans in a large bowl and cover with about 4 inches (10 cm) of water. Soak for 4 to 8 hours. Drain, rinse, and transfer the beans to a medium pot.

Add 4 cups (about 1 L) water and ½ teaspoon of the salt to the pot with the beans. Cover with the lid ajar and bring to a boil over medium-high heat. Cook for about 10 minutes, then reduce the heat to medium-low and cook until the beans are tender. Remove the beans from the heat, then strain out and reserve the cooking liquid.

Add the coconut milk, the remaining ½ teaspoon salt, and the cloves to the pot of beans and bring to a boil over medium-high heat. Cover with the lid ajar, reduce the heat to medium-low, stir, and cook until the beans absorb some of coconut milk, about 30 minutes. Remove from the heat and let cool for 30 minutes.

VARIATION

Frejon for dessert: In a blender, combine 1 cup (240 ml) each frejon and water, 2 cups (480 ml) coconut milk, 3 tablespoons sugar, ¼ teaspoon ground cloves, and 4 ice cubes. Blend on high until creamy. Pour into a bowl, cover, and refrigerate for at least 2 hours. Sprinkle with ground cloves or cinnamon and serve.

Working in batches, scoop the beans and coconut milk mixture into a blender or food processor. For every 2 cups (480 ml) of mixture, add 2 or 3 ice cubes. Puree until smooth. Pour the blended mixture through a fine-mesh strainer back into the pot. Add the sugar and cinnamon. Cover the pot with the lid ajar, and cook for about 15 minutes, stirring frequently and carefully—it will splatter—until the mixture thickens a bit. Taste and adjust with additional salt, sugar, and/or cinnamon.

GARAU GARAU
RICE AND BEANS

FOR THE BEANS AND RICE

1 cup (6¾ ounces/190 g) dried black-eyed peas, picked over and rinsed

1 teaspoon fine sea salt, plus more as needed

1 small red onion, diced (optional)

2 cups (380 g) converted long-grain rice, rinsed and drained

1 cup (240 ml) groundnut oil (see page 267) or peanut oil

1 medium red onion, diced

1 tablespoon chopped fresh ginger

1 tablespoon chopped garlic

FOR SERVING

2 large Roma (plum) tomatoes, diced

1 cup (100 g) shredded white cabbage

1 cup shredded butter lettuce (55 g) or iceberg lettuce (70 g)

1 small red onion, diced

½ medium cucumber, diced (not seeded)

½ small green bell pepper, diced

4 large hard-boiled eggs, left whole, quartered, or sliced into rings

Basic Yaji (page 26)

2 beef stock cubes (in their wrappers)

Garau garau is a gift from the North West composed of white rice, boiled beans, vegetables, yaji (typically a coarse blend), beef stock cubes, seasoned oil, and protein such as hard-boiled eggs or fried fish. This dish is sweet and spicy and easy to make now now (meaning "right now," also "quickly"—remember our fondness for reduplicated words?).

You can cook the rice and beans together from the start or build this plate from leftover rice and boiled beans. Make some delicious spiced oil; be sure to chop (not mince) the ginger and garlic so you get crunchy bits. Serve the rice and beans hot, with the cool sides.

Place the beans in a large bowl and cover with about 4 inches (10 cm) of water. Soak for 4 to 8 hours. Drain, rinse, and transfer the beans to a medium pot.

Add 1½ quarts (about 1.4 L) water, ½ teaspoon of the salt, and the small onion (if using) to the pot with the beans. Cover with the lid ajar and bring to a boil over medium-high heat. Cook for about 10 minutes, then reduce the heat to medium-low and cook until the beans are somewhat soft but not cooked through, about 10 minutes.

Add the rice and stir. Reduce the heat to low, cover, and cook until the rice and beans are cooked through and tender, 15 to 20 minutes more. Taste and season with salt as needed.

In a small pot or pan, heat the oil over medium heat for 1 to 2 minutes. Add the medium onion, ginger, garlic, and remaining ½ teaspoon salt. Stir gently and cook until fragrant and golden, with some crunchy bits, about 10 minutes. Remove from the heat and let cool. The onion oil can be stored in an airtight container at room temperature for up to a week, or refrigerated for up to 3 months—you may need to warm the oil before use.

To serve, lay out all the sides in individual bowls or plates. Spoon a portion of the beans and rice onto a plate, then add small portions of the vegetables and eggs. Pile on a spoonful of yaji between the beans and rice and the vegetables. If you like, unwrap a stock cube, break it up with your fingers, and sprinkle it over your food. Drizzle with the oniony oil and tuck in.

RICE AND ITS HISTORY

The history of rice in Nigeria and West Africa stretches back centuries. Historians believe that African rice (*Oryza glaberrima*) evolved from *Oryza barthii*, a variety of wild rice that grew inland in Mali, around the Niger Delta and in the Niger valleys. From there it spread westward across the Grain Coast, from Nigeria through to Senegal, long before Asian rice, *Oryza sativa*, was brought to West Africa through the trans-Saharan connection with North Africa or by the Portuguese in the sixteenth century. In the era of chattel slavery, people from the West African region were targeted for enslavement for their knowledge of various rice-growing systems, particularly swamp-based ones, and helped establish not only rice crops in the American South but also the knowledge systems that sustained them. This knowledge played a foundational role in the success of rice in the Carolinas.

Rice is everyday food in Nigeria today, but this wasn't always the case. Fifty or sixty years ago, it was a dish for special occasions and celebrations, and mostly limited to the regions where it was grown. That changed after the country's independence from Britain in 1960, when the economy transitioned from agriculture to oil exploration. Rice is the only crop grown across all the planting regions in Nigeria, from the dry regions of the uppermost north to the swampy southern region.

Broken grains are steamed and enjoyed as one might couscous. Whole grains are cooked and served in both sweet and savory dishes, including sabban, cooked rice folded into sweetened yogurt; and basise, a rice pudding similar to Arosidosi (page 296).

There are a number of contemporary rice celebrations. There is World Jollof Rice Day, created by two Instagrammers, @asoebiafrica and @westafrikanman, in 2015, who planned to celebrate it on the third Saturday of August, which fell on August 22 that year. That date has stuck, and around the world, various events and celebrations are held showcasing jollof rice not only on the day but during that whole week.

Another contemporary celebration, Ofada Rice Day, or Ofadabration, was created in Lagos in 2018 by Tobi Fletcher, a Nigerian entrepreneur who comes from the Ofada region. During the celebration, a mix of arts and culture is showcased in music, dance, food, and drink with a variety of Ofada dishes, from rice to sauce.

ASSORTED

OF MEAT
AND MORE

P SOFT	13000	8000	4000
LL CHK	13500	6500	3250
P OROBO	14000	6750	3000
NORMAL	13000	7000	NO
G HARD	15000	6500	3250
SOFT	13000	7500	3750
GIZZ	13000	6500	3250
GIZZ	18000	7500	NO
SOFT	17000	9000	4500
SAGE	16000	8500	NO
4-C	13000	8000	4000
LA	000	6500	3250
		8500	4250

09033 26858
07035 411

"This soup get plenty obstacles."

TRANSLATION: "THIS SOUP HAS A LOT OF PROTEIN THAT
SETS UP A DELICIOUS, ENJOYABLE OBSTACLE COURSE AS I FEAST."

NIGERIANS LOVE PROTEIN, AND THAT CUTS ACROSS TRIBE,
belief system, and geography: rainy-season locusts,
grasshoppers, grubs, game (fondly known as bushmeat);
chicken, guinea fowl, turkey, beef, goat meat, ram (mutton);
shrimp and prawns, periwinkles, oysters, whelks, clams,
and crabs; and fish. Nose-to-tail eating of "assorted"—an
assortment of animal parts, both flesh and offal (see page 19)—
is also important. Cowskin, tripe, intestines, tongue, liver,
kidney, heart, and more are delightful "obstacles" in steaming
bowls of soups and stews.

The north of Nigeria has a long tradition of excellence
in meat preparation, from balangu (also known as balango),
grilled strips of boneless beef or ram cooked in their juices
and confited in groundnut oil; to denderu, seasoned, fall-
off-the-bone-tender meat from the Kanuri and Shuwa Arabs,
traditionally cooked for 24 hours in underground ovens;
kilishi, similar to jerky (sheets of seasoned beef dried until
chewy-crispy); and dambun nama.

The eastern Igbo people dish up nkwobi, of cow leg, and
isi ewu, of goat head, in emulsified, aromatic sauces. In the
South South, piom piom—periwinkles—are served in similar
aromatic sauces. And then there's grilled fish and whole
roasted fish basted in seasoned red palm oil and covered in
pepper sauce or yaji (page 26).

There are other proteins like wara, a soft, squeaky cow's-
milk cheese, and fried awara, aka Nigerian tofu (page 181).
Plant-forward ingredients like mushrooms and textured cakes
made of ẹ̀gúsí are enjoyed on their own or as meat replacements.

CLOCKWISE FROM LEFT: *Women in the lagoon, selling fish at Epe; kilishi, dried meat;
miniature calamari, prawns, and fish; a butcher selling goat meat at Oniru New Market*

FEATURED IN THESE RECIPES

1. **Aidan fruit.** Also known as aridan, uyayak (Ibibio), yanghanyanghan (Itsekiri), prekese (Twi, Ghana), and lauded as "soup perfume" for its warm notes of brown butter, toffee, and bitter chocolate. Available fresh, dried, and powdered.

2. **Atili oil.** A rich, earthy oil from atili fruit, also known as ube okpoko, ube osa, or ube mgba in the east. Substitutes include pumpkin seed oil and extra-virgin olive oil.

3. **Black beniseeds.** Also known as black sesame seeds or benne seeds. Nigeria is among the top ten producers in the world.

4. **Black stone flower**. Also known as dagad phool. It comes in curly, brittle, papery, black-gray bits. Its earthy, smoky flavors bloom in oil.

5. **Cameroon pepper.** These smoke-dried yellow and red Scotch bonnets and habaneros are available whole or ground.

6. **Country onion.** Also known as rondelles. These super-hard, round, mustard-colored seeds with papery dark-brown skins have a strong allium-garlic flavor and are available whole or ground.

7. **Gbafilo.** Also known as igbafilo (Itsekiri). This large (1½- to 2-inch/4 to 5 cm) egg-shaped nut has a brittle, sandpaper-like surface that houses an edible kernel.

8. **Omilo.** Also known as umilo, cocoplum, paradise plum, or abajeru. This hard-shelled spice sports a honeycomb pattern outside and a soft, oily kernel inside.

9. **Njangsa.** Oily, bitter, spicy seeds of the *Ricinodendron heudelotii* tree with notes of fresh fruit and chocolate.

10. **Uda.** Also known as grains of Selim. Small black pods with earthy, smoky, and musky notes, similar to black cardamom. Substitute a mix of black cardamom seeds and black peppercorns.

11. **Yaji.** A spice blend used in soups, stews, sauces (see page 26).

12. **Yajin kuli.** A nutty and coarse spice blend made with kulikuli (see page 26).

FRIED FISH

1 tablespoon Curry Powder
(page 25)

1 tablespoon dried thyme

1 teaspoon fine sea salt

1 teaspoon dry pepper
(see page 22)

2 whole firm-fleshed fish
(about 1½ pounds/680 g
total), cleaned, cut into
pieces, and patted dry (see
Note)

Neutral oil, for frying

NOTE: *To cut the cleaned
fish, place the fish on a
cutting board. Beginning
with the head, cut down
1 inch (2.5 cm) from the
mouth. Cut off the tail
portion 3 to 4 inches (7.5 to
10 cm) from the bottom. If
the middle section is shorter
than 5 inches (12.5 cm), leave
it as is; if it's longer, cut it
in half.*

Cut into steaks and deep-fried until crisp on the outside but still
moist and tender inside, fried fish is an institution in Nigeria, in homes
and on the streets, where you'll find trays of fish stacked and ready
to serve. Croaker, mackerel (also known as titus), tilapia, hake, fresh
cod, and snapper are popular fish for frying.

Fried fish can be enjoyed on its own or with sides, tossed in Ata
Dindin (page 332), or added to stews or soups.

In a small bowl, stir together the curry powder, thyme, salt, and dry
pepper. Season the fish inside and out with this spice blend. Place
them on a tray, cover, and refrigerate for 30 minutes to 2 hours.

When ready to fry the fish, fill a wok or Dutch oven with 1½ to
2 inches (3.8 to 5 cm) of oil and heat over medium heat to 350°F
(175°C). Line a large colander or strainer with paper towels.

Working in batches, use a fish spatula or tongs to add the fish to the
hot oil, being careful not to overcrowd the pan. Fry on one side for
about 4 minutes, until it is golden around the edges. Carefully flip
the pieces over and cook the second side for 3 to 4 minutes. With a
slotted spoon, transfer the fish to the lined strainer. Repeat with the
remaining fish, allowing the oil to return to temperature between
batches.

Serve hot, warm, or cold.

VARIATION

To air-fry the fish, spread the seasoned fish over the air fryer tray.
With a brush, baste the fish with oil. Air-fry at 390°F (200°C) for
15 minutes, or until the fish is golden, turning the fish with tongs
halfway through the cooking.

STEWED GIZZARDS

2 pounds (900 g) cleaned chicken gizzards, each cut into 2 or 3 pieces

4 cups (about 1 L) hot water

2 teaspoons fine sea salt, plus more as needed

1½ cups (360 ml) Curry Stock (page 333)

3 medium red onions: 1 coarsely chopped, 2 thinly sliced

4 medium Roma (plum) tomatoes, coarsely chopped

4 red tatashe peppers, coarsely chopped

1 medium green bell pepper, halved: ½ coarsely chopped, ½ finely diced

1 or 2 Caribbean seasoning peppers

½ to 1 Scotch bonnet or habanero pepper, minced

1 cup (240 ml) neutral oil

2 dried bay leaves

1 tablespoon Curry Powder (page 25), plus more as needed

1 teaspoon dried thyme, plus more as needed

½ teaspoon freshly ground black pepper, plus more as needed

NOTES: *You can use turkey gizzards, if you have them. Cut them into smaller (2-inch/5 cm) pieces before use.*

Undersalt stewed gizzards until they are cooked through, then taste and season as needed; they can easily become oversalted and abrasive.

Dishes of stewed or peppered gizzards are relatively young in Nigerian culinary history. In the past, chickens were sold whole, meaning there was only one gizzard per bird, which was often reserved for the head of the home, typically the father. Today, though you can buy chicken gizzards packaged by the pound, they are still appreciated.

I love the peculiar chewy-crunch of gizzards cooked just right. You want the base sauce to be partly chunky and partly saucy, so it cooks quickly. The spice level is up to you, so adjust accordingly.

In a medium pot, combine the gizzards, hot water, and ½ teaspoon of the salt. Cover with the lid ajar and cook over medium-high heat until the gizzards firm up, lose their rawness, and turn pale, 7 to 8 minutes. Remove from the heat, drain the gizzards, and rinse off the froth and scum with cold water.

Return the gizzards to a clean medium pot and add the curry stock. Set over high heat, cover, and bring to a boil. Reduce the heat to low, stir, and simmer until the gizzards are cooked but still crunchy, about 15 minutes. Separate the meat and stock, reserving both.

Meanwhile, make the sauce: In a blender or food processor, combine the chopped onion, tomatoes, tatashe, chopped bell pepper, seasoning pepper(s), and Scotch bonnet. Pulse until a coarse but uniform mixture forms.

Line a strainer with paper towels.

In a wok, large pan, or Dutch oven, heat 2 tablespoons of the oil over medium heat until it shimmers, 2 to 3 minutes.

Working in batches, add the gizzards to the hot oil, cover with a splatter screen, and fry until lightly brown, shaking every couple of minutes, 4 to 5 minutes total. Lift the gizzards from the oil with a spider or slotted spoon, gently shaking to remove excess oil, and transfer to the prepared strainer. Repeat with the remaining gizzards, adding 2 tablespoons of oil for each batch.

Add the remaining oil to the pan, then add the sliced onions and ½ teaspoon of the salt. Stir well and cook until the onions soften, about 3 minutes. Season with 1 teaspoon salt, the bay leaves, curry powder, thyme, and black pepper and cook until aromatic, about 1 minute. Add the tomato-pepper mixture. Increase the heat to high and cook uncovered, stirring often until the liquid evaporates, oil pools on top and at the sides, and the sauce is chunky, about 10 minutes.

Reduce the heat to low. Add the cooked gizzards to the sauce, loosening the sauce with 1 cup (240 ml) of the reserved stock. Cover and simmer, stirring often so the gizzards absorb some sauce and the flavors blend, until some oil floats to the top and sides, 8 to 10 minutes.

Taste and adjust the seasoning with more salt, curry powder, thyme, or black pepper, if needed, then reduce the heat to maintain a simmer, cover, and cook until just tender, 8 to 10 minutes. Taste and cook longer if you want softer gizzards.

Remove from the heat. Add the diced bell pepper and stir to combine well. Cover and let stand for a few minutes before serving.

Serve the stewed gizzards on their own, or make some Gizdòdò (recipe follows).

Gizdòdò

SERVES 4 TO 6

1 recipe Dòdò (page 120), diced

1 recipe Stewed Gizzards (opposite)

1 small green bell pepper, finely diced

1 small red onion, diced

White rice for serving (optional)

Sweet, fried ripe plantains tossed in stewed gizzard sauce is a dish that's become popular in the past fifteen to twenty years—a gift from the Nigerian diaspora in North America, now a continental favorite. The combination of "chicken," plantain, and vegetables is similar to the Cameroonian dish called poulet DG (Directeur Général chicken).

In a large pan, combine the dòdò, gizzards, bell pepper, and onion. Cook over medium heat until the pepper and onion soften a touch and the mixture is heated through, about 5 minutes.

Serve on its own, or with rice.

KÀZĀN RĪDĪ

SESAME CHICKEN

1 cup (140 g) raw black sesame seeds, rinsed and drained (see Note)

½ teaspoon black stone flower (optional)

2 tablespoons Basic Yaji (page 26), plus more as needed

2 teaspoons fine sea salt

1 teaspoon dry pepper (see page 22)

1 medium red onion, sliced, plus 1 small red onion, sliced into thin strips or rings

1 or 2 red Scotch bonnet or habanero peppers, stemmed

½ small green bell pepper, coarsely chopped

1 or 2 thumb-size pieces fresh ginger, peeled

2 medium garlic cloves, peeled

4 bone-in, skin-on chicken legs (8 to 10 ounces each), thighs and drumsticks separated, or 4 drumsticks and 4 thighs

1 tablespoon Curry Powder (page 25)

¼ cup (60 ml) atili oil (see Note)

1 small red bell pepper, diced

NOTES: *For best results, add some white or brown sesame seeds to the black ones before toasting—use them to monitor the toasted seeds' color.*

Substitute 3 tablespoons grassy extra-virgin olive oil plus 1 tablespoon toasted sesame oil for the atili oil.

I fell in love with kàzān rīdī, black sesame chicken, a Plateau state specialty, in 2018. My friend Madey made it for Christmas lunch, with stewing chickens. For a quicker cook, use softer chickens (broiler/fryer/roasters), or other proteins such as beef or lamb, which can be boiled, grilled, roasted, or fried.

In a large skillet, dry the sesame seeds over medium heat, stirring, until the moisture evaporates, about 12 minutes. Toast until the seeds smell nutty and begin to pop, 4 to 5 minutes more. If using the black stone flower, add and toss with the sesame seeds for 1 minute more. Transfer to a plate to cool.

Working in batches, add the toasted seed mix, the yaji, 1 teaspoon of the salt, and the dry pepper to a spice grinder or food processor. Grind until broken down and dark—don't overprocess the mixture; you want "flour," not butter. Set aside.

In a food processor or blender, combine the sliced medium onion, Scotch bonnet, green bell pepper, ginger, and garlic. Process or pulse to form a coarse mixture.

In a stockpot, combine the onion mixture, chicken, curry powder, and remaining 1 teaspoon salt. Cover and cook over medium heat, stirring often, until the chicken loses is no longer raw and yields its juices and the mixture begins to boil, about 10 minutes. Add 2 cups (480 ml) water, cover, and cook until the chicken is tender but not falling apart, 15 to 20 minutes.

Remove the chicken to a plate to cool a bit, about 15 minutes. You can leave the chicken skins on or remove them.

Put the atili oil in a large bowl and carefully add the chicken. Toss to coat each piece in the oil. Sprinkle half the black sesame mixture over the chicken and toss well to coat, adding more as needed.

Transfer the chicken to a serving platter. Top with the small sliced onion and the red bell pepper. Serve with any remaining black sesame mixture.

DAMBUN NAMA

BEEF FLOSS

2 pounds (900 g) lean beef sirloin or tenderloin, cut into 4-inch (10 cm) chunks

2 teaspoons fine sea salt

1 large red onion, chopped

2 thumb-size pieces fresh ginger, peeled

2 tablespoons Basic Yaji (page 26)

1 beef stock cube

¼ cup (60 ml) neutral oil

SIX TYPES OF DAMBU YOU CAN MAKE

1. Chicken (dambun kaza): Use broiler/ fryer/roaster chickens. Cook the meat on the bone, then shred.
2. Duck (dambun agwagwa): Use the same process as for chicken.
3. Guinea fowl (dambun zabuwa): Use the same process as for chicken.
4. Goat (dambun akuya): Bone-in shoulder meat works well. Cook the meat on the bone, then shred.
5. Ram (dambun rago): Use the same process as for goat.
6. Fish (dambun kifi): Use skinless fillets from your favorite fish.

Dambun nama is the Hausa name for shredded meat floss. Your choice of beef is important. Lean meat without fat or sinew is generally preferred. Don't overseason in the early stages. You want to cook the meat low and slow until it falls apart—use a pressure cooker, if you like.

In a medium pot, combine the beef, 1 teaspoon of the salt, and 6 cups (1.4 L) water. Bring to a boil over high heat. Cover with the lid ajar, reduce the heat to medium-high, and cook until the beef firms up, loses its rawness, and turns pale, about 12 minutes. Remove from the heat, drain the cooking liquid, and rinse the meat and the pot with cold water. Return to the heat. Add the onion, ginger, 1 tablespoon of the yaji, and the stock cube. Fill the pot with water to about ½ inch (1.3 cm) above the meat. Cover and cook until the meat is soft and can be pulled into strings with ease, 1½ to 2 hours. With a slotted spoon, transfer the meat to a plate and let cool, about 20 minutes. Strain and reserve the cooking liquid (use it instead of water in Mīyan Taushe, page 255).

Transfer the cooled meat to a large mortar. With a pestle, pound the meat so it separates into strands. Alternatively, seal the meat in a large zip-top bag, set it on a cutting board, and flatten it with a rolling pin.

In a heavy nonstick wok or pan, combine the remaining 1 tablespoon yaji, the remaining 1 teaspoon salt, the oil, and the shredded meat. Cook over low heat, stirring often, making small circular motions with the meat. Continue until the mixture stops steaming and is a bit dry to the touch, about 20 minutes. Remove from the heat and let rest for 20 minutes, then return to low heat and cook, stirring often so it doesn't burn, until the floss is completely dry, fluffy, and brown, about 20 minutes. Spread the beef floss over a platter to cool completely.

If your floss isn't dry, position a rack in the center of the oven and preheat the oven to 270°F (130°C). Spread the floss across a baking sheet and bake, checking every 5 to 10 minutes, until it is dry.

Store in an airtight container in the refrigerator for up to 2 weeks or in the freezer for up to 6 months—although the meat floss never really freezes. Remove and let it come to room temperature before using.

BEEF SŪYA

NUTTY SPICED BEEF SKEWERS

1 pound (450 g) beef fillet, sirloin, or blade steak

3 tablespoons neutral oil, plus more for the grate

⅓ cup (35 g) Basic Yaji (page 26), plus more as needed

FOR SERVING

½ cup (88 g) Yajin Kuli (page 26)

Thinly sliced red onions

Sliced tomatoes

SIX OTHER WAYS TO ENJOY SŪYA

1. In a shayi burger (see page 80)
2. With bread to make a sandwich
3. With Soaked Garri (page 72)
4. Added to (instant) noodles
5. With Nigerian Salad (page 97)
6. In a stir-fry, with Māsà (page 85) and vegetables

Sūya is Nigerian street food at its finest—think flame-grilled, nutty, spicy meat cradled in paper with a side of fresh tomatoes, sliced red onions, sometimes fresh Scotch bonnets or habaneros, cabbage, and some extra yajin kuli for dipping.

The dish originated with the Hausa in the north, where the knowledge and mastery of meat is unparalleled. Though sūya is often thought to be meat skewers, it is an umbrella name for grilled or roasted meat. There are two common types: tsire, yaji-seasoned skewered meat cooked over a glowing fire or on a charcoal grill; and balangu (or balango), long strips of meat, often ram, roasted in wet, thick butcher's paper in a confit of oil, such as groundnut oil.

Some popular cuts of beef for sūya include tenderloin (fillet), flank steak, sirloin, blade steak (also known as top blade), round, round top, and, in Nigeria, tozo, a fatty-tender marbled cut from the hump of a zebu (a relative of the American Brahman cattle breed). It is soft, chewy, and utterly delicious.

I recently learned—thanks to my friend Hauwa—that sūya is prepared with basic or "normal" yaji and, once grilled, served with a different blend, yajin kuli (also known as yajin tsire, sūya spice, or sūya pepper; see page 26). Growing up in the south of Nigeria, all I knew was yajin kuli and, until recently, I used it both to season and to serve with sūya, but there's a risk of burning the meat as a result.

Mai sūya (see page 176) typically grill the meat, allow it to rest for a few hours, and reheat it once people are ready to buy; this twice-cooked process intensifies the flavors.

The combination of sūya with Māsà (page 85) is a favorite.

If using wooden skewers, soak them in water for at least 30 minutes before grilling so they don't burn on the grill.

Wrap the beef tightly in plastic wrap and place on a plate or small baking sheet. Freeze for 15 to 30 minutes, until the beef is partially frozen and firm to the touch.

Unwrap the meat. With a sharp chef's knife, slice the meat against the grain into strips that are 2 inches (5 cm) long, 1 inch (2.5 cm) wide, and ⅛ inch (3 mm) thick. The easiest and most efficient way to do this is to start by portioning the beef into pieces that are

S IS FOR SŪYA AND A HOST OF OTHER STREET-GRILLED MEATS

Most cultures feature grilled meat on sticks, often as part of their street food culture, and interestingly, the names of many of these grilled skewers begin with S. The list includes Nigerian sūya, South African sosatie, Indonesian saté, Balinese satay, Greek souvlaki, spiedies from upstate New York, and shish kebab, which originated in Turkey but is now typical of West Asian and Eastern Mediterranean cuisines.

2 inches (5 cm) wide and 1 inch (2.5 cm) thick, and then cutting those pieces crosswise into ⅛-inch-thick (3 mm) strips.

Put the strips of meat in a large bowl and drizzle the oil over them, then sprinkle with 2 tablespoons of the yaji. Carefully toss and massage the yaji into the beef until the meat is evenly coated. Season with another 2 tablespoons of the yaji.

Working with one piece of beef at a time, thread it onto a metal or wooden skewer, piercing each piece through twice to secure it, then spread the meat out on the skewer so it will cook evenly. Leave 2 inches (5 cm) of the skewer exposed at either end. Place the completed skewer on a platter and repeat with the remaining beef. Once all skewers are assembled, sprinkle the remaining yaji on both sides. Cover and refrigerate the skewers for at least 30 minutes and up to 8 hours before grilling.

If using a charcoal grill, light a chimney starter full of charcoal. When the coals are hot and covered with gray ash, carefully spread them onto one side of the grill. If using a gas grill, set the burners on one side of the grill to high (leave the other side off). Cover and preheat for 5 to 10 minutes. Clean and oil the grilling grate.

Place the skewers on the grill over direct heat and cook for about 8 minutes, turning them over once, until charred on both sides and cooked through. Transfer to a serving platter and let rest for 2 to 3 minutes before serving. (Alternatively, let the skewers rest for 1 to 2 hours, then reheat as needed.)

Serve the skewers with the yajin kuli, onion, and tomatoes.

SŪYA FACTS

Sūya is prepared by mai sūya, Hausa men from the north of Nigeria trained in the art of spice and meat preservation. I've not yet come across a non-Hausa man or woman sūya maker/seller in all my years. The origins of sūya are linked to pastoral nomads who traveled with cattle, living and trading. Thanks to their journeys, every nook and cranny of every Nigerian city is blessed with a "sūya spot."

Ordering sūya is easy—you say what you want, and the sūya is selected and reheated, then served in newspaper, on the skewers or removed from them, with a sprinkling of yaji or yajin kuli, fresh tomato wedges, red onion, cabbage, and, for the brave, slices of fresh hot red Scotch bonnets or habaneros.

When I was young, sūya was rarely made by home cooks, although you could invite the mai sūya to cater a meal. If you were far away from your birthland and hankering after the meats, then, and only then, was it okay to make sūya at home. Furthermore, you could buy it only in the evening, at sūya spots, after the mai sūya had spent all day prepping— slicing the meat, dredging it in yaji, threading it on skewers, and grilling it. At 4 or 5 p.m., the sūya spots suddenly transformed into hives of activity, welcoming everyone regardless of creed or bank balance.

Nigerians joke that sūya not sold at night or in newspaper isn't real sūya. Today, sūya is widely available, sold at all times of day, and more and more people are making it at home—and we're all better off for it.

OTHER NAMES FOR COW LEG

There are many names for cow (and goat, and ram) legs and feet, from "marching ground" (or "matching ground"), a literal expression describing the act of stepping or walking on the ground; to "homework," which alludes to the intricacies of extracting the fleshy bits and marrow from the cooked feet.

In Brazil, you'll find it as mocotó (with etymological roots in mbokotó, from the Kimbundu language), similar to bokotó (Yorùbá).

NKWOBI

COW LEG IN CREAMY PALM OIL SAUCE

2 pounds (900 g) cow leg, washed and cut into 2-inch (5 cm) pieces

2 teaspoons fine sea salt, plus more as needed

3½ quarts (3.3 L) hot water

2 medium red onions: 1 chopped, 1 cut into thin rings

1 or more red Scotch bonnet or habanero peppers, minced, plus more as needed

½ teaspoon Cameroon pepper (see page 164) or dry pepper (see page 22), plus more as needed

2 beef stock cubes, plus more as needed

1 tablespoon Nkwobi Spice Blend from Scratch (recipe follows) or Quick Nkwobi Spice Blend (recipe follows)

¼ cup (60 ml) red palm oil

2 tablespoons Alkaline Water (page 334)

½ cup (about 1.6 ounces/ 45 g) ugba, rinsed and drained

2 tablespoons chopped fresh utazi or scent leaves (see page 20), for garnish

1 small tatashe or red bell pepper, diced, for garnish

NOTE: *Cow leg is also sold as cow foot, cow heel, or cow's trotters. Seek out butchers that cater to African, Asian (Filipino, Indonesian), Caribbean (Jamaican, Trinidad and Tobago), and Eastern European (Armenian, Turkish) customers.*

A gift from the east of Nigeria, nkwobi is a delightful combination of meat and spices tossed in creamy ṅcha sauce and famously served in a shallow wooden mini mortar called an okwa (Igbo). The dish is piled high in the bowl, giving an illusion of a more-than-one-can-finish golden tower of spiced and seasoned cow leg.

Small serving bowls work well for the nkwobi. It's not traditional, but a sprinkle of sliced or diced sweet red peppers adds a nice contrast. Serve with palm wine.

In a large pot, combine the cow leg, 1 teaspoon of the salt, and 2 quarts (1.9 L) of the hot water. Cover with the lid ajar and bring to a boil. Remove from the heat. Drain the cow leg, rinse with cold water, and return to the pot.

Add the remaining 1½ quarts (1.4 L) hot water and the remaining 1 teaspoon salt to the pot, cover, and bring to a boil over high heat. Reduce the heat to low and cook, adding water to the pot as needed to keep the meat covered, until the meat is soft but still has some bite, 1½ to 2 hours, or longer if you want the meat to be softer. Remove from the heat.

Drain the cow leg (reserving the cooking liquid) and return it to the pot. Add the chopped onion, Scotch bonnet (to taste), Cameroon pepper, stock cubes, nkwobi spice blend, and oil. Stir, cover, and cook over low heat until warmed through, about 10 minutes. Remove from the heat.

Stir in the alkaline water; the color of the sauce will change to a bright yellow-orange and it should thicken. Add the ugba and stir. If you want a looser sauce, add some of the reserved cooking liquid ¼ cup (60 ml) at a time. Stir well to coat all the pieces of meat.

Taste and adjust the seasoning with more salt, Scotch bonnet or Cameroon pepper, or seasoning cubes, if needed.

Ladle into individual bowls and top with the sliced onion, fresh utazi or scent leaves, and tatashe or red bell peppers.

RECIPE CONTINUES →

Nkwobi Spice Blend from Scratch

MAKES ABOUT ¼ CUP (60 G)

2 medium gbafilo seeds (see page 164), shelled

7 ehuru seeds (see page 25), shelled

1½ teaspoons whole uziza peppercorns (see page 95)

11 njangsa seeds (see page 164)

4 whole uda pods (see page 164)

5 omilo seeds (see page 164), shelled

2 country onion seeds (see page 164; ½ teaspoon ground), or ¼ teaspoon dried onion and ¼ teaspoon granulated garlic

1 (1-inch/2.5 cm) piece aidan fruit (see page 164)

1½ teaspoons ground ginger

Country onions are really hard and may not blend smoothly if left whole, so crack them with a mallet or in a mortar and pestle before they go into the spice grinder.

In a small stainless-steel or cast-iron skillet, combine the gbafilo, ehuru, uziza peppercorns, njangsa, uda, omilo, country onion, and aidan fruit. Toast the spices over medium-low heat, stirring and swirling the pan frequently, until fragrant—you might hear popping sounds—5 minutes. Remove from the heat, transfer the mixture to a plate, and let cool to room temperature, about 10 minutes.

Transfer the toasted spices to a spice grinder, add the ground ginger, and grind as fine as you can—you should end up with a cross between fine coffee grounds and tea granules. Empty the ground spices into an airtight container and cover. Let stand for 2 to 3 days, then regrind (and pass through a sieve to remove any larger pieces, if you like). Store in an airtight container away from light and heat, for up to 6 months.

Quick Nkwobi Spice Blend

MAKES 1 TABLESPOON

2 teaspoons Pepper Soup Spice Blend (page 240)

½ teaspoon ground ginger

¼ teaspoon garlic powder

¼ teaspoon onion powder

Combine the spices in a small bowl.

Store in an airtight container away from light and heat, for up to 6 months.

FRIED AWARA

FRIED TOFU

12 ounces (350 g) extra-firm tofu, drained and patted dry

Neutral oil, for frying

2 tablespoons Basic Yaji (page 26), plus more for serving

1 teaspoon fine sea salt

¼ cup cornstarch (30 g), rice flour (35 g), or potato starch (40 g)

In the north, Awara is the name for tofu, and is enjoyed as a source of protein on its own and in stews, sauces, and soups. It's not uncommon to find people making plain and spiced awara from scratch, but store-bought extra-firm tofu works equally well.

I don't press my extra-firm tofu, so it stays moist and juicy. If all you have access to is medium-firm tofu, you may want to press it by weighing it down so it releases some of its liquid before using. Alternatively, and untraditionally, do as my friend food writer and journalist Naomi Duguid recommends: Freeze 1-inch (2.5 cm) cubes of tofu and then defrost to create chewier, spongier chunks (see Variation).

Serve as a snack, or add to stews or soups.

Cut the tofu into roughly 1-inch (2.5 cm) cubes, drizzle with 2 tablespoons oil, and rub gently so the cubes are evenly coated. Add more oil by the tablespoon if some of the cubes aren't well coated.

In a large bowl, stir together the yaji and salt. Add the tofu cubes and toss gently until evenly coated. Cover and let stand on the counter for 30 minutes or in the fridge up to 2 days.

When ready to fry, in a wok or large Dutch oven, heat 1½ inches (4 cm) of oil over medium-high heat to 350°F (175°C). Line a rimmed baking sheet with a wire rack or paper towels.

Spread the cornstarch in a shallow bowl. Toss the seasoned tofu in the starch to coat.

Working in batches, and with a slotted spoon, shake off any excess starch and add the tofu to the hot oil, being careful not to overcrowd the pot. Fry until golden and crisped all over, turning partway through so they cook evenly, 6 to 7 minutes.

Use the slotted spoon to lift the fried tofu from the oil, gently shaking off any excess, and transfer it to the the prepared baking sheet to drain further. Repeat with the remaining tofu, allowing the oil to return to temperature between batches.

RECIPE CONTINUES →

Let sit for about 5 minutes before serving hot or warm, with more yaji on the side.

VARIATIONS

For a chewier texture, cut the drained tofu (no need to press it) into 1-inch (2.5 cm) cubes. Spread them on a rimmed baking sheet in a single layer and freeze for about 2 hours, or until solid. If you're not using them right away, seal them in a freezer bag to prevent freezer burn and freeze for up to 3 months. When ready to use, place them in a strainer in the sink and run warm water over them until they defrost. Gently squeeze and pat dry, then season and fry as directed.

To air-fry the tofu: Combine ¼ cup (60 ml) oil, the salt, and yaji in a large bowl and whisk well. Add the tofu and toss well so each piece is evenly coated. Sprinkle evenly with the cornstarch. Cover and let stand on the counter for 30 minutes or in the fridge for up to 2 days. When ready to cook the tofu, working in batches, arrange the cubes in a single layer on the air fryer tray and air-fry at 400°F (205°C), turning the tray partway through so they cook evenly, until golden and crisped all over, 10 to 12 minutes. Remove from the air fryer and repeat with the remaining tofu. Let sit for about 5 minutes before serving.

PLANT-FORWARD PROTEINS

There are some unusual plant-forward ingredients in Nigerian cuisine that provide protein, texture, or both. Many of them feature in soups and stews, either on their own or alongside meat and seafood.

Across the country, mushrooms are enjoyed fresh, sun-dried, smoked, or fermented to make umami-rich condiments and are used instead of meat in some dishes. The Yorùbá of the South West have a whole catalog of mushrooms, describing them by flavor, shape, texture, growing location, and more.

In the southeastern states of Abia, Anambra, and Imo, ofe achara with mgbam is a ceremonial version of Ègúsí Soup (page 253). Common at parties, weddings, New Yam festivals, and other events, the soup includes tender hearts of achara, a perennial grass, and mgbam, a textured cake made from ground ègúsí seeds and ground ero ósú (also known as mushroom ósú or king tuber mushroom). Ero ósú, like truffles, grows in and around mushrooms during the rainy season but is larger, with skin that resembles the brown bark of yam and a spongy white interior. It is prized not for the hint of earthy flavor and aroma but for its strength as a binder in making mgbam.

In the Central and South South regions, sun-dried unripe pawpaw shreds and chunks are rehydrated, developing a chewy texture, perfect for soups. Igyande mbwue ha ishwa, made from sesame seeds, is one version from the Tiv people. The calyxes of white *Hibiscus sabdariffa* flowers star in Margi special, a stew from the Margi community of the North East, often part of celebratory meals, and in ọbè ishapa, a Yorùbá soup. Èfọ́ elégede features not only pumpkin leaves but sun-dried chunks of pumpkin.

From north to south, beans feature in a variety of forms—smoked cowpeas are added to soups like owho esha, a specialty of the Urhobos in the South South, enjoyed at the new year; dried pretzel bean skins are rehydrated and form the bulk of adenge soup, from the Tivs; and a variety of cowpeas, nseme, go into a special okro soup, nseme otong. Chewy, shredded ugba (see page 95) brings delightful texture to okwuru ugba, a version of okro soup.

ALL-TIME
FAVORITES

STEWS AND
SAUCES

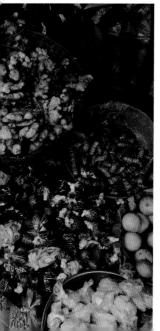

SOUPS, STEWS, AND SAUCES—THE THREE S'S OF Nigerian cuisine—are their own language. Stews and sauces are served with rice, pasta, and cooked vegetables. We sop up our stew with soft bread like the Italians do.

You'll find stews everywhere—roadside food stalls, palaces, homes, restaurants—in a range of consistencies from thick (like classic stew) to light (like omi ọbẹ̀). Stew is sometimes combined with soups—like Ewédú (page 244)—and can be used as an ingredient if you don't want to make stew bases from scratch for Egg Sauce (page 84) or quick (what Nigerians call "emergency") jollof rice (page 143).

There are four or five key elements for most stews: base, stock (not necessary in all cases, like in Palm Oil Stew), seasoning, oil, and protein. The base can be tomato- or pepper-led (see page 335). The stock and seasoning tend to pair traditional flavor bases with palm, groundnut (peanut), or ẹ̀gúsí oil; crayfish; dry pepper; and irú or other seasoning like ogiri. Nontraditional bases, like in classic stew, feature vegetable oils and seasonings like curry powder, dried thyme, ginger, and garlic.

Sauces tend to be on the chunky end of the spectrum, with the main ingredient and base combined in a number of ways. For example, in both garden egg sauce and chicken curry, the vegetables are sliced and chopped, and remain distinct through to the end, and the protein is in bite-size chunks.

Feel free to explore different proteins in the different bases, from meat to mushrooms and more.

CLOCKWISE FROM LEFT: *"Pepper" being processed at a community grinder; sombo pepper; white garden eggs; an array of fresh and dried spices*

FEATURED IN THESE RECIPES

1. **Bay leaves.** Both Indian and Mediterranean varieties are popular, for stews and stocks.

2. **Crayfish.** Use it whole or ground for a fishy essence.

3. **Dry fish.** Catfish is a popular fish in Nigeria, enjoyed dried (and fresh). Its popularity and availability have grown in the past decade or two. It is used whole, or deboned and broken into bits and chunks.

4. **Dried prawns.** These reddish prawns are often used "whole," head-on or off. Occasionally, the heads are removed, blended, and used as you would crayfish.

5. **Dried thyme.** It has been popular in Nigeria since the early 1900s and remains so today.

6. **Irú woro.** These fermented locust beans sport a pasty ash coating over the seeds. Buying them (and using them from) frozen is a great way to extend their lifespan.

7. **Red Roma (plum) tomatoes.** Similar to the plum variety of tomatoes in Nigeria and known as both Tomato Jos and (Dan) UTC tomatoes (after the now-defunct Union Trading Company). They are prized for their textural and taste characteristics: firmness, thick flesh, long shelf life, and good flavor.

8. **Smoked mackerel.** Popular in sauces like Garden Egg Sauce (page 204) and often bought in the open market in Nigeria. It is also a popular ingredient in Polish cuisine, so check out Polish grocers and supermarkets for hot-smoked whole mackerel. Substitute fillets or even tinned fish.

CLASSIC STEW

6 medium red Roma (plum) tomatoes, coarsely chopped

6 red tatashe peppers, or 3 red shepherd peppers, coarsely chopped

3 medium red onions: 2 coarsely chopped, 1 thinly sliced

1 or more Scotch bonnet or habanero peppers, stemmed

4 cups (1 L) Curry Stock (page 333), plus more as needed

3 teaspoons Curry Powder (page 25), plus more as needed

3 teaspoons dried thyme, plus more as needed

2 teaspoons fine sea salt, plus more as needed

1 cup (240 ml) neutral oil

2 or 3 dried bay leaves

½ teaspoon freshly ground black or white pepper, plus more as needed

⅓ cup (80 g) tomato paste

2 pounds (900 g) Fried Meat (page 330)

PAIRINGS WITH STEW

1. Agege bread (see page 75) or other soft bread
2. Cooked plantains, yams, or sweet potatoes
3. Soups
4. Pasta

When you say "stew" to Nigerians, one thing comes to mind: an aromatic red dish made with a seasoned blend of tomatoes, red onions, and peppers, similar to Italian ragù. Considered mother sauce and staple, stew is known far and wide, in every nook, cranny, creek, and grassland of the land. If you have stew on hand, you have most of a meal.

Use your favorite protein (typically parcooked)—beef, chicken, goat meat, offal, Fried Awara (tofu; page 181), or seafood. Serve with white rice.

Working in batches, combine the tomatoes, tatashe peppers, coarsely chopped onions, Scotch bonnet (to taste), and 2 cups (480 ml) of the curry stock in a blender. Puree until smooth; you should have about 2½ quarts (2.4 L) of stew base.

Pour the stew base into a 4-quart (4 L) or larger stockpot or saucepan. Add 1 teaspoon each of the curry powder, thyme, and salt, cover with the lid ajar, and bring to a boil over medium-high heat, about 8 minutes. Reduce the heat to medium-low and cook, stirring and scraping the bottom occasionally, until the stew base has reduced by at least a third (to about 2 quarts/1.9 L), about 40 minutes. Transfer to a heatproof large bowl.

In the same pot, heat the oil over medium heat. When the oil is shimmering, add the sliced onion, bay leaves, black pepper, and the remaining 2 teaspoons curry powder, 2 teaspoons thyme, and 1 teaspoon salt. Cook, stirring, until the mixture is fragrant and the onion has softened slightly, about 2 minutes.

Add the tomato paste and cook, stirring, until it darkens, sweetens, and splits in the oil, about 4 minutes. Add the stew base and the remaining 2 cups (480 ml) curry stock and stir well. Reduce the heat to low or medium-low, cover with the lid ajar, and cook until the mixture has reduced by a third and oil comes to the surface, about 25 minutes (be careful when you check on the stew, as it may splatter). Taste and adjust the salt, pepper, and spices as needed.

Stir in the fried meat and cook, covered, until some oil floats to the top, 15 minutes more. If the stew is too liquid, keep cooking to reduce it further; if it is too thick, add more stock or water to thin it. Remove from the heat and discard the bay leaves before serving.

OMI ỌBẸ̀
LIGHT TOMATO STEW

1 pound (450 g) stewing beef, cut into 2-inch (5 cm) chunks

3 medium red onions: 1 thinly sliced, 2 halved

2 tablespoons ground crayfish (see page 23)

1 teaspoon dry pepper (see page 22)

2 teaspoons fine sea salt, plus more as needed

3 large red Roma (plum) tomatoes, halved

3 red tatashe peppers, or 1 to 2 red shepherd peppers, cut into large chunks

2 sombo peppers, Thai red chiles, or Fresno peppers, stemmed

1 or more Scotch bonnet or habanero peppers, stemmed

½ cup (120 ml) red palm oil

¼ cup (60 ml) peanut oil or other neutral oil

2 teaspoons fresh, frozen, or dried irú (see page 25)

7 ounces (about 200 g) pomo (cowskin; see page 21), cut into small pieces (1 cup)

7 ounces (about 200 g) cow shaki (tripe), prepared (see page 21) and cut into 2- to 3-inch (5 to 7.5 cm) pieces (1 cup)

The name of this smooth, light stew translates to "water of the stew." Also known as buka stew, it is made with the classic stew ingredients along with a blend of oils and irú for seasoning, and features an assortment of meat and offal. Omi Ọbẹ̀ is one of the quartet of dishes that make up àbùlà (see sidebar, page 243). You can skip the tripe and pomo and use more beef, or substitute cooked kidney, liver, goat, or another protein of your choosing.

The vegetables go in to the pot whole or in chunks so they can be removed with ease to be blended, strained, and returned to the pot.

In a medium pot, combine the stewing beef, sliced onion, ground crayfish, dry pepper, 1 teaspoon of the salt, and 4 cups (about 1 L) water. Bring to a boil over high heat, 7 to 8 minutes.

Add the onion halves, tomatoes, tatashe, sombo, and Scotch bonnet (to taste) to the pot. Reduce the heat to medium and cook until the vegetables soften, about 20 minutes. With a slotted spoon, transfer the softened vegetables to a plate and let cool for about 10 minutes.

Set the Scotch bonnet aside. Peel the tomatoes, removing as much of their skin as possible, then transfer the flesh to a blender with the onion, tatashe, and sombo. Blend until smooth, then pass the mixture (you should have about 4 cups/1 L) through a fine-mesh strainer back into the pot with the meat; discard any bits left in the strainer. Rinse out the blender with ½ cup (120 ml) water and pass that through the strainer, again discarding any bits left.

Return the pot to low heat. Add the palm oil, groundnut oil, irú, and 1 teaspoon of the salt to the stew and stir until incorporated. Cover and simmer so the ingredients come together, about 10 minutes. Taste and adjust the seasoning—add salt if needed, and if you'd like more heat, add the reserved Scotch bonnet, whole or chopped. Cook over low heat until the beef is just tender, about 15 minutes more, or until the meat is cooked to your liking. Add the pomo and shaki and cook until they absorb the sauce and oil pools on top and around the sides, 15 minutes more.

Remove from the heat and serve.

TOMATOES

In addition to delivering sweet and tart flavors, tomatoes are high in glutamate, making them one of the best plant-based sources of umami. Nigeria is the second-largest grower of tomatoes in Africa (after Egypt), and several varieties are grown in the country, including Tomato Jos, a highly prized cultivar similar to the Roma (plum), as well as beefsteaks and heirlooms.

In some areas, tomatoes are sun-dried for export, but fresh tomatoes are typically harvested just before market day and packed in baskets made of raffia, much like the wicker baskets used in many parts of Africa and Asia and the flat baskets of Italy. These are lined with dry grass and straw to cushion the tomatoes. Once full, they are covered with newspaper or cement paper (heavy-duty butcher's paper), wrapped with twine, and transported to markets around the country. Tomatoes are sold in bowls and baskets by volume, not by weight. Nearly every street corner has a little wooden table or stall with pyramidal stacks of tomatoes in various stages of ripening, red onions, and Scotch bonnets or habaneros.

GROUNDNUT STEW

4 cups (about 1 L) Curry Stock (page 333)

3½ teaspoons fine sea salt, plus more as needed

2 tablespoons grated fresh ginger

1 tablespoon minced garlic

½ teaspoon dried thyme

½ teaspoon freshly ground black pepper

1 pound (about 450 g) boneless or bone-in chicken thighs, cut into 2-inch (5 cm) pieces

1 pound (about 450 g) boneless or bone-in beef chuck, cut into 2-inch (5 cm) pieces

3 medium red onions: 2 coarsely chopped, 1 sliced

2 large red Roma (plum) tomatoes

½ cup (120 ml) groundnut oil (see page 267)

2 dried bay leaves

1½ cups (8 ounces/225 g) Roasted Groundnuts, skinned (recipe follows)

1 whole Scotch bonnet or habanero pepper, poked 2 or 3 times with a knife

½ to 1 teaspoon dry pepper (see page 22; optional)

White rice for serving

NOTE: *You'll find shelled red groundnuts (peanuts) in many stores, in packs sometimes described as Spanish red peanuts.*

My friend 'Layide introduced me to this stew when we lived in the Netherlands. She ordered a large batch from a Nigerian caterer, and when the creamy, darker-than-beige-but-not-quite-brown stew came, she split it with me. We savored the creaminess, nuttiness, and spice, ladling spoonfuls over freshly boiled rice, and enjoyed it as part of a groundnut chop spread (see page 140).

In a large bowl or container, combine the curry stock and 1 cup (240 ml) water to thin the stock (you should have 5 cups/about 1.2 L thinned stock). Set aside.

In a separate large bowl, combine 3 teaspoons of the salt, the ginger, garlic, thyme, and black pepper. Add the chicken and beef and rub it well so the meat is seasoned properly. Set aside.

In a blender, combine the chopped onions and the tomatoes with 1 cup (240 ml) of the thinned curry stock and blend until smooth; you should have about 3 cups (720 ml) stew base total. Set aside.

In a large heavy-bottomed pan or Dutch oven, heat ¼ cup (60 ml) of the groundnut oil over medium heat. When the oil is shimmering, add the chicken and beef. Increase the heat to high and cook, stirring every now and again, until the meat loses color, about 15 minutes. With a slotted spoon, transfer the meat to a bowl; cover to keep warm.

In the same pan, combine the remaining ¼ cup (60 ml) groundnut oil, the sliced onion, the remaining ½ teaspoon salt, and the bay leaves and stir. Reduce the heat to medium and cook until the onion softens, about 5 minutes. Add the stew base and 2 cups (480 ml) of the thinned stock, stirring and scraping up any browned bits from the bottom of the pan. Increase the heat to high, cover with the lid ajar, and cook until just reduced, 20 to 25 minutes.

Meanwhile, in a blender, combine the peanuts with 1 cup (240 ml) of the thinned stock. Blend on high until creamy (a touch of grit is okay); you should have about 2 cups (480 ml). Transfer to a bowl.

When the stew has reduced, carefully transfer 1 cup (240 ml) of the stew to the peanut paste and stir until well combined. Add this mixture to the pot with the stew and stir well. Cook for about 5 minutes, then return the meat to the pot. Add the remaining

1 cup (240 ml) thinned stock and the Scotch bonnet and stir well. Reduce the heat to low, cover with the lid ajar, and cook, stirring often, until the meat is soft and tender, and oil pools around the sides and on top, 25 to 30 minutes. Taste and adjust with more salt, if needed. If you want more heat, add some dry pepper.

Remove from the heat and let stand for about 10 minutes; it will thicken. If desired, thin the stew with water ¼ cup (60 ml) at a time and season as you desire. Serve with rice.

RECIPE CONTINUES →

Roasted Groundnuts

MAKES 1½ CUPS (225 G)

4 cups (about 1 L) boiling water

1 cup (5½ ounces/160 g) raw groundnuts (peanuts), rinsed and drained

2 teaspoons fine sea salt

NOTE: *To remove the skins, rub the groundnuts until most of the skins come off. Transfer the groundnuts to a colander set on a tray and shake it so the broken skins fall through the holes. Continue rubbing as needed. Discard the skins and store the groundnuts.*

In a heatproof bowl, combine the boiling water, groundnuts, and salt. Stir, cover, and let sit at room temperature (or, once cool, in the fridge if the weather's hot) for 4 to 8 hours. The soaking liquid will thicken and color.

Drain the groundnuts in a colander, rinse, and gently pat them dry—leave the skins on, as they protect the groundnuts while they cook.

Spread the groundnuts on a rimmed baking sheet and set aside to air-dry for 1 to 2 hours.

Microwave roasting: Cook the groundnuts in batches. Be careful during this process as the dish will get hot.

Place a single layer of groundnuts in a microwave-safe dish. Microwave at full power, uncovered, in 1-minute bursts, stirring and resting for up to 1 minute after each burst. The groundnuts will go from oily-wet to translucent and opaque. You might hear popping and crackling. The groundnuts are ready when some skins turn papery and slip off with ease and the nuts take on golden hues. If you split one in half, you should see patches of light brown. This should take 6 to 8 minutes total.

Remove the dish from the microwave and set on a rack. You will hear more popping and crackling as the groundnuts continue to cook, then cool, shrink, and turn crunchy, about 30 minutes. Repeat with the remaining groundnuts.

Oven roasting: Position a rack in the center of the oven and preheat the oven to 350°F (175°C).

Roast the peanuts on a rimmed baking sheet, checking them and stirring every 5 minutes until they're lightly golden brown and fragrant, about 20 minutes. You might hear the occasional pop and crackle. They may not look dark, but they continue to cook as they cool. Remove the baking sheet from the oven and set it on a wire rack. Let cool for about 30 minutes—there will be more popping and crackling as the peanuts cool and shrink.

Store the groundnuts in an airtight container for up to 4 weeks at room temperature, 3 months in the refrigerator, and 6 months in the freezer.

SERVES 4

PALM OIL STEW

2 large red onions: 1 coarsely
chopped, 1 thinly sliced

2 medium red tatashe
peppers, coarsely chopped

1 Scotch bonnet or habanero
pepper, or more as needed,
stemmed

1 cup (240 ml) red palm oil

1 tablespoon fresh irú (see
page 25)

2 teaspoons ground crayfish
(see page 23)

1½ teaspoons fine sea salt

1 whole dry fish (about
150 g), 5 to 6 inches (12.5 to
15 cm) in diameter, or
2 small dry fish, 2½ to
3 inches (6.3 to 7.5 cm)
in diameter, cleaned (see
page 23)

This stew features dry fish cooked in a base of onions and sweet
and hot peppers. Some people add tomatoes, but I think their acidity
doesn't work well with palm oil.

You can make the stew with whole dried or smoked fish, steaks,
or flaked and broken bits. If you don't want to cook the fish head-
on, remove the head and save it for making dry fish powder (see
page 23); replace it with more fish (the head is typically a third of
the total weight of the fish). Other dried and smoked proteins, like
smoked turkey, work well here.

Serve with white rice or boiled vegetables.

In a blender or food processor, combine the chopped onion, tatashe,
Scotch bonnet, and ¼ cup (60 ml) water. Blend on medium to high
speed to form a slightly coarse mixture (you should have about
2½ cups/600 ml). Pour the mixture into a medium bowl, then rinse
out the blender with ½ cup (120 ml) water and add the contents of
the blender to the bowl to make 3 cups (720 ml) total.

In a medium pot, heat the palm oil over medium heat. When the oil
is shimmering, add the sliced onion, the irú, ground crayfish, and
1 teaspoon of the salt. Stir well and cook until the onion is somewhat
softened, translucent, and orange-tinged, 4 to 5 minutes.

Stir in the pureed onion-pepper mixture. Reduce the heat to low,
cover, and cook until the sauce thickens and oil floats to the top,
about 15 minutes. Taste and add some or all of the remaining
½ teaspoon salt and more Scotch bonnet, if desired.

Add the fish to the pot and stir to coat it with the sauce. Cover and
cook until the fish absorbs some of the sauce and warms through, and
oil bubbles to the surface and around the sides, 8 to 10 minutes.

Remove from the heat and let stand for 10 to 15 minutes before
serving.

THE ETYMOLOGY OF CURRY

The origin of the word "curry" is கறி, *kari*, "black" in Tamil, related to black pepper, *Piper nigrum*. Before the 1500s, in Indian cuisine, black pepper was the spice by which all other spices were defined and described. Thus, "curry" means "spiced," referring to dishes once seasoned with black pepper but now embracing other similarly hot, pungent spices, chiles, and, by extension, blends like curry powder.

CHICKEN CURRY

1 pound (450 g) boneless, skinless chicken thighs, cut into 1- to 2-inch (2.5 to 5 cm) chunks

1½ teaspoons fine sea salt, plus more as needed

1 teaspoon grated fresh ginger

1 teaspoon minced garlic

¼ cup (60 ml) peanut oil or other neutral oil

3 medium red onions, cut into 1-inch (2.5 cm) chunks

2 dried bay leaves

1 teaspoon Curry Powder (page 25)

1 teaspoon dried thyme

2 medium starchy potatoes (such as Yukon Gold or russets), peeled and cut into 1-inch (2.5 cm) chunks

2 carrots, cut into 1-inch (2.5 cm) chunks

1 small red bell pepper, cut into 1-inch (2.5 cm) chunks

1 small green bell pepper, cut into small dice

½ teaspoon freshly ground black pepper

½ teaspoon ground turmeric

1 cup (240 ml) Curry Stock (page 333) or water

2 tablespoons sifted all-purpose flour

This vibrant and delicious dish connects Nigeria, Japan, and Korea by way of British colonialism to "curry powder" from India. Swap the chicken for beef, mushrooms, or your favorite vegetables. Whatever you do, don't skip the green bell peppers—they add flavor and fragrance to the sauce.

Serve with white rice or spaghetti.

In a medium bowl, combine the chicken, 1 teaspoon of the salt, the ginger, and the garlic. Rub the seasonings into the chicken, then cover and refrigerate for 30 minutes.

In a large sauté pan, heat the groundnut oil over medium heat until it shimmers. Add half the onions, the bay leaves, and the remaining ½ teaspoon salt. Cook until the onions soften and brown, about 8 minutes. Stir in the curry powder and thyme. Cook until aromatic, 1 to 2 minutes, then add the chicken, potatoes, and carrots. Cook, stirring well every now and again, until the chicken loses its raw look and yields its juices and the liquid begins to boil, about 10 minutes.

Add the remaining onions, the red bell pepper, half the green bell pepper, the black pepper, turmeric, curry stock, and 1 cup (240 ml) water and stir. Reduce the heat to low, cover, and cook until the chicken is tender, about 15 minutes.

In a small bowl, whisk together the flour and 1 cup (240 ml) water to form a smooth slurry. Add the slurry to the pan and stir to incorporate, then cook until the sauce starts to thicken, about 5 minutes.

Add the remaining green bell pepper and cook for 5 minutes more, until they brighten in color and soften a touch. Taste and add more salt, if needed. Discard the bay leaves before serving.

GARDEN EGG SAUCE

About 1½ pounds (750 g) garden eggs (see page 95), rinsed (see Notes)

1 teaspoon fine sea salt, plus more as needed

¼ cup (60 ml) red palm oil

3 medium tomatoes, cored and thinly sliced

1 large red onion, thinly sliced

1 Scotch bonnet or habanero pepper, thinly sliced

¼ cup (55 g) smoked mackerel, deboned, skin-on if you like, and cut into chunks (see Notes)

2 teaspoons ground crayfish

1 teaspoon dry pepper (see page 22; optional)

NOTES: *I like to leave the stems on the garden eggs, which makes peeling them easier.*

Thai eggplants can be substituted for the garden eggs. And if those aren't available, use an equivalent weight of whatever eggplants you can find.

If smoked mackerel— including tinned—is not an option, use dry fish (see page 23) or any firm, oily fish like herring, sardines, or salmon (fresh, smoked, or tinned).

This combination of garden eggs, soft sweet onions, tomatoes, and some heat from the Scotch bonnet reminds me of ratatouille. Smoked or dry fish provides nuggets of rich flavor in the sauce without making it fishy or overly rich. You can skip both the crayfish and the fish, or replace them with mushrooms; fresh oyster, button, or king mushrooms work well, though rehydrated dried mushrooms such as shiitake or black fungus would provide great texture.

Serve with boiled plantain (page 125), white rice, or Dòdò (page 120).

Place a steaming rack on the bottom of a pot. Fill the pot with hot water just to the top of the rack. (Alternatively, you can use a steamer basket or a heatproof plate that fits inside the pot.) Add the garden eggs to the rack and lightly season them with salt. Cover and steam until fork-tender, 25 to 30 minutes; be sure to maintain the water level as they cook. Remove them from the steamer and let cool for about 10 minutes, then remove the stalks and peel off the skin in strips from top to bottom, as you might a banana.

Place the peeled garden eggs in a large bowl and mash them with a fork or potato masher until just chunky; you should have about 2 cups (450 g). (Alternatively, you can use an immersion blender.)

In a large sauté pan, heat the palm oil over medium heat. When the oil is shimmering, add the tomatoes, onion, Scotch bonnet (to taste), and 1 teaspoon salt. Cook, stirring so the vegetables don't scorch, until they soften a bit, a couple of minutes.

Add the mackerel and ground crayfish and cook for 2 to 3 minutes. Stir in the garden egg mash, reduce the heat to low or medium-low, cover with the lid ajar, and cook for 4 to 5 minutes, until the flavors come together and the mix is saucy. Taste and add more salt and the dry pepper, if desired.

If you want a smoother mix, puree some of the sauce, then return it to the pan and reheat. You can thin it with water.

SPICES AND SPICE PARTNERS

A stunning array of spices and spice blends from fruits and seeds are uniquely African. The list includes calabash nutmeg (*Monodora myristica*), alligator pepper (*Aframomum melegueta*), uda or grains of Selim (*Xylopia aethiopica*), efu (*Byrsocarpus dinklagei*), uziza peppercorns (*Piper guineense*), as well as the more common ginger (*Zingiber officinale*). Nigeria is one of the top producers and exporters of ginger in the world, and also exports black stone flower (dagad phool, a lichen with earthy flavors), garlic, turmeric, and chile. These spices create a range of flavor profiles—bitter, sweet, herby, astringent—and are fragrant and aromatic. They are used in both savory and sweet applications, in therapeutic remedies, and for spiritual purposes.

Names are important in Nigerian culture, and a child's introduction to the world is feted with a naming ceremony from the eighth day after birth. Guests bring symbolic gifts of spices and nuts (from alligator pepper to kola nut), sugar, sugarcane, honey, red palm oil, water, salt, alcohol (from palm wine to gin to schnapps), a holy book (the Bible or the Koran), and more. Each ingredient represents a specific prayer and wish for the child; for instance, each pod of alligator pepper has numerous seeds, symbolizing abundance and fertility.

Spices are also central to healing broths from Chicken Pepper Soup (page 239), enjoyed across the country, to aju mbaise, a healing broth made by steeping aju, a donut-shaped parcel of herbs, barks, and spices including uziza seeds, aidan fruit, and ginger; these broths are used for colds and flus, postpartum recovery, and more.

Across the country, indigenous spices are used daily. In the north in particular, due to Arabic influence, cooks also use green cardamom, cinnamon, and cloves, known collectively as kāyan ƙanshī, sweet-smelling things. This mix, in many ways, resembles the tea masalas of India and Kenya. Here they bring spice and warmth, for spiced water, Hausa koko (Àkàmù, page 76), tea, and other sweet treats.

Though the spice blends can be complex, some combinations work so well in pairs—I think of them as spice partners.

- Try ehuru (calabash nutmeg) and uda (grains of Selim) in Chicken Pepper Soup—they bring fresh, citrus, smoky, earthy, and slightly bitter flavors.

- Ground ehuru (calabash nutmeg) and uziza peppercorns in combination deliver fresh, nutty, floral, bright, and spicy flavors.

- The combination of ataiko and rigije, commonly for Banga Soup (page 257), packs a delightful punch—think small in quantity but mighty—highly flavorful with fresh eucalyptus notes and scented so that only a small amount is needed (in banga). Ataiko is a close relative of alligator pepper, but not as hot. It is commonly sold as seeds and is used almost exclusively in banga and pepper soups (they work brilliantly in sweet blends for bakes and drinks—think green cardamom). The notes in rigije combine muted eucalyptus with undertones of coffee and almond.

MORE THAN JUST FUFU

CHEWS AND SWALLOWS

SWALLOWS ARE THE STAFF OF LIFE, EATEN FOR LUNCH,

but also other meals, paired with soups or stews.

These soft, unleavened cooked doughs, similar to Nepali dhindo, Indian ragi mudde, and Czech houskové knedlíky, are made from grains, roots, and tubers and used fresh, or dried and ground into meal or flour. For fresh-ingredient swallows, fruits or vegetables are boiled, processed, or cooked from wet mashes or slurries. Meals and flours are made from dried, fermented, or smoke-dried ingredients.

Fufu (or foofoo) is a swallow, but not all swallows are fufu. Across West Africa and in the diaspora, fufu means different things. In Nigeria, it is a soft, chewy dough made from fermented wet-milled cassava, cooked in water and stirred or pounded. Sweet, tangy, and pungent, it is packed with probiotics and filling—hence the name "six to six," a reference to keeping one full from 6 a.m. to 6 p.m.

Swallows can be made with a single ingredient, such as semolina (also known as semo), or a combination of ingredients like cornmeal and cassava flour (uka) or àmàlà iṣu and Guinea corn paste (okapete). In the north, they are largely made from cereals—rice, millet, wheat, Guinea corn, and corn; in the central, western, and southern (coastal) regions, they are made from fruits, vegetables, roots, and tubers, such as yams and plantains; and inland to the east, they are made with cassava, breadfruit, and Bambara beans.

The myth of swallows being bland is an annoying one. They have unique flavors and textures, from soft, stretchy, and fluffy (pounded yam) to slightly gritty (tūwōn masàr̄ā), chewy (tapioca starch) and sticky (tūwōn shinkafa).

CLOCKWISE FROM LEFT: *Wrapped fufu; dried plantain for àmàlà; yellow garri, rice, and beans; yam*

FEATURED IN THESE RECIPES

1. **Èlubọ́.** Also known as àmàlà flour. It is milled from skin-on or peeled sun-dried yam (èlubọ́ iṣu), unripe plantain (èlubọ́ ògèdè), or cassava (èlubọ́ gbaguda or láfún).

2. **Garri.** Toasted cassava granules. Garri is the name of both the ingredient and, in some parts of southern and eastern Nigeria, the dish itself.

   Different processing styles and fermentation periods create a variety of tastes and textures—Ijebu garri from the southwest is sour and comes in fine, light yellow granules, perfect for Soaked Garri (page 72); yellow garri is a sunny color and tends to be less sour and starchier, and is great for Ẹba (page 216).

3. **Igbakọs.** These scoops, whether traditional triangular ones cut from calabash gourds or aluminum or plastic ones, are used to shape and scoop the finished dough. Use any small saucer, rice cooker spoon, or other serving spoon you have on hand.

   Before you use them, dip them in water or lightly grease with neutral oil so the soft doughs slip off easily and the portions end up with somewhat smooth surfaces.

4. **Ọmọrogun.** Also known as ẹba stick, turning garri, or turning stick. These are strong wooden tools with wide/flat bottom sections that taper toward the top, making it easy to work and knead the dough.

5. **Tapioca starch.** In Nigeria, you'll find tapioca starch sold in semisolid blocks, but despite its form, it is the same ingredient as powdered tapioca starch or tapioca flour. Tapioca starch is gluten-free.

TŪWŌN SHINKAFA

2 cups (400 g) shinkafan tūwō or Thai jasmine rice, rinsed and drained (see Note)

4 cups (about 1 L) hot water, plus more as needed

NOTES: *If you can, soak the rinsed rice for 30 minutes before cooking; the rice will cook faster and will be more aromatic.*

If you plan to use a handheld mixer, make sure your pot doesn't have any layers that can be stripped off, such as with a nonstick or lined one.

This swallow, popular across the north of Nigeria, is made with shinkafan tūwō, intentionally overcooked and then worked into a sticky dough. Serve fresh with Mīyan Taushe (page 255) or Gbẹ̀gìrì (page 243). Refrigerate leftovers and enjoy as dumamé, also known as damé, meaning "double-fire," or twice cooked. To make dumamén tūwōn shinkafa, cut into chunks, combine with some soup (such as mīyan wākē, similar to Gbẹ̀gìrì), reheat, and serve with Basic Yaji (page 26) and Clarified Mân Shānū (page 18).

In a medium pot, combine the rice and 3 cups (720 ml) of the hot water. Stir well, cover, and bring to a boil over high heat, then cook for 2 minutes. Reduce the heat to low and cook until the rice is soft, 10 to 15 minutes. If there's still water at the bottom of the pot, continue cooking until the rice is dry and and there's no water left, checking every 2 to 3 minutes.

If the rice isn't cooked through, add more water ½ cup (120 ml) at a time. The rice should be soft and overcooked and smear easily when pressed between your fingers.

Using a sturdy wooden spoon, mash the rice against the side of the pot and stir until it breaks down and becomes sticky. Alternatively, using a handheld mixer at medium speed, mix until the rice breaks down and becomes sticky. It won't be smooth, but there should be no distinct grains.

Cover and cook for about 3 minutes to heat through.

Serve in individual portions or family style.

ẸBA

SWALLOW OF TOASTED CASSAVA GRANULES

3 cups (720 ml) boiling water, plus more as needed

2 cups (280 g) white or yellow garri, plus more if needed (up to ½ cup/70 g)

Ẹba is a cooked dough made from garri (toasted cassava granules). Garri is the name of both the ingredient and, in some parts of southern and eastern Nigeria, the dish itself.

When I was growing up, we made ẹba with my maternal grandmother's perfectly toasted sunny yellow garri, made from cassava grown on her farm in Uzere. When it came to soaked garri, it was garri from my dad's hometown, Igarra—sour, light yellow with crunchy grains perfect with Roasted Groundnuts (page 200).

Some people love cold leftover ẹba with hot soups and sauces, similar to dumamé made with Tūwōn Masàřā (page 221), with Ẹ̀gúsí Soup (page 253), or with Geisha-brand canned mackerel or sardines in tomato sauce, a combination popularly called ẹbange and a favorite of Nigerian students in boardinghouses. The Igbos enjoy nri öra or nnli öla, leftovers. The soup is gently reheated in a clay pot, to which the swallow is added, until warmed through. The best way to enjoy it? Directly from the pot!

Pour the boiling water into a medium pot or heatproof bowl. In a circular motion, evenly sprinkle the garri over the surface of the water. Add 1 tablespoon of hot water at a time to any dry patches. Cover and let stand until the water has been absorbed and the mixture has thickened, become glossy, and begun turning translucent, about 5 minutes.

With an ọmọrogun, sturdy wooden spoon, or spatula, stir until the dough comes together, 1 to 2 minutes. You may find it easier to work the dough in small portions before combining it all together. The dough should be cohesive and firm, slightly sticky, and easy to scoop. If it is too soft and wet, stir in additional garri 1 tablespoon at a time until it holds. If the dough is too hard, stiff, or dry (crumbly, with uneven wet and dry patches), stir in more boiling water 1 tablespoon at a time until it holds together nicely.

Serve family style or in individual portions.

RECIPE CONTINUES →

To make ahead, create wraps. Line a small bowl with a piece of plastic wrap, letting it hang over the sides. With the ọmọrogun, spoon a portion of the dough into the lined bowl. Pull the hanging edges of the plastic wrap to cover the dough and gently shape it into a ball. Keep warm, seam-side down in an insulated dish or warmer. Repeat with the remaining dough. The ẹba will hold for 1 to 2 hours.

Enjoy with soup.

VARIATION

To make stovetop ẹba, pour 3 cups (720 ml) boiling water into a medium pot and set over low heat. With a circular motion, evenly sprinkle the garri all over the surface. With an ọmọrogun, sturdy wooden spoon, or spatula, stir the mixture until the dough comes together, 1 to 2 minutes. It will be slightly sticky and easy to scoop. Adjust the texture accordingly, adding more garri or boiling water by the tablespoonful to achieve the desired texture.

PREPARING TO EAT SWALLOWS

Some people eat swallows with clean hands, others with cutlery. If eating by hand, it's not uncommon to provide guests or elders with two "wash hand" bowls—one for washing with soap, and a second for rinsing with clean water—and napkins to dry their hands.

There's an order and rhythm to eating swallows that begins with pinching off a morsel from one side—largely an aesthetic decision, so the swallow isn't soup-kissed or "stained"— rounding it, and, if you desire, making a dent in it before dipping it into soup and finally eating it. Think of the process as pinch, roll, dip, and eat. The slightly shorter sequence using cutlery is to scoop-cut from one side, dip, and eat.

Purists say swallows should not be chewed, but chew them if you wish. Some people are one-bowlers, who eat their swallow and soup from the same plate or bowl, the swallow to one side and the soup to the other, or with the soup poured over the swallow. Two-bowlers place the swallow in its own dish to keep it separate from the soup. And there's a third group who pick and choose when they want to be one- or two-bowlers.

ÌMÓYÒ ẸBA

3 cups (720 ml) seafood stock from Ìmóyò Ẹlẹ̀ja (page 107)

2 tablespoons red palm oil

1 teaspoon tomato paste

2 cups (280 g) white or yellow garri, plus more as needed

½ to 1 cup (120 to 240 ml) boiling water

AROUND THE WORLD IN CASSAVA MEAL

Garri is also popular in the Caribbean, Central America, South America, and Europe, where it goes by (a combination of) different names related to farina (Latin), meaning meal or powder, and manioc or mandioca (Tupi), meaning cassava.

There's farinha de mandioca in both Brazil and Portugal; cassava farine in Trinidad, Dominica, Grenada, Saint Lucia, and a few other Caribbean Islands; and farine in Guyana.

This popular Easter dish is the traditional food of the Aworis of Ogun state and Lagos state in southwest Nigeria. It is one of a handful of Nigerian swallows made with a seasoned seafood stock and is enjoyed with Ìmóyò Ẹlẹ̀ja (page 107) and other imóyos.

It is similar to gari pinon, pinon rouge, or pinor in Togo and Ghana, daƙouin (served with fish) in Benin, and Brazilian pirão de peixe.

In a large pot, combine the stock, palm oil, and tomato paste. Bring to a boil over high heat and cook for about 5 minutes, then reduce the heat to medium-low. In a circular motion, sprinkle the garri evenly over the surface of the stock. Let stand until the stock has been absorbed, no dry garri remains, and the mixture has thickened, become glossy, and begun turning translucent, about 5 minutes.

With an ọmọrogun, sturdy wooden spoon, or spatula, stir until the dough comes together, 1 to 2 minutes. Drizzle in ½ cup (120 ml) of the boiling water over the top and knead with the wooden spoon for 2 to 3 minutes more. The dough should be cohesive and firm, slightly sticky, and easy to scoop. If it is too soft and wet and refuses to form a cohesive mass, stir in additional garri 1 tablespoon at a time until you get a consistency that holds together. If the dough is too hard, stiff, or dry (crumbly, with uneven wet and dry patches), stir in more boiling water 1 tablespoon at a time until it holds together nicely.

Serve in individual portions or family style.

VARIATION

In Warri, it is common to combine garri and hot strained curry stock to create a couscous-like dish that is enjoyed as a snack. You'll need 1 part garri topped with 2 parts hot stock. Stir them together with a fork to combine and separate until mixed and fluffy.

TŪWŌN MASÀR̃Ā

2 cups (250 g) white corn flour, sifted

1 cup (240 ml) hot water

White corn flour is the star here. For best results, make some targe, a water roux. The process is similar to making Chinese tangzhong or Japanese yudane. The targe keeps the tūwō soft as it cooks. However, you can skip this step and slowly work the corn flour into the water.

In a small bowl, whisk together ½ cup (65 g) of the corn flour and 1 cup (240 ml) room-temperature water to make a smooth slurry.

Pour 3 cups (720 ml) warm water into a medium pot and set over low heat. Make a circular stirring motion in the water with a wooden spoon, sturdy ladle, or whisk and gradually drizzle in the slurry. Cook, stirring, for 1 to 2 minutes, until smooth and beginning to thicken, then cover and cook until the mix gelatinizes and bubbles on top, 7 to 8 minutes.

Carefully uncover and stir the mixture well. Gradually add the remaining 1½ cups (188 g) corn flour, stirring until it is all incorporated. Cook, stirring and pressing the dough against the side of the pot to smoothen out any lumps, 2 to 3 minutes more.

Make 5 or 6 holes in the mixture, then pour in the hot water—don't stir. Cover and cook for 7 to 8 minutes more. Uncover and stir well to form a soft, smooth dough. Remove from the heat.

Serve in individual portions or family style and enjoy with soup.

SIMILAR VERSIONS AND VARIATIONS

In Nigeria, variations include tūwōn toka, made with alkaline-rich water (from being soaked in ashes) before cornmeal is incorporated, and tūwōn dawa, featuring Guinea corn (sorghum) flour and a pinch of akaun (potash; see page 95).

Across the world, ground corn flour and cornmeal are made into soft doughs similar to tūwōn masàr̃ā, from Guyanese fufu to Puerto Rican funche; fungee in Anguilla, Antigua, and Barbuda; Kenyan ugali; Malawian nsima; Zambian nshima; and Ugandan posho.

COLLECTIVE NAMES FOR SWALLOWS AROUND NIGERIA

Swallow names vary across the regions; the Yorùbás call them òkèlè, meaning mountain or hill, from the word òkè, "morsel." Both pay tribute to the way swallows are usually served mounded on the plate. In Hausa, swallows are called tūwō, meaning "porridge" or "mash." The Igbos in the east have a variety of names for swallows, from ütara to nni onuno to nri olulo, soft doughs that, like Japanese mochi, turn glutinous after pounding or kneading. In the North Central region, the Tiv people call them ruam, while the Idoma call them oje.

TAPIOCA STARCH

2 cups (320 g) tapioca starch

2 tablespoons red palm oil, or more as needed

This swallow is made from cassava starch, also known as tapioca starch or tapioca flour, the same starch used to make boba. Cooked with red palm oil, which gives it a bright orange color and a touch of earthiness, starch, like boba, has a chewy texture. But unlike boba, it is served as an accompaniment to savory soups, like Chicken Pepper Soup (page 239) and Banga Soup (page 257).

Starch is not eaten with cutlery, and because of its elasticity when cooked, it requires a unique cutting method, which I call the three Ps—pinch, press, pull. Set your thumb and index finger around the periphery of your ball of starch. With a twisting motion, **pinch** a small piece, then **press** your thumb and index finger together or press down into the plate to sever, and **pull** the morsel away from the larger ball—that's it, you're ready to dip it into your soup.

In a large, shallow nonstick skillet, combine the tapioca starch and 3 cups (720 ml) room-temperature water. Mix well until the starch dissolves and forms a slurry; it should have the consistency of lump-free crepe batter.

Set the pan over low heat and add the palm oil. With a wooden spoon or sturdy spatula, start stirring in one direction, making sure to reach the bottom of the pan, where the mixture will thicken first. Stir continuously to prevent scorching. As the opaque mixture thickens, you will see the orange of the oil meld into the starch in swirls, to form a dimpled rough dough ball.

Work the dough with the spoon, kneading it against the bottom and side of the pan to smooth out any lumps. Cook, stirring and working the mixture, until a smooth, glossy, and translucent orange ball forms, about 5 minutes. Cook for 3 to 4 minutes more, flipping the dough ball halfway through. Remove from the heat.

Cool briefly, 2 to 3 minutes.

Using your thumb and forefinger (see headnote), divide the dough into portions and serve.

ÀMÀLÀ IṢU

2 cups (200 g) èlubọ́ iṣu
(sun-dried yam flour; see
page 212), sifted

4 cups (about 1 L) hot water

**HOW TO USE
LEFTOVERS**

Àmàlà adagbona, like
dumamé (see page 221),
is all about reheating
leftover cold àmàlà,
cut up with Ewédú
(page 244) or okro,
stew, protein, and some
seasoning.

Three types of àmàlà are made from èlubọ́, the fine flour that
defines the dish: àmàlà iṣu, from sun-dried slices of skin-on or peeled
yam; àmàlà láfún, from fermented and dried cassava; and àmàlà
ògèdè, from sun-dried unripe plantains. All three variations are
prepared in similar ways, and each has a certain sweetness.

The texture of well-made àmàlà iṣu is soft and velvety, and its
brown color is attributed to the oxidation of the yam slices during
the drying process. Enjoy it in àbùlà, a one-bowl delight featuring
bright green Ewédú (page 244), red Omi Ọbẹ̀ (page 194), and orange-
tan Gbẹ̀gìrì (page 243); it's best eaten hot with a spoon to get the
ideal ratio of swallow to soup.

In a medium pot combine the èlubọ́ iṣu with 4 cups (about 1 L)
warm water. Pass the mixture through a fine-mesh strainer into a
3-quart (3 L) saucepan, pressing out any lumps; discard anything left
behind in the strainer.

Add 2 cups (480 ml) of the hot water to the pan and cook over low
to medium heat, stirring with a wooden spoon, until the mixture
thickens and begins to gelatinize, and you can form a dough mass,
5 to 6 minutes. Cook, mixing and working the dough so it stays
smooth, until it becomes even more cohesive, 3 to 4 minutes more.

Add the remaining 2 cups (480 ml) hot water, cover, and cook over
low heat until the dough turns from opaque to more translucent,
about 5 minutes. Spread the dough into an even layer over the
bottom of the pot, then poke three or four 1-inch-wide (2.5 cm)
holes with a wooden spoon and pour in 1 cup (240 ml) room-
temperature water. Immediately cover and cook until what's left of
the water (if any) is hot, 2 to 3 minutes. Uncover and cook, stirring
continuously, until soft, smooth, and stretchy, 2 to 3 minutes more.

To serve, dip an igbakọ, small saucer, or spoon into water and scoop
portions, placing each one on a plate or in a bowl. Serve with your
favorite soup.

POUNDED YAM

1½ pounds (680 g) West African yams, peeled, sliced into 1-inch-thick (2.5 cm) rounds, and rinsed

NOTES: *I don't advise using the food processor's metal S-blade for this, as it makes it much harder and riskier to remove the pounded yam safely. Instead, use the plastic dough blade.*

Leave the chute lid off so steam can escape.

Feel free to start and stop the food processor a couple of times, pulsing for 30 seconds to a minute each time.

The taste of freshly pounded yam is heavenly—its sweetness and soft, fluffy texture will convert you. Poundo made from yam flour is a good substitute.

When my sisters, brothers, and I were young, my parents created an after-church routine that included eating pounded yam and Ẹ̀gúsí Soup (page 253) for some Sunday lunches, followed by a treat of our favorite sweet drinks, and then some Nintendo NES time, before we finally had a nap, or siesta, as we call it. Ah, core memories.

In Nigeria, we generally don't weigh yam before boiling and pounding. It's common to judge portions by eye: two or three 1-inch (2.5 cm) rounds of yam per person, plus a few extra. Peel, rinse, cut into chunks, and boil.

Traditionally, pounded yam is made using a mortar and pestle, but the ease with which it comes together in a food processor makes that my method of choice. It is best eaten hot or warm, as cold pounded yam loses its fluffy texture and can become dry and sometimes crumbly. The good thing is, it reheats to perfection. In a microwave-safe bowl, combine pounded yam and hot water, 1 tablespoon water per cup (250 g) of yam. Microwave in 1-minute bursts, checking after each minute, for up to 4 minutes, until piping hot. For 1-cup portions, restore the texture by kneading the yam using a small spoon. For larger portions, pulse in a food processor to restore the texture.

Place the yams in a large pot and add cold water to cover by at least 2 inches (5 cm). Cover and bring to a boil over high heat. Cook for about 10 minutes; it will foam and froth. Reduce the heat to medium and cover with the lid slightly ajar. Cook until the yams are fork-tender, 12 to 15 minutes.

Set the pot on the lowest heat possible so the yam and the thick, starchy cooking liquid stay warm.

To pound the yams, you can use a food processor with the dough blade (see Note), a mortar and pestle, or a stand mixer.

Food processor: With a slotted spoon, transfer the yam pieces to the food processor, reserving the cooking liquid. Process until the yam comes together and begins to form a sticky dough, about 3 minutes. Check the consistency; if you like, you can stop here. If you'd prefer it softer, with the motor running, gradually add reserved cooking liquid by the tablespoon and process, stopping to check after each addition, until the pounded yam is soft, fluffy, and stretchy.

Mortar and pestle: Fill a large bowl with hot water and set it nearby. With a slotted spoon, transfer the yam pieces to the mortar, reserving the cooking liquid; if you are new to this, start with just half the pieces. With the pestle, mash the yam, then continue pounding to smooth out any lumps, pushing the yam against the sides of the mortar as you work it into a sticky, cohesive dough. If the pounded yam sticks to the pestle, dip the pestle into the hot water. When the yam is smooth and without lumps, add a tablespoon of the reserved cooking liquid. Gently work it into the dough, adding more cooking liquid 1 tablespoon at a time, until the pounded yam is soft, fluffy, and stretchy.

Stand mixer or handheld mixer: With a slotted spoon, transfer the yam pieces to the bowl of a stand mixer fitted with the flat beater attachment. Set it on low speed and beat until yam crumbles form, 1 to 2 minutes, then increase to medium speed and beat until smooth and without lumps. Increase the speed to high and add a tablespoon of the reserved cooking liquid. Continue beating and adding more cooking liquid by the tablespoon until the pounded yam is soft, fluffy, and stretchy.

Serve in individual portions or family style.

VARIATION

Iyán ànòmó is a specialty in the North Central region of Kwara (particularly in the city of Ilorin), Kogi, and Benue states, typically enjoyed during festive periods. It is made with a combination of yam, sweet potatoes, and sweet cassava; the tubers are peeled, rinsed, and boiled, then separated by type, pounded individually, and finally combined. Iyán ànòmó goes well with okro soup (page 247).

HOW TO USE LEFTOVERS

In the North Central region, leftover pounded yam is sliced, dried, crumbled, and incorporated into stir-fries, soups, and pottages. The Okun people of Kogi state make a soup called ọbẹ epa with preserved pounded yam, and then enjoy it with fresh pounded yam. They say, "Muyán rún yán" ("We're eating pounded yam with pounded yam"). And they love it, declaring, "Ọmọ ewú iyán d'ọmú ó dòtun" ("The remake is in no way inferior to the fresh one").

CASSAVA AND INGENUITY

If yam is the king of crops, then cassava is the undisputed queen. While there isn't a historic annual cassava festival across the country, it is celebrated daily in the ways it is cooked, eaten, and enjoyed.

Nigeria is the largest producer of cassava in the world, and it is embedded in the fabric of our food culture, but surprisingly, the tuber isn't indigenous to Nigeria. Also known as yuca or manioc, cassava likely originated in Brazil, Bolivia, or El Salvador, and was first introduced to West Africa by Portuguese explorers and enslavers sometime in the sixteenth century. It did not take root until the late nineteenth century, possibly because processing methods were not well known (some varieties of cassava are toxic if processed incorrectly). Circa 1888, when chattel slave trade was abolished in Brazil, the West African returnees came home to the continent, bringing with them knowledge of processing cassava and its uses. Subsequent colonialists encouraged cultivation of cassava for its hardy nature.

Varieties of cassava are classified by levels of toxicity: Bitter varieties are more toxic than sweet. In Nigeria, you will find both varieties. In Europe and North America, the sweet varieties are more common. Like cocoyam (taro), all parts of the cassava plant—roots, skins, and leaves—are toxic raw. But the roots can be boiled, roasted, fried, and frittered, ground into flour, fermented, and more. All these methods start with peeling and rinsing the cassava, then soaking it for varying lengths of time.

Some ways cassava is used include dried (then rehydrated) shreds for Àbàchà Ncha (page 103), chips enjoyed as a snack with coconut, and tapioca granules cooked in coconut milk to make mingau (page 301). Kpokpogari, hard cassava biscuits popular in southern Nigeria, are a fibrous by-product of making Tapioca Starch (page 223).

Unfermented and fermented cassava flours are different from tapioca flour (also known as tapioca starch). Unfermented flour is typically made the same day the cassava is harvested; the tubers are peeled, washed, ground, pressed, and dried. Fermented cassava flour can be plain or smoked. Peeled cassava is soaked for a few days to ferment, then wet milled or mashed and drained to make uncooked fufu. This wet-milled cassava can be shaped into balls and smoked to make pupuru (also known as ikwurikwu), a specialty of the riverine people in the east, south, and western regions of Nigeria. The balls are smoked until they are dry and dark brown-black layers form. They are stored to be ground and used later. Pupuru can be prepared like ẹba, on the counter or stovetop. Láfún, also known as white àmàlà, is a flour made by drying the fermented cassava, then grinding it into flour.

While cassava flour contains both fiber and starch, tapioca flour is mostly starch, like cornstarch (versus cornmeal). Prepared cassava is ground with water, then passed through a fine-mesh strainer with more water and collected in a container; the starch is left to separate from the water and settle to the bottom of the container. The water is decanted and the starchy residue dried to make tapioca flour. In Nigeria, the starch is either dried, or left wet and stored with a covering of water.

LUNCH AND DINNER OF CHAMPIONS
(SOMETIMES BREAKFAST, TOO)

SOUPS

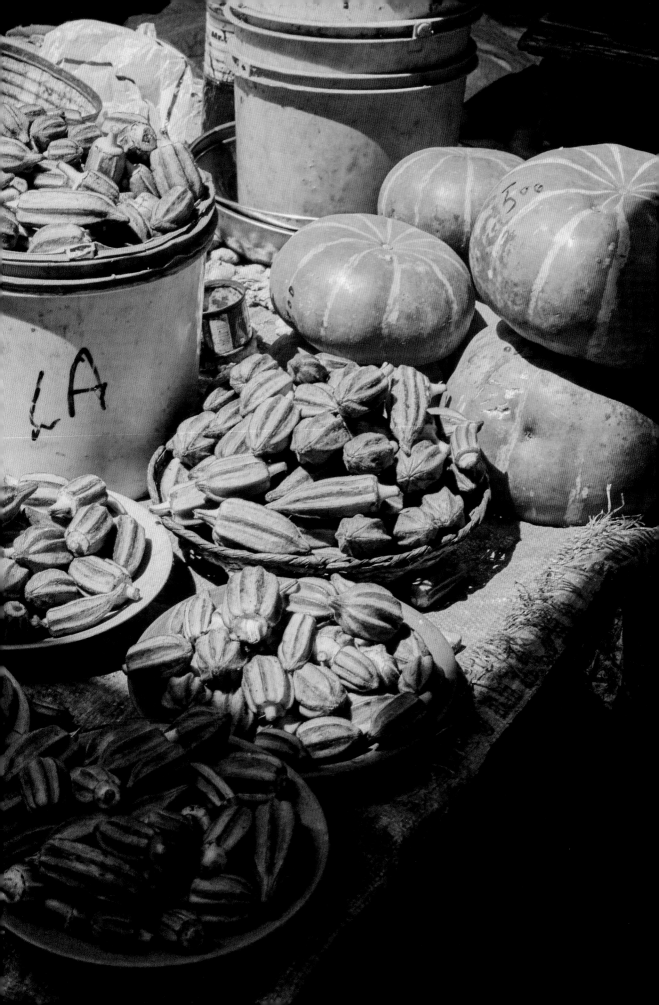

"Better soup, na money kill am."

TRANSLATION: "MONEY MAKES A GOOD POT OF SOUP."

SOUPS, LIKE SWALLOWS, ARE A PILLAR OF NIGERIAN cuisine. Though you can pair most swallows with any soup, there are some iconic pairings: banga and Tapioca Starch (page 223), ègúsí soup and Pounded Yam (page 226), mīyạn taushe and Tūwōn Shinkafa (page 214). You can also enjoy soups with white rice or boiled vegetables.

Nigerian soups are often surf and turf. We have "drinking" soups and "eating" soups—barely cooked, light, and thick. Soups typically have four or five elements: a soup base, seasoning, thickeners, greens, and oils. The soup base could be water, stock, or a stew base with some added protein. The seasoning typically includes salt, dry pepper, ground crayfish, fermented seeds and nuts, and, less commonly, fresh ginger, turmeric, and garlic. Thickeners are used fresh, dried, or ground, sometimes in combination. They include nuts, seeds, fruits, vegetables, cereals, roots and tubers, pulses, legumes, gums, flours, flowers, and greens, whether herby, leafy, aromatic, or bitter. And finally, most soups require some oil: red palm oil, groundnut oil, shea butter, and mân shānū (see page 18) are common.

Federal Character is a combination of three soups: ègúsí; okro; and èfọ́ rírò with stew and "assorted" meats. Named for the 1997 constitutional principle of Federal Character in Nigerian law—"to promote national unity, foster national loyalty and give every citizen of Nigeria a sense of belonging to the nation, notwithstanding the diversities of ethnic origin, culture, language or religion which may exist and which is their desire to nourish and harness to the enrichment of the Federal Republic of Nigeria"—it is the ultimate soup mash-up.

CLOCKWISE FROM LEFT: *Two women, Oniru New Market, Lagos; pomo, cowskin; whelks, periwinkles, washed bitter leaves and palm nuts; blue crabs*

FEATURED IN THESE RECIPES

1. **Alligator pepper.** Named for its bumpy, alligator-skin-like pod. The seeds are nutty, citrusy, and fragrant—think cardamom and ginger—with a slight numbing effect.

2. **Banga.** Also known as palm nut cream or concentrate, and sauce graine. Banga cream is different from red palm oil, just as coconut cream is from coconut oil. It is rich and creamy with sweet and earthy flavors.

3. **Banga stick.** African licorice, also known as oburunbebe. Use whole or strip off the bark and use that.

4. **Bonga fish.** Smoked flat fish with gold-streaked skin.

5. **Dàddawā.** Fermented dried locust beans or soybeans, ground and in balls.

6. **Ẹ̀gúsí.** Also called bitter melon seeds, you'll find them in the shell with inedible mustard-yellow skins; shelled, by hand or machine, to reveal creamy-white seeds; and dry-milled, with the texture of almond meal. Substitutes include Indian margaz, pumpkin seeds, and Salvadoran pepitas.

7. **Irú.** See page 25.

8. **Lemongrass leaves.** Commonly used instead of the stalks (fresh or dried). If leaves aren't available, substitute 1 large stalk, cut and bashed, for a small bundle (10 leaves).

9. **Makrut lime leaves.** An alternative to Persian lime leaves, which my mom uses, these are sold fresh and frozen in Asian markets.

10. **Mân shānū.** See page 18.

11. **Ọ̀gbọ̀nọ̀ seeds.** The seeds of the native African mango, sold split or ground.

12. **Periwinkles.** Beautiful turquoise and silver sea snails coiled inside spiraled dark brown-black shells. You'll find them fresh, frozen, dried, and smoked. Remove the "eyes," small brown discs attached to one end—they are unpleasant.

13. **Stockfish bits.** Bits, shavings, or chunks of dried fish—cod, haddock, saithe, or tusk.

14. **Whelks.** A variety of sea snails, also known as ngolo. Sold fresh, frozen, dried, and smoked. Substitute clams or cockles.

IRHÍBÓTỌ
UNCOOKED SOUP

3 teaspoons ground crayfish
(see page 23) or dry fish
powder

2 teaspoons ground ehuru
(see page 25)

2 whole uda pods (see
page 164), seeded and
toasted

1 Scotch bonnet or habanero
pepper, minced, or
½ teaspoon dry pepper

½ teaspoon fine sea salt,
plus more as needed

4 cups (about 1 L) just-boiled
water

Dry pepper (see page 22;
optional)

8 ounces (250 g) whole dry
fish, bonga fish or catfish
(see page 23)

Irhíbótọ is an uncooked soup, the preserve of Nigerian grandmothers.
It is prepared in a wood-hewn mortar, rather than on the stovetop.
The mortar is both pot and serving dish, with the pestle acting as a
blender.

This is a quick, inexpensive, and aromatic soup with spices,
thickened with nuts, seeds, vegetables, tubers, and sometimes fish.

Have everything ready to start the meal (including drinks, sides,
and clean hands), and everyone ready to eat it, so you can feast and
enjoy the true essence, as "e dey hot," as it is freshly made.

Serve with Boiled Yam (page 124), boiled plantain (page 125), Ẹba
(page 216), or Tapioca Starch (page 223). While it is not traditional to
do so, you can refrigerate and reheat leftovers.

In a small pan, combine the ground crayfish and ehuru. Gently toast
them over medium heat, stirring, until warm and aromatic, 1 to
2 minutes. Remove from the heat and transfer the mixture to a large
mortar. Add the uda, and a bit of the Scotch bonnet—you can add
more later. With the pestle, pound the mixture until it has broken
down and is well combined.

Add the salt and stir well to combine. Gradually drizzle in 2 cups
(480 ml) of the boiled water, stirring carefully with the pestle until the
paste dissolves and the mixture is incorporated. Add the remaining
2 cups (480 ml) boiled water and stir well to incorporate. Taste and
add more salt and Scotch bonnet and/or dry pepper as needed.

Holding the fish with tongs, pass it over a medium-high flame on
a gas stovetop, toasting it from head to tail on both sides, until the
fish is roasted and aromatic, 3 to 4 minutes. (Alternatively, position
an oven rack 6 inches/15 cm from the broiler element and preheat
the broiler. Place the fish on a baking sheet and broil until heated
through and aromatic, 1 to 2 minutes on each side.)

Carefully transfer the fish to the soup. Stir well, gently pressing the
fish down so it is submerged—it will sizzle. Let stand for a minute
to allow the fish to absorb some liquid and soften. Flip the fish and
submerge, then let stand for 1 minute.

Enjoy the soup family style, straight from the mortar, or in individual
bowls.

OFE NSALA
THICKENED SPICED SOUP

2 large white onions,
coarsely chopped

1 Scotch bonnet or habanero
pepper, or as needed,
minced, or ½ teaspoon dry
pepper

2 tablespoons whole
crayfish (see page 23)

1 thumb-size piece fresh
ginger, peeled and finely
chopped

1 teaspoon ogiri isi (see
page 25; optional)

½ stewing chicken (about
1 pound/450 g), cut into
6 pieces

1 teaspoon fine sea salt, plus
more as needed

1 tablespoon ground ehuru
(see page 25)

½ teaspoon ground uziza
peppercorns (see page 95)

1 (1-inch-thick/2.5 cm) yam
round (about 125 g total),
peeled and quartered

½ teaspoon dry pepper
(see page 22), or to taste

2 (1-inch-thick/2.5 cm) dry
fish steaks, deboned (asa is
a favorite)

1 to 3 teaspoons shredded
fresh uziza leaves or
scent leaves (see page 20;
optional)

I learned how to make this soup from a mama in the market. Nigerian mamas, or "market women," as we call them, are like your friendly, knowledgeable grocer or butcher. They'll sell you what you need to cook a meal and deliver lessons on how to cook it.

Pounded Yam (page 226) is the most popular accompaniment to nsala and is commonly used to thicken and add body to the soup base. The yam is often cooked in a separate pot and timed so that it is ready to be pounded around the same time the soup is ready to serve. If you aren't using the pounded yam or don't want to worry about the timing, boil the yam in the soup as directed here.

In a blender, combine the onions, Scotch bonnet (to taste), crayfish, ginger, and ogiri (if using). Add 1 cup (240 ml) water and puree until smooth. Add more water as needed so you have 1½ quarts (1.4 L) soup base total.

Transfer the soup base to a large pot, then add the chicken and stir to coat. Season with the salt, ehuru, and ground uziza. Cover and bring to a boil over high heat, about 8 minutes, then reduce the heat to low and cook until the chicken begins to soften and oil pools on the surface, about 45 minutes.

Add the yam pieces to the pot, cover, and cook until the yam is fork-tender, about 15 minutes. Use a slotted spoon to transfer the yam to the blender. Add 2 cups (480 ml) water and blend until smooth, then pour the pureed yam into the soup and stir well. Cover and cook until the soup thickens, 10 minutes more. Taste and adjust the seasoning with salt and the dry pepper, if needed. Add the dry fish, cover with the lid ajar, and cook until the dry fish is heated through, 10 to 15 minutes more. Remove from the heat.

Stir in the uziza leaves, if desired. Cover the soup and let rest for 3 to 4 minutes before serving.

VARIATION

Swap half the chicken for bone-in beef or goat meat, adjusting the cooking time as required, or use your favorite proteins.

CHICKEN PEPPER SOUP

1 (2.2-pound/1 kg) stewing chicken, cut into 2-inch (5 cm) pieces

2 tablespoons Pepper Soup Spice Blend (recipe follows)

2 teaspoons ground crayfish (see page 23) or dry fish powder (optional)

2 teaspoons fine sea salt, plus more as needed

½ to 1 teaspoon dry pepper (see page 22), plus more as needed

2 small bundles lemongrass (see page 235)

1 Scotch bonnet or habanero pepper (optional)

2 or 3 sprigs scent leaves or uziza leaves, finely chopped

2 fresh makrut lime leaves (optional)

½ medium red tatashe pepper or red bell pepper

LEMONGRASS BUNDLES

Gather about 10 leaves into a small bundle and make knots by tying two or three times.

To use, rub the leaves with clean hands to bruise them and release their scent, then add the bundle to the pot.

Pepper soup, the traditional drinking soup of Nigeria, is an aromatic, spiced, herby one-pot broth with protein that will warm your bones. It is our comforting chicken soup, similar to Yemeni hawaij-spiced soup or South Indian rasam. The flavor notes are sweet, earthy, nutty, bitter, woodsy, and floral. Versions abound, but this recipe, from the Niger Delta in the South South, is my favorite.

The soup is flavorful and the bite-size pieces of protein are easy to eat with a spoon. Bowls are typically accompanied by saucers or plates for discarding the bones. Sometimes, you need to eat with your hands to make the most of the protein.

You can make your own spice blend or use store-bought. Your finished pot of pepper soup will have ground spices in the broth and at the bottom. Though not common, you can use a spice bag or strain the soup at the end.

The serving size and manner of serving changes depending on where and when you're eating it. Small bowls are perfect as an appetizer; out and about in a pepper soup joint, large bowls are common; and when served alongside white rice, Boiled Yam (page 124), boiled plantain (page 125), other tubers, or bread rolls, medium bowls work well.

In a stockpot, combine the chicken, 1 tablespoon of the spice blend, the ground crayfish (if using), 1 teaspoon of the salt, and dry pepper to taste. Cover and cook over medium to high heat, stirring now and again, until the chicken loses its raw color and sweats out its juices, and the liquid begins to boil, about 10 minutes.

Add 1 cup (240 ml) water and 1 lemongrass bundle and stir. Reduce the heat to low, cover, and cook until the chicken renders some of its fat, 20 minutes more.

Add 6 cups (1.5 L) water, the remaining 1 tablespoon spice blend, remaining 1 teaspoon salt, and the Scotch bonnet (if using; you can poke it before adding it so it releases some heat) to the pot and stir. Cover and simmer until the chicken is cooked through and tender, about 30 minutes, or until the chicken is cooked to your liking.

Add the remaining lemongrass, half the scent leaves, the lime leaves (if using), and the tatashe pepper. Stir well and cook for about

10 minutes. Taste and adjust the seasoning with salt and dry pepper, if needed, then let the soup stand for 10 minutes so the flavors can develop. Remove the lemongrass and lime leaves (you can rinse them and freeze in a freezer-safe container to use for future recipes, or discard them).

Serve the soup family style or ladle the soup and chicken into individual bowls; top with the remaining scent leaves before serving. Leftovers can be stored in an airtight container in the refrigerator for up to 5 days or in the freezer for up to 3 months.

Pepper Soup Spice Blend

MAKES ABOUT ¼ CUP (25 G)

8 whole uda pods (see page 164), seeded

6 ehuru seeds (see page 25), shelled

2 gbafilo seeds (see page 164), shelled and coarsely chopped

2 omilo seeds (see page 164), shelled and coarsely chopped

½ teaspoon alligator pepper seeds (see page 235)

½ teaspoon whole uziza peppercorns (see page 95)

1 (4-inch/10 cm) piece aidan fruit (see page 164)

Some people add crayfish and fish powder to this mix, grinding them with the toasted spices.

In a small stainless-steel or cast-iron skillet, combine the uda, ehuru, gbafilo, omilo, alligator pepper, uziza, and aidan fruit. Toast the spices over medium-low heat, stirring and swirling the pan frequently, until fragrant, about 5 minutes. Remove from the heat, transfer to a plate, and let cool to room temperature, about 10 minutes.

Transfer the toasted spices to a spice grinder and grind into a crumbly, coarse powder, 2 to 3 minutes. Transfer to a jar with a lid. Seal the jar and set aside to rest for 2 to 3 days, then regrind.

Return the spice blend to the jar and store at cool room temperature, away from light and heat, for up to 6 months.

PEPPER SOUP, IN THREE

Pepper soup can be a drinking soup, a pottage, or an "eating soup."

For drinking soups, the type of protein used gives the pepper soup its name: Chicken Pepper Soup (page 239), fresh fish pepper soup, dry fish pepper soup, and so on. Bone-in cuts are commonly used, as they deliver the most flavor. Chicken pepper soup, for instance, is often made with whole chickens, both broilers and stewing hens; of the two, stewing hens tend to make more flavorful pots, though soups made with broilers take less time to cook. That said, when you only have a short time to prepare a pot, use chicken chunks.

Goat meat pepper soup is a party favorite, and in Nigeria, skin-on goat meat (lightly smoked as part of the butchering process) is the default. Another popular pepper soup for parties is assorted meat pepper soup, also known as farfesun kayan ciki (Hausa), made with meat (goat meat is popular) and offal (tripe, intestines, liver, kidney, lung, heart, and more). You can make turkey pepper soup with fresh or smoked turkey, ram or lamb pepper soup, and more. Depending on your choice of protein, you will need to adjust the cooking times. Regardless of what you choose, the protein should always be cooked through, with textures varying from soft and tender to chewy.

Fresh fish pepper soup is the most common seafood version, though lobster, prawns, and shrimp work well, too. The fish is mostly of the firm-fleshed variety, like catfish, croaker, snapper, tilapia, barracuda, or smoke-dried fish.

For the pepper soup pottages, vegetables, and tubers, commonly unripe or just-ripe plantains, and/or yams are cooked in the pepper soup base as the meat boils. The result is a thickened, spiced, saucy mix of meat and vegetables. Ukodo, with chunks of plantain and/or yam, is one version from the Niger Delta region. Oto ebighe is a similar soup, seasoned with uyayak and other spices; water yam is processed and portioned into dumplings that are poached in the soup base.

Finally, there are eating soups that use pepper soup as their base, such as okro pepper soup, thickened with chopped, sliced, or grated okro; and ẹ̀gúsí pepper soup, thickened with ground ẹ̀gúsí. Both versions are enjoyed with swallows.

GBẸ̀GÌRÌ
LIGHT COWPEA SOUP

1 cup (4.9 ounces/138 g) washed (see page 67) black-eyed peas or other cowpeas, drained

1 tablespoon red palm oil, plus more if needed

1 tablespoon finely ground crayfish (see page 23), or a mix of ground crayfish and fish powder

1 teaspoon fine sea salt, plus more as needed

½ teaspoon fresh irú pete (see page 25)

¼ teaspoon dry pepper (see page 22), plus more as needed

NOTE: *You can cook the beans in a pressure cooker following the manufacturer's directions.*

Gbẹ̀gìrì is a bright yellow-orange bean soup made with dried black-eyed peas or brown beans. It is an essential component of àbùlà from the South West, along with àmàlà (page 224), Ewédú (page 244), and Omi Ọbẹ̀ (page 194).

In a 2- to 3-quart (2 to 3 L) pot, combine the beans with water to cover by at least 1 inch (2.5 cm). Cover the pot with the lid ajar and bring to a boil over high heat, about 8 minutes. Reduce the heat to low and cook until the beans are soft and give when pressed, about 1 hour.

Drain the beans, reserving the cooking liquid (you should have about 3 cups/720 ml cooking liquid).

Transfer the beans and 2 cups (480 ml) of the reserved cooking liquid to a blender. Add the palm oil, ground crayfish, salt, irú, and dry pepper. Let cool for about 10 minutes, then blend until the mixture is smooth, creamy, and of pouring consistency. Pour the mixture back into the pot. If desired, add 1 to 3 teaspoons more palm oil so the gbẹ̀gìrì is more orange. Taste and add salt and dry pepper, if needed.

Cook over medium-high heat, stirring well, until heated through, 5 to 6 minutes. Remove from the heat and serve hot.

THE SERVING OF ÀBÙLÀ

Àbùlà is a quartet of brown àmàlà (see page 224), yellow-orange Gbẹ̀gìrì, green Ewédú (page 244), and red-orange Omi Ọbẹ̀ (page 194). A variety of proteins is often the crowning glory.

To compose a serving, get a wide bowl, a couple of inches (about 5 cm) deep (like for pasta); the goal is to have one plate that shows off all the colors of the dishes you're serving. Scoop and spread the àmàlà so it takes up two-thirds of the bowl, making a crater in the center. Ladle in the gbẹ̀gìrì, ewédú, and omi ọbẹ̀, and finish with the protein. Serve with a spoon.

EWÉDÚ
JUTE LEAF SOUP

½ teaspoon fine sea salt, plus more as needed

1 teaspoon fresh irú (see Note, and page 25)

4½ ounces (125 g) fresh ewédú leaves (see page 20), rinsed

1 tablespoon ground crayfish (see page 23)

NOTES: *Stir with a wooden spoon, cook over low heat, leave the pot open once the leaves are blended, and watch your timing so you don't overcook the soup, otherwise you may end up with a thin, watery soup without the draw.*

Irú pete is soft and dissolves into the soup, but use whatever irú you have or leave it out.

This draw soup (see sidebar, opposite) is made with ewédú leaves; the same greens used in Egyptian molokhia soup. To break down the greens after they've poached in the seasoned base, blend or reach for an ijabe—a traditional broomlike whisk solely reserved for ewédú and other dishes.

Serve as part of àbùlà (see page 243).

In a medium pot, combine 1 cup (240 ml) water and the salt. Cover and bring to a boil over high heat, then reduce the heat to low.

Add ½ teaspoon of the irú and the ewédú leaves. Cover with the lid ajar and cook until the ewédú changes color, softens, and gives off a fresh vegetal aroma, about 6 minutes. Remove from the heat and let cool for about 10 minutes, then transfer to a blender. Blend until the leaves are broken down and the mixture is viscous.

Pour the blended soup back into the pot with the ground crayfish and the rest of the irú.

Cook until the soup thickens, 4 to 5 minutes. Stir, taste, and add salt, if needed. Serve as part of àbùlà.

VARIATION

To make buka ewédú, ewédú ẹlẹgúsí, hydrate 2 tablespoons ground ègúsí (see page 235) in ¼ cup (60 ml) room-temperature water. Add this right after the blended ewédú leaves. Cook for 4 to 5 minutes, to lose the rawness of the ègúsí, then whisk and finish as directed in the recipe.

DRAW SOUPS

One way to describe Nigeria's viscous draw soups is to think of the pull of melted cheese, but with more liquid. Soups are named after their "draw ingredient," and they are among the first foods fed to weaning babies. The source of the draw can be fruit kernels and nuts like ọgbọ̀nọ̀ (see page 235); fruits treated as vegetables like fresh young green cocoa pods and okro (fresh, or dried and ground); gums from plant stalks like okoho; dargaza; leafy greens used dry, like kuka (baobab leaves), or fresh, like ewédú.

Eating draw soups without creating a web of soup everywhere requires an understanding of how to cut the draw. Scoop the amount desired from the pot or bowl. Draw the rounded base of the spoon across the edge of the vessel as you remove it, as you might with a jar of honey. If you're eating with your fingers, pinch them together once you've dipped or scooped the soup.

SEAFOOD OKRO SOUP

1 large onion, coarsely chopped

1 yellow Scotch bonnet or habanero pepper, or more as needed, or ½ teaspoon dry pepper (see page 22)

2 tablespoons ground crayfish (see page 23)

⅓ cup (80 ml) red palm oil

2 teaspoons fine sea salt

4 blue crabs (about 1 pound/450 g total), cleaned and left whole or cut in half

1 pound (450 g) fresh head-on prawns, peeled and deveined, heads and shells reserved

1 pound (450 g) cleaned whole tilapia, cut into head, tail, and crosswise into center steaks that are 1 to 2 inches (2.5 to 5 cm) thick

4 ounces (115 g) cleaned and shelled fresh periwinkles (see page 235)

4 ounces (115 g) cleaned and shelled fresh ngolo (whelks; see page 235)

1 pound (450 g) fresh okro, grated, sliced, or a mix

1.75 ounces (50 g) fresh ugu (see page 20), rinsed and finely chopped

1 red tatashe pepper, bell pepper, or Italian sweet pepper, seeded and finely diced

There's plain okro, made like Ewédú (page 244), and there's this deluxe version, made with a combination of seasoned protein, broth, and palm oil. It is similar to the okra gumbos of the American South, but made without a roux. Adjust the amount of broth for your preferred consistency.

Firm, white-fleshed fish like tilapia, barracuda, croaker, and cod are the bare minimum for seafood okro. You could use crabs, lobster, clams, or squid, too.

Serve with Ẹba (page 216).

NOTES: *Yellow and orange Scotch bonnets have beautiful aromas and flavors that work well here, but use red ones if they aren't available.*

This recipe calls for ugu (pumpkin leaves). If you can't find it, use fresh spinach or skip it altogether. You can also add 2 to 3 tablespoons chopped or shredded Nigerian herbs of your choice, like uziza or scent leaves.

In a food processor or a blender, combine the onion, Scotch bonnet, and ground crayfish. Pulse to form a coarse but uniform mixture. (You'll be using the food processor again soon, so don't put it away—you don't need to rinse it between uses.)

In a large pot or Dutch oven, heat the palm oil over medium heat. When the oil is shimmering, add the blended onion mixture and cook until softened, 3 to 4 minutes, then add 4 cups (1 L) water and 1 teaspoon of the salt. Stir well, cover, and cook until the mixture emulsifies, about 5 minutes.

Reduce the heat to low, add the crabs, and stir well. Cover and cook until the crabs turn orange, about 5 minutes. Use tongs to transfer the crabs to a plate to cool.

Gather the prawn heads and prawn shells in a wide slotted spoon or strainer and carefully lower them into the pot. Cook until the heads and shells turn a peachy orange, about 4 minutes. Lift out the spoon or strainer and transfer the heads and shells to the food processor or blender. Add 1 cup (240 ml) of the broth from the pot and 1 cup (240 ml) water. Let the mixture cool for about 5 minutes, then process until the shells have broken down. Strain the prawn stock through a fine-mesh strainer set over a bowl and discard the solids.

RECIPE CONTINUES →

Add half the prawn stock to the pot. Cover with the lid ajar and cook for about 10 minutes to allow the flavors to meld. Stir in the fish, periwinkles, and ngolo and cook until the seafood is just tender, about 10 minutes.

Add the okro, prawns, and remaining prawn stock. Stir well, cover with the lid ajar, and cook until the okro just softens and begins to draw, 8 to 10 minutes more. Add the ugu leaves and the red pepper. Cook until the leaves begin to wilt and darken in color, about 2 minutes, then stir them in.

Taste and adjust the seasoning, adding some or all of the remaining 1 teaspoon salt before serving.

VARIATIONS

You can make a version of mixed okro soup with meat instead of seafood. Beef is common; chicken, not so much. Tripe, oxtail, tongue, and other animal parts are welcome.

Nigerians joke a lot about how common it is to find "seafood okro" that is actually surf and turf, with snails, pomo (cowskin), and even beef included; the combination of proteins makes for a rich and delicious pot of soup.

WHAT'S IN A SOUP'S NAME?

In Nigerian languages, many soups have two-part names. First is the word for soup: *ofe* in Igboland across the South East, *miya* in the North East and North West (which becomes the particular *mīyạn* when speaking about a specific type, like mīyạn taushe of pumpkin and greens), and ọbẹ̀ in the South West, among others.

Second is the soup's specific name. Some soups are named after the protein used, such as Chicken Pepper Soup (page 239). Several are named after the main ingredient—for example, Ẹ̀gúsí Soup (page 253), named for the creamy-white seeds used to make it. Some soups, like Ofe Nsala (page 237), also known as white soup, were all about thrift, cooked without (historically) expensive ingredients like red palm oil and thus lacking the orange tint that the oil would have imparted. And then there are those named for the technique used to make them, like Ẹ̀fọ́ Rírò (page 250), meaning "mixed," and Irhíbótọ (page 236), which describes soups made in mortars set on the ground instead of on the stovetop and flavored with pepper and spices.

EDIKANG IKONG
SOUP OF LEAFY GREENS

2 large onions, coarsely chopped

1 Scotch bonnet or habanero pepper, or as needed

1 cup (70 g) ground crayfish (see page 23)

1 pound (450 g) bone-in or boneless beef, cut into 2-inch (5 cm) pieces

1 teaspoon sea salt, plus more as needed

1 teaspoon dry pepper (see page 22), plus more as needed

4 ounces (115 g) dry fish, rinsed, deboned

4 ounces (115 g) cooked stockfish flakes (see page 24)

1 cup (240 ml) red palm oil

4 ounces (115 g) cleaned and shelled fresh periwinkles

1 pound (450 g) ugu (see page 20), chopped

1 pound (450 g) waterleaf (see page 20), chopped

1 to 2 red tatashe peppers, seeded and finely diced

This soup of mixed greens from the South South where the Efik, Ibibio, and other tribes make their home is a combination of ugu (pumpkin leaves) and waterleaf. Good edikang ikong is all about shredded and cooked greens that turn soft and silky, bound together with good-quality red palm oil so you don't end up with a mound of greens to one side of the pot and a pool of stock on the other.

Some people press out the mucilage from the waterleaf, but you don't have to for this recipe. Just be sure to allow it to wilt and soften before finishing the soup. Substitute spinach for the waterleaf and lacinato or curly kale for ugu. Serve with Ẹba (page 216) or another swallow of your choice.

In a food processor or blender, combine the onions, Scotch bonnet (to taste), and ⅓ cup (23 g) of the ground crayfish. Pulse to form a coarse mixture.

Transfer half the onion mixture to a stockpot and add the beef, salt, and dry pepper. Cover and cook over medium-high heat, stirring now and again, until the beef loses its raw look and yields its juices and the liquid begins to boil, 10 to 12 minutes.

Top with 2 cups (480 ml) water and stir well, then taste and adjust the seasoning. Cover and return to a boil for 2 to 3 minutes. Reduce the heat to low and cook until the meat softens but retains some resistance and oil pools around the edges of the pot, 15 minutes. Taste the stock and adjust the seasoning with more salt and/or dry or fresh pepper, if needed.

Add the dry fish, stockfish flakes, remaining onion mixture, the palm oil, ⅓ cup (23 g) of the ground crayfish, and the periwinkles. Reduce the heat to low, cover, and cook until the palm oil and stock emulsify, about 10 minutes.

Add the ugu, waterleaf, tatashe peppers, and the remaining ⅓ cup (23 g) ground crayfish. Cover and cook until some oil bubbles on the surface and around the edges, 5 to 6 minutes more. Uncover and stir, then taste and adjust the salt and dry pepper before serving.

Ẹ̀FỌ́ RÍRÒ

STEWED GREENS

3 medium red onions:
2 coarsely chopped, 1 thinly sliced

8 ounces (225 g) bone-in or boneless beef, cut into 2-inch (5 cm) pieces

2 tablespoons ground crayfish (see page 23)

½ teaspoon dry pepper (see page 22), or more as needed

2½ teaspoons fine sea salt, plus more as needed

4 red tatashe peppers or 2 medium red shepherd peppers, coarsely chopped

2 teaspoons irú (see page 25), plus more as needed

2 pounds (900 g) fresh ẹ̀fọ́ sọkọ (see page 20), leaves plucked and rinsed (see Note)

½ cup (120 ml) red palm oil

1 Scotch bonnet or habanero pepper, minced

8 ounces (225 g) cooked protein, such as pomo (cowskin; see page 21), snails, or shaki (honeycomb tripe; see page 21)

About 3½ ounces (100 g) smoked or dry fish, rinsed, deboned, and broken into bite-size pieces

1 small package (100 g) cooked stockfish flakes (see page 24; optional)

The beauty of ẹ̀fọ́ rírò is the sweet and spicy stew base into which sọkọ, soft, silky greens, are stirred. Sọkọ, shortened from sọkọyọkọtọ, means "make husband robust and fresh," testament not only to layered, delicious flavors but also superpowers. "Ẹ̀fọ́ rírò" combines two Yorùbá words: ẹ̀fọ́, meaning "leafy greens," and rírò, meaning "stirred" or "mixed," alluding to both the technique used and the combination with other ingredients. It is treated as both soup—to be enjoyed with chews and swallows—and stew, perfectly paired with vegetables or rice and beans.

If using fresh greens, wash, blanch, chop, and press them to extract excess moisture before incorporating. If you can, use ẹ̀fọ́ sọkọ; otherwise, use sweet potato greens or a 50/50 combination of ẹ̀fọ́ tẹ̀tẹ̀ (amaranth greens) and spinach. Frozen chopped spinach will also work.

Serve with Ẹba (page 216) or your favorite swallow.

In a food processor or blender, pulse the coarsely chopped onions until finely chopped. Transfer half of the finely chopped onion to a stockpot and add the beef, 1 tablespoon of the ground crayfish, the dry pepper, and 1 teaspoon of the salt. Cover and cook over medium-high heat, stirring now and again, until the beef loses its raw look and begins to yield its juices and the liquid begins to boil, about 10 minutes.

Top with 2 cups (480 ml) water and stir well. Cook until the meat is almost soft, 10 to 15 minutes more; some oil from the meat, depending on the cut, might pool around the sides. Remove from the heat and, using a slotted spoon, scoop out the beef from the stock, reserving both (you'll need at least 1 cup/240 ml stock).

In a food processor or blender, combine the remaining finely chopped red onions with the tatashe peppers, 1 teaspoon of the irú, and ½ cup (120 ml) water and pulse just long enough to form a thick, coarse puree. Set the pepper mixture aside.

In a medium or large pot of salted boiling water, blanch the ẹ̀fọ́ shoko until soft and dark, 1 to 2 minutes. Drain the greens in a fine-mesh sieve in the sink, then set the strainer over a large bowl. Spread out the greens in the strainer and let cool for about 10 minutes. Squeeze the greens to remove excess moisture, reserving the liquid. Transfer the greens to a cutting board and finely chop.

NOTES: *Two pounds of fresh greens will give you about 2 cups (560 g) defrosted and drained frozen greens.*

This recipe uses beef and variety meats, but you can use fresh seafood like fish or prawns, sautéed mushrooms, or dried or smoked proteins like catfish, chicken, or turkey instead; adjust the cooking times accordingly.

In a medium pot, heat the palm oil over medium heat. When the oil is shimmering, add the sliced onion, season with ½ teaspoon of the salt, and cook, stirring often, until the onion becomes tinged with orange and it has softened but not browned, about 3 minutes. Add the remaining 1 tablespoon ground crayfish and the remaining irú. Cook until fragrant, 1 to 2 minutes. Stir in half the chopped Scotch bonnet. Cook, stirring often, until the pepper has softened slightly, 2 to 3 minutes. Taste and add more of the Scotch bonnet, if you like.

Add the pepper mixture, season with the remaining 1 teaspoon salt, and increase the heat to high. Cover with the lid ajar and cook, stirring occasionally, until hot and bubbling, 4 to 5 minutes. Stir in 1 cup (240 ml) of the reserved stock, the beef, cooked protein, smoked or dry fish, and stockfish flakes (if using). Cover with the lid ajar and cook, stirring often, until the stew has slightly reduced and thickened and all the proteins are cooked to your desired tenderness, about 10 minutes; there should be oil pooling on the surface around the sides.

Stir in the chopped greens until well incorporated. Taste and adjust the seasoning, adding more irú as desired. If you prefer a looser stew, stir in more of the reserved stock, the reserved liquid from the greens, or water in ¼-cup (60 ml) increments. Cover and cook for 2 to 3 minutes, so the greens cook with and soak up some of the sauce. Remove from the heat.

Let stand for 10 minutes before serving. Leftover èfọ́ rírò can be stored in an airtight container in the refrigerator for up to 3 days or in the freezer for up to 6 weeks. Defrost overnight in the refrigerator and reheat gently before serving.

ÈGÚSÍ SOUP
MELON SEED SOUP

2 cups (300 g) ground ègúsí seeds (see page 235)

1½ teaspoons fine sea salt, plus more as needed

2 large onions, coarsely chopped

1 Scotch bonnet or habanero pepper, or as needed

1 cup (70 g) ground crayfish (see page 23)

1 pound (450 g) bone-in or boneless beef, cut into 2-inch (5 cm) pieces

1 teaspoon dry pepper (see page 22), plus more as needed

1½ cups (360 ml) red palm oil

1 tablespoon irú (see page 25; optional)

4 ounces (115 g) dry fish, rinsed

4 ounces (115 g) cooked stockfish flakes (see page 24)

4 ounces (115 g) cleaned and shelled fresh periwinkles

1¾ ounces (50 g) fresh ugu (see page 20), finely chopped

1¾ ounces (50 g) fresh waterleaf (see page 20), finely chopped

1 tablespoon finely chopped fresh or dried bitter leaf

1 small red tatashe pepper, coarsely chopped

The fluted pumpkin gourd that is the source of ègúsí seeds has historic significance in Nigerian cuisine. It is depicted in terra-cotta sculptures made by the Nok culture, a civilization that thrived between 500 BCE and 200 CE. Named for the seeds that thicken and flavor it, this dish is considered both a national soup and a regional one, with variations on how it's prepared.

Gently toasting the ègúsí deepens its nuttiness. Serve hot or at room temperature, with Pounded Yam (page 226). See page 20 for substitution ideas for the greens.

In a large skillet, combine the ground ègúsí and ½ teaspoon of the salt, spreading the mixture into an even layer. Toast over medium heat, stirring, until golden and fragrant, 6 to 7 minutes. Transfer to a plate and spread the mixture out to cool.

In a food processor or blender, combine the onions, Scotch bonnet (to taste), and ⅓ cup (23 g) of the ground crayfish. Pulse to form a coarse mixture. Transfer half the onion mixture to a stockpot and add the beef, the remaining 1 teaspoon salt, and the dry pepper. Cover and cook over medium-high heat, stirring now and again, until the beef loses its raw color and sweats its juices and the liquid begins to boil, about 10 minutes.

Top with 3 cups (720 ml) water and stir well. Cover and cook until the meat is cooked through but retains some resistance and oil pools around the edges, 10 to 15 minutes. Taste the stock and adjust the seasoning accordingly with salt and/or dry pepper.

Meanwhile, in a medium bowl, make a paste by combining the remaining onion mixture, the toasted ègúsí, and ¼ cup (60 ml) water. Stir well to form a creamy paste.

In a large pot, heat 1 cup (240 ml) of the palm oil over low heat for 1 minute. Stir in the irú (if using) and cook until aromatic, about 2 minutes. Gradually add the stock to the pot, then add ⅓ cup (23 g) of the ground crayfish. Cover and bring to a boil over medium heat.

RECIPE CONTINUES →

Reduce the heat to low. Add the ègúsí paste into the stock and stir. Cover and cook, stirring and gently scraping the bottom of the pot occasionally, until the ègúsí paste looks crumbly, about 25 minutes; patches of orange-red palm oil may bubble on the surface or around the edges.

Add the remaining ½ cup (120 ml) palm oil, the beef, dry fish, stockfish flakes, and periwinkles and stir gently to break up any cooked ègúsí curds. Taste and season with salt and dry pepper. Cook until the beef is heated through and tender and some of the orange-red palm oil pools on top, about 10 minutes.

Mound the ugu and waterleaf on top of the soup, but do not stir them in. Add the remaining ⅓ cup (23 g) ground crayfish. Cover and steam until the greens have wilted, about 2 minutes, then stir them into the soup. Add the bitter leaf and tatashe pepper, cover with the lid ajar, and cook until the greens soften, about 8 minutes.

Stir, taste, and season with salt and dry pepper, if needed. Serve.

VARIATIONS

Across the country, versions of ègúsí soup are made with the same base ingredients and thickeners but using different techniques and featuring different greens and vegetables, including okro, dried unripe papaya, pumpkin, and ìṣápa—white *Hibiscus sabdariffa* calyxes. In parts of the South South, ègúsí soup might feature balls and curds of ègúsí, thick with greens. In the South East, it might be more of a creamy soup with a garnish of greens, and in the South West, it might be made with ground toasted ègúsí but without greens, known as ègúsí Ijebu.

MĪYAṆ TAUSHE
PUMPKIN SOUP

4 medium onions: 2 coarsely chopped, 2 thinly sliced

1 Scotch bonnet or habanero pepper, or 1 teaspoon dry pepper (see page 22), plus more as needed

1 (2-inch/5 cm) piece fresh ginger (about 15 g), peeled and finely chopped

1 pound (450 g) bone-in beef and brisket bones, cut into 2-inch (5 cm) or larger pieces

1 tablespoon plus 2 teaspoons fine sea salt, plus more as needed

1 large Roma (plum) tomato, coarsely chopped

1 red tatashe pepper (about 150 g), coarsely chopped

1 tablespoon dàddawā (about half a locust bean disc; see page 24; optional)

¾ cup (180 ml) groundnut oil (see page 267)

¼ cup (60 ml) red palm oil

1 pound (450 g) ripe orange pumpkin, peeled, seeded, and cut into 2-inch (5 cm) chunks

½ cup (2.6 ounces/75 g) Roasted Groundnuts (page 200), skinned and coarsely ground

3.6 ounces (100 g) alayyahu (amaranth greens), rinsed and finely chopped (about 2 cups)

Clarified Mân Shānū (page 18), for drizzling

Fresh pumpkin and groundnuts (peanuts) star in this comforting, sweet, and nutty soup with roots in the city of Kano in the North West. Ripe orange-fleshed pumpkins are the gourds of choice; outside Nigeria, kabocha and butternut squashes make good substitutes. Once cooked, mash the pumpkin for a chunky base as directed in the recipe, or blend it to make a smooth puree.

Mīyaṇ taushe thickens as it cools, but you want it to be loose and soupy so your māsà (page 85) can soak up the liquid for a comforting meal. You can also serve it with Tūwōn Shinkafa (page 214). Don't forget to finish with a drizzle of mân shānū.

In a blender, combine half the chopped onions, the Scotch bonnet, the ginger, and 1 cup (240 ml) water. Blend until smooth. You should have about 3 cups (720 ml); add 1 cup (240 ml) more water so you have 4 cups (about 1 L) in total.

Transfer the mixture to a stockpot. Add the beef and 1 tablespoon of the salt. Stir and bring to a boil over high heat, 6 to 8 minutes. Reduce the heat to low, cover, and cook until the beef softens, about 30 minutes.

In a blender, combine the remaining chopped onions, tomato, tatashe pepper, dàddawā (if using), and ½ cup (60 ml) water. Pulse to break down the vegetables and create a thick mixture. You should have about 2½ cups (360 ml) of soup base.

In a 4- to 5-quart (4 to 5 L) pot, warm the groundnut and palm oils over low heat until fragrant, 2 to 3 minutes. Add half the sliced onions and season lightly with 1 teaspoon of the salt. Stir, then cook until the onions are evenly orange in color and softened but not browned, about 3 minutes.

Add the soup base, increase the heat to high, cover with the lid ajar, and cook, stirring occasionally, until the mixture has reduced, about 15 minutes. Add the pumpkin and season with the remaining 1 teaspoon salt. Reduce the heat to medium, cover, and cook, stirring now and again, until the pumpkin is fork-tender, about 15 minutes.

RECIPE CONTINUES →

Remove from the heat. With a potato masher, coarsely mash the pumpkin, leaving the soup chunky.

Return the pot to low heat and add the beef and stock. Cover with the lid ajar and cook, stirring often, until the soup is slightly reduced and thickened, oil pools on the surface and around the edges, and the meat is tender (or cooked to your preference), about 10 minutes.

Add the groundnuts. Stir well, cover with the lid ajar, and cook, stirring now and again so the bottom doesn't scorch, until the soup is slightly thicker, about 10 minutes. Taste and adjust the seasoning with salt and/or pepper, if needed.

Add the alayyahu and the remaining sliced onions on top of the soup, but do not stir them in. Cover and cook until the greens are just wilted, about 3 minutes, then stir the greens and onions into the soup and cook until heated through, 2 to 3 minutes more. Taste and add more salt and/or dry pepper, if needed. Remove from the heat.

Serve the soup with some mân shānū drizzled over the top.

TIPS FOR MAKING SOUP

- Start with a flavorful soup base (see Ofe Nsala, page 237)
- Alternatively, begin by dry-frying seasoned meat, stirring every few minutes, until it is no longer flesh-colored, then cover the pot to steam the meat so it produces its own juices. Allow it to cook in the juices before you add any liquid.
- Use a pressure cooker to save time for hardy cuts like cow leg, shaki (tripe), stockfish, etc. Follow the manufacturer's recommendations, being especially careful when releasing the pressure after cooking.
- If storage space allows, prep large batches of protein and portion them into freezer-safe containers to freeze for future soups.
- Use palm nut cream instead of palm oil for a different flavor.
- Explore different greens by adding combinations you like and varying the amounts.
- Lean into plant-forward soups, many of which are standard in Nigeria, using dried unripe papaya, dried pumpkin or other squash, mushrooms, tofu, beans, and more.

BANGA SOUP
PALM NUT SOUP

1 or 2 whole tilapia (about 1 pound/450 g), cut crosswise into center steaks 1 to 2 inches (2.5 to 5 cm) thick

1 tablespoon plus 2 teaspoons fine sea salt

2 medium red onions, coarsely chopped

2 or more red or yellow Scotch bonnet or habanero peppers, stemmed

1 (28-ounce/800 g) can palm nut cream

¼ cup (35 g) ground crayfish (see page 23)

2 tablespoons Banga Soup Spice Blend (recipe follows)

1 tablespoon dried bęlęntięntięn (see page 20)

1 (5-inch/12.5 cm) banga stick (see page 235), rinsed (optional)

10½ ounces (300 g) fresh head-on large prawns, peeled and deveined, heads and shells reserved (optional)

½ stewing chicken (about 1 pound/450 g), cut into 6 pieces

8 ounces (230 g) bone-in or boneless beef, cut into 2-inch (5 cm) pieces

2 small bundles lemongrass (see page 235)

1 or 2 fresh makrut lime leaves (optional)

1 teaspoon shredded fresh bitter leaf

NOTE: *Undersalt your soup and adjust later, as it's often reheated and reduced before serving, which concentrates the flavors.*

Popularly called banga, this spiced rich soup of the Niger Delta is made with palm nut cream, fresh or canned (as I've used here), and aromatic spices.

The first time I made this soup, I rang my mum—the expert—for directions. I may not have listened carefully when she told me what to do with the blended prawn heads and shells. I cooked up a delicious pot, and added all of the blended heads and shells. The seafood essence came through beautifully, as did the grit from the heads and shells. So learn from my mistake: Strain the prawn broth, and discard the bits!

Serve with Tapioca Starch (page 223).

Place the fish in a medium bowl, and rub all over, inside and outside, with 1½ teaspoons of the salt. Refrigerate for 15 minutes to 1 hour before cooking.

In a food processor or blender, combine the onions, Scotch bonnets (to taste), and 1 cup (240 ml) water. Puree until smooth.

In a large pot, combine the onion mixture, palm nut cream, 2 quarts (about 2 L) warm water (use some to rinse out the palm nut cream can), the ground crayfish, banga soup spice blend, bęlęntięntięn, banga stick, and 1 tablespoon of the salt. Stir well, cover the pot with the lid ajar, and cook over high heat until some oil bubbles to the top and around the sides, about 15 minutes.

Reduce the heat to medium. If using, gather the prawn heads and shells in a wide slotted spoon or strainer and carefully lower them into the pot. Cook until the heads and shells turn a peachy orange, about 4 minutes. Lift out the spoon or strainer and transfer the heads and shells to a blender. Add 1 cup (240 ml) warm water and the remaining ½ teaspoon salt, then blend until the shells have broken down and the mixture is creamy. Strain the prawn stock through a fine-mesh strainer set over a bowl and discard the solids.

Add the chicken, beef, half the prawn stock, and 1 bundle of the lemongrass to the pot, stir well, and cover with the lid ajar so the mixture doesn't boil over. Bring to a boil over medium heat, then reduce the heat to medium-low and cook until the meat is tender and cooked through but retains some resistance and the soup has reduced by a quarter to a third, about 30 minutes more; some oil should pool on the surface and around the edges.

Reduce the heat to low and add the remaining bundle of lemongrass, the lime leaves (if using), salted fish, and bitter leaf. Stir gently, cover with the lid ajar, and cook for about 5 minutes, then add the remaining prawn stock and the prawns, ensuring they are submerged in the soup. Stir gently, being careful not to break up the fish, and cook for 6 minutes more, until the prawns are cooked through. Remove from the heat and let stand for a few minutes before serving. Remove the lemongrass and banga stick—both can be reused.

For a thicker soup, spoon the portion to be served into an evwere (see below) or cast-iron skillet and cook until it reaches the desired consistency.

Banga Soup Spice Blend

MAKES ABOUT ¼ CUP (36 G)

2 tablespoons (25 g) ataiko (see page 207)

1 tablespoon rigije (see page 207)

Spices—aromatic, resinous, antiseptic—cut through grease in the same way lemon juice and other acids cut through fatty foods.

Combine the ataiko and rigije in a spice grinder and grind until a fine, speckled powder forms, 2 to 3 minutes. Transfer to a jar with a lid. Seal the jar and store at cool room temperature, away from light and heat, for up to 6 months.

SERVING BANGA SOUP IN AN EVWERE

Reheating and reducing the banga prior to serving in a single-portion or family-sized evwere, a clay pot (like Korean ttukbaegi), is part of its tradition.

If you have a small amount of soup left over, without any meat or protein, do as the people in Warri do: Gently reheat the leftovers in an evwere over low heat. Crack an egg or two into a bowl, lightly season it with salt, whisk, and pour it into the soup. Cook, undisturbed, for 2 to 3 minutes, then gently stir from the bottom up so it doesn't scorch. You could also try adding boiled eggs to the soup as it reheats, turning them often so they get evenly coated in the soup.

GREENS AND OTHER LEAFY VEGETABLES

Greens are true mainstays of the Nigerian kitchen. They are abundant and easily accessible, and are used in dishes and drinks depending on their flavor, shape, texture, moisture content, and consistency.

On any given day, in any given Nigerian market, you will find many kinds of leaves, including ugu (pumpkin), cocoyam (taro), sweet potato, cassava, sesame, cowpea, jute mallow, and more. You'll find them fresh; dried, to be used as is or rehydrated; or, in the case of sesame leaves and baobab leaves, dried and ground into powder (these latter two leaves are viscous).

The Fulani, a nomadic group, crush the leaves and stalks of bomu bomu, a plant in the milkweed family, and stir them into warm fresh milk to curdle it in the making of wara, a soft dairy cheese.

The water content of some greens, like waterleaf, changes with the seasons. Bitter and sour greens are also important. These include bitter leaves, so called for the intense bitterness of the fresh leaves, which can be tempered by sun-drying for a few days, then hand-washing the greens until they lather or froth; yakuwa, leaves from *Hibiscus sabdariffa*, which add a distinct sourness; and garafuni, dried balsam apple leaves, which add bitter, earthy notes.

Inedible, food-safe, and waterproof leaves, like plantain or banana leaves and the leaves of the miracle fruit plant (*Thaumatococcus daniellii*), are used to wrap food, imparting sweetness in the process, thanks to the protein thaumatin. Some of these leaves are also popular as fermentation vessels for seeds and legumes, in the making of irú, ogiri igbo, and ugba. They are also used as lids for pots bubbling away over heat, and as plates and platters to serve food.

Some leaves are used as edible wrappers for starchy vegetables, like in ekpang nkukwo, a dish of the southern Efik and Ibibio people in which grated water yam and cocoyam (taro) are spooned into red cocoyam leaves, rolled and wrapped into cigar shapes, then stewed with protein, palm oil, seasoning, and more until soft and luscious.

Herbs are used raw, in salads like àbàchà (page 103) and as the main vegetables in soups like omoebe (black soup) from the southern region of Edo, where fragrant scent leaves are blended with greens for the base of the soup.

Watching ọ̀kazị̄ being shredded for afang soup is like watching art. Here the skill of a mama (market vendor) is evident as she shreds the tightly rolled and gathered leaves into the finest chiffonade. First, knives are sharpened, be it on the concrete pavement, with another knife, or at the hands of a professional sharpener, then the wooden chopping block, shaped like a brick, is set on a wide enamel tray. Clean leaves are marshaled and rolled into a plump cigar, 2 to 3 inches (5 to 7.5 cm) across. The cigar gets cut in half across the length and the halves get stacked, one on top of the other, and then the shredding begins, with precision and speed. The end result is a tray full of thin, green ribbons that can be used as is, pounded, or dried and rehydrated.

THINGS TO KEEP THE MOUTH MOVING

SNACKS

NIGERIA HAS A RICH SNACKING CULTURE. THE YORÙBÁS call snacks *ìpápánù*, which means "playthings for the mouth to enjoy." This playground has a lot to offer: an assortment of cookies, sweetmeats, and other confections, perfect for the times in between meals when you're feeling peckish.

All-purpose flour, corn flour, toasted rice, groundnuts (peanuts), and coconut are the most common ingredients for these confections. They are as much childhood treats as they are adult delights, and are mostly sold on the streets and, these days, in grocery stores. If ever there were a headquarters of ìpápánù in Nigeria, it would be on Lagos Island, where there are snack stalls from Igbosere to Balogun market and under the bridge at Apongbon. It's no wonder the treats are often called Lagos Island snacks.

Snacks are a great way to welcome guests. Two popular ones to serve are plantain chips and ọkwu ọjị, a spicy groundnut butter served with fresh garden eggs or cucumbers.

Nuts shine in snacks—including groundnuts, cashews, and tiger nuts. They are roasted, boiled, coated, ground, and incorporated into a variety of bites including sweetmeats— mixtures of soft and sandy truffle-size balls.

Chin Chin, sold in a variety of shapes, is one of the most common ìpápánù available year-round and especially at Christmastime. To present it to guests, you might lay out a selection of bites in small bowls, like you would mezze: Chin Chin; Rock Buns, and crunchy Kulīkulī.

Having snacks is a great thing for you, as the host; make enough so there's some left for you when your guests leave.

CLOCKWISE FROM LEFT: *Woman selling spices; chin chin bits; lemons and limes; roasted groundnuts and candied groundnuts in recycled bottles*

FEATURED IN THESE RECIPES

1. **Groundnuts.** These legumes, also known as peanuts, are popular in Nigeria, where you'll find them in various forms—in and out of the shell—boiled, roasted, fried, ground, and transformed.

2. **Groundnut oil.** A popular cooking oil across the country, especially in the north, made from roasted, ground, and pressed groundnuts. Used in cooking, dressings, and more. The flavor is strong, as is the aroma—rich and nutty. Use North American peanut oil or any other neutral oil if you can't find Nigerian-style groundnut oil.

3. **Powdered peanut butter.** This fine shelf-stable flour is made from roasted groundnuts, defatted through a pressing process that removes most of the oil. It is a great substitute for Kulīkulī (page 277), which traditionally requires an arduous manual process to create defatted groundnut dough.

CHIN CHIN
FRIED DOUGH BITS

⅔ cup (5 ounces/160 ml) cold dairy or nondairy milk

1 teaspoon vanilla extract

3 cups plus 2 tablespoons (13.3 ounces/375 g) all-purpose flour, plus more for dusting

½ cup (100 g) sugar

1½ teaspoons baking powder

1 teaspoon fine sea salt

½ teaspoon freshly grated nutmeg

2 teaspoons finely grated lemon zest or orange zest

About ½ cup (4 ounces/ 100 g) cold unsalted butter

Neutral oil, for frying

I can't imagine a Christmas season without making or eating chin chin. As kids, we got all our chin chin from Mrs. Amadi, my mum's friend, who made the best diamond-shaped chin chin in the world (okay, in *my* world). Chin chin is made from stiff, kneaded dough, rolled out by hand or machine, then cut into the shape of your choice: small and chunky cubes, thin strips, diamonds, knots, or flakes. The small, delicately sweet fried dough shapes crunch like a cookie and taste a little like cake made with warming spices.

Enjoy chin chin on its own, with tea, coffee, Champagne, or your favorite beverage. You can also eat it as you might cereal (think Cinnamon Toast Crunch) or crumble some over ice cream.

In a liquid measuring cup, whisk together the milk and vanilla until well combined.

In a large bowl, whisk together the flour, sugar, baking powder, salt, nutmeg, and lemon zest until thoroughly incorporated. Using the large holes of a box grater, grate the butter into the flour mixture. Using clean hands, quickly toss the flour and butter together just until the butter is evenly distributed, then rub to form pea-size pieces.

Make a wide well in the center of the butter-flour mixture. Slowly pour the milk into the well. Using a flexible spatula or wooden spoon, gradually stir until combined. Using your hands, knead the dough against the sides of the bowl or on a lightly floured work surface until it comes together in a soft, but not sticky, ball. Cover with plastic wrap or a clean kitchen towel and let rest for 10 minutes. (Alternatively, shape the dough into a flat disc, wrap in plastic wrap, and refrigerate for up to 2 days or freeze for up to 6 months; bring to cool room temperature, about 68°F/20°C, before rolling.)

Lightly flour your work surface, rolling pin, and a rimmed baking sheet. Unwrap the dough, divide it into 4 equal portions (about 195 g each), and shape each into a ball. Working with one at a time, roll out each ball to form a 5-inch (12.5 cm) round that's about ¼ inch (6 mm) thick, adding flour as needed to prevent sticking. Using a sharp knife or pizza wheel, cut the round into ½-inch-wide (1.3 cm) strips, dipping the wheel or knife in flour as needed to keep the dough from sticking. Cut each strip on the diagonal into ½-inch (1.3 cm) diamond shapes. Transfer to the baking sheet, lightly dust with flour, and gently toss to prevent sticking.

Fill a wok or large Dutch oven with 1½ to 2 inches (3.8 to 5 cm) of oil; it should come no more than halfway up the vessel. Heat the oil over medium-high heat to 360°F (180°C). Line a large fine-mesh strainer with paper towels.

Divide the dough pieces into three or four batches. Working with one batch at a time, use a spider or slotted spoon to add the dough to the hot oil. Cook, turning the pieces with the spider, until golden brown all over, about 3 minutes; they will puff up during cooking. Transfer the chin chin to the lined strainer to drain. Repeat with the remaining dough, allowing the oil to return to temperature between batches.

Transfer the chin chin to a serving bowl and serve warm, or let cool completely for 15 to 20 minutes before serving.

AROUND THE WORLD IN CHIN CHIN

Could chin chin be related to Italian cenci, the crispy ribbons of fried dough dusted with confectioners' sugar? When pronounced, "chin chin" sounds like "cenci," and the doughs are similar, with some variations in flavorings and spices.

There are many fried-dough snacks around the world, made from stiff, non-yeasted, kneaded dough, similar to chin chin. On the African continent, you'll find them in Togo and Benin, where they are known as atchomon; in Ghana, as achomo; in Cameroon, as croquettes Africaines, petits atchomon, or ross; and in Guinea, as gâteaux secs. In parts of the United States, they go by the name angel wings. In Europe, Italian chiacchiere are popular at Easter (during Carnival, as are merveilles in the southwest of France, bugnes Lyonnaises, and Andalusian pestinos, which are deep-fried in olive oil and glazed with honey or cinnamon sugar). There are Czech bozi milosti and Slovenian fánky, both meaning "God's grace." In Southeast Asia, there are paara in Hindi (shakkar paara are sweet, dipped in syrup; namkeen paara are savory, often with herbs like dried fenugreek and ajwain kneaded in). In Guyana, there is the similar mithai (aka kurma in Trinidad), which comes crunchy or soft and is drizzled with a sugar syrup that crystallizes.

MAKES 12 TO 15 COOKIES

ROCK BUNS

½ cup (4 ounces/113 g) cold unsalted butter, plus 1 tablespoon for the pan, if needed

1¼ cups (5.3 ounces/150 g) all-purpose flour

½ teaspoon baking powder

½ teaspoon Mixed Spice (recipe follows) or freshly grated nutmeg

½ teaspoon fine sea salt

½ teaspoon finely grated lemon zest

½ teaspoon finely grated orange zest

⅓ cup (2.4 ounces/67 g) sugar

2 tablespoons dairy or nondairy milk, or more as needed

1 large egg

1 teaspoon vanilla extract

1 tablespoon raisins

These shaggy-looking treats are my son's favorite. Cookies with British roots, they started life as "rock cakes" or "rock buns," similar to scones, but are now more like round cookies with rough edges.

You can include dried fruit, commonly raisins but also currants, and candied citrus. Sometimes a single raisin (or piece of dried fruit) is placed in the center and other times they are incorporated into the dough. Enjoy with tea or your favorite beverage.

Preheat the oven to 350°F (175°C). Line a rimmed baking sheet with parchment paper or grease it with 1 tablespoon butter.

Sift the flour, baking powder, mixed spice, and salt into a medium bowl.

Using the large holes of a box grater, grate the butter into the flour mixture. Using clean hands, quickly toss the flour and butter together just until the butter is evenly distributed, then rub to form pea-size pieces.

In a separate bowl, combine the lemon and orange zests and the sugar and rub them together until moist and fragrant. Stir the sugar mixture into the butter-flour mixture and make a well in the center.

In a liquid measuring cup, whisk together the milk, egg, and vanilla until combined, then pour into the well. Mix well, forming a stiff dough. If it is too dry, add more milk 1 tablespoon at a time.

Scoop tablespoonfuls of dough onto the prepared baking sheet, spacing them about 1 inch (2.5 cm) apart. Press a single raisin into the center of each one. Bake for 14 to 16 minutes, rotating the pan from front to back halfway through, until golden brown.

Remove from the oven and let cool on the baking sheet for 8 to 10 minutes, then transfer the buns to a wire rack. Let cool for about 10 minutes more before serving, or let cool completely and store in an airtight container at room temperature for up to 1 week.

MAKES ¼ CUP (20 G)

1 teaspoon ground Ceylon cinnamon

1 teaspoon ground allspice

½ teaspoon ground coriander

½ teaspoon ground ginger

½ teaspoon freshly grated nutmeg

½ teaspoon ground mace

¼ teaspoon ground cloves

NOTE: *To make the spice blend with whole spices, gently toast each spice individually until fragrant, then let cool. Grind and pass through a fine-mesh strainer to remove any big bits. Regrind, if need be, then store as directed.*

Mixed Spice

Mixed spice is similar to any blend of warming spices for sweets and cakes, like pumpkin pie spice. To keep each batch fresh, it's best to make it in small quantities. Mixed spice works well in pancake batter (page 79), Chin Chin (page 269), and other bakes. Use your favorite cinnamon if you don't want to use the Ceylon variety.

In a container with a tight-fitting lid, combine all the ingredients. Seal and shake until well blended.

Store at cool room temperature, away from light and heat, for up to 6 months.

KOKORO
CRUNCHY CORN STICKS

2½ cups (about 375 g) corn flour, sifted, plus more as needed

3 tablespoons sugar

1 teaspoon fine sea salt

1 teaspoon ground ginger

½ teaspoon onion powder

½ teaspoon dry pepper (see page 22)

½ teaspoon garlic powder

½ teaspoon ground cloves

Neutral oil, for frying

This pencil-thin snack with tapered ends and a thicker middle tastes a bit like crunchy toasted corn tortilla chips. It is sold in a variety of lengths, from 4 to 24 inches (10 to 60 cm). If you're ever on Lagos Island and see an enamel tray of thin, long sticks, buy some, wrapped in newspaper.

Both yellow and white corn flour work here. You can also convert leftover Tūwōn Masàřā (page 221) to kokoro. Feel free to halve the recipe.

In a medium bowl, whisk together 1 cup (125 g) of the corn flour, the sugar, salt, ginger, onion powder, dry pepper, garlic powder, and cloves.

In a small bowl, whisk together ¼ cup (about 30 g) of the corn flour mixture and ½ cup (120 ml) room-temperature water until smooth to form a slurry.

Place 1 cup (240 ml) warm water in a medium pot over low heat. Make circular stirring motions with a wooden spoon, sturdy ladle, or whisk, then slowly drizzle the slurry into the center, stirring continuously as you go. Cook, stirring, for 1 to 2 minutes, then cover and cook until the mix gelatinizes and bubbles vigorously on top, 7 to 8 minutes.

Gently remove the lid and give the mixture a thorough stir, then slowly add the remaining corn flour mixture, stirring continuously until it is fully incorporated. Cook, stirring vigorously, for 2 to 3 minutes in order to smooth out any lumps. Cover the pot, remove it from the heat, and set aside until the mixture has cooled, about 20 minutes.

Sprinkle a rimmed baking sheet with 2 tablespoons of the corn flour to prevent sticking. Sprinkle 1 to 2 tablespoons corn flour on a clean counter and scoop the cooked corn flour mixture out of the pot onto the counter. About ½ cup (62.5 g) at a time, knead the remaining 1 cup (125 g) corn flour into the cooked dough. Divide the dough into two equal pieces and flatten one piece into a 5 by 10-inch (12.5 by 25 cm) rectangle. Cut a 1-inch (2.5 cm) grid to make 50 squares and set aside. Repeat with the other piece.

RECIPE CONTINUES →

Dust your work surface with more corn flour, if needed. Take a piece of the dough and roll it against the surface until pencil-thin. Classic kokoro tapers at both ends, so each piece should be about 4 inches (10 cm) long and ⅓ inch (8.5 mm) wide at its thickest, with the ends rolled very thin. Place the rolled-out dough on the prepared baking sheet and repeat with the remaining dough.

Line a rimmed baking sheet with a wire rack or paper towels. Fill a wok or large Dutch oven with about 2 inches (5 cm) of oil; it should come no more than halfway up the vessel. Heat the oil over medium-high heat to 350°F (175°C).

Working in batches, add the kokoro to the hot oil, being careful not to overcrowd the pan. Fry, frequently moving the pieces around with a slotted spoon to cook evenly on all sides, until golden brown, about 4 minutes total. Use the slotted spoon to transfer the kokoro to the prepared baking sheet. Repeat with the remaining kokoro, allowing the oil to return to temperature between batches.

Allow the kokoro to cool completely; they will harden and firm up as they cool. Cover and allow them to rest for 6 hours or overnight.

The next day, preheat the oven to 300°F (150°C). Transfer the kokoro to a clean rimmed baking sheet. Bake for 5 to 10 minutes, until heated through. Transfer the sticks to a wire rack to cool completely.

Enjoy on their own or with a drink. Leftovers can be stored in an airtight container at room temperature for 4 weeks or in the freezer for up to 3 months.

KULĪKULĪ

1½ cups (5.3 ounces/150 g) powdered peanut butter, sifted, plus more for dusting

1 tablespoon sugar

1½ teaspoons dry pepper (see page 22)

1½ teaspoons ground ginger

½ teaspoon fine sea salt

½ teaspoon ground cloves

¾ cup (180 ml) hot water

½ cup (75 g) Roasted Groundnuts (page 200), ground to an even, coarse meal

Peanut oil, for frying

These crunchy groundnut (peanut) cookies are a specialty of the Nupe people of North Central. They are sometimes sweet, often spicy, and come in a variety of shapes, including flat cookies, rings, sticks, and roundish balls.

Traditionally, kulīkulī is made with roasted groundnuts with some fats and oil extracted in a skilled, technical process. This simplified recipe calls for powdered peanut butter, which also has some of the fat removed (look on the ingredient list for partially defatted peanuts, which produce excellent results). The kulīkulī is twice-cooked to enhance both flavor and texture.

Enjoy kulīkulī as a snack, on its own or with Soaked Garri (page 72); or grind it and use it as a salad topping (page 102) or to make Yajin Kuli (page 26).

In a medium bowl, combine the powdered peanut butter, sugar, dry pepper, ginger, salt, and cloves. Whisk well, then slowly add the hot water, stirring to combine. Let cool for about 10 minutes, then knead the dough, adding the ground groundnuts as you knead, until well combined.

Divide the dough into 4 pieces. Work with one piece at a time, and portion it with a teaspoon scoop.

With a light hand so the dough stays nice and airy, shape each scoop into a ⅓-inch (8.5 mm) stick, a flattish cookie (1½ inches/4 cm wide), or a ring (this shape is the trickiest). Repeat with the remaining 3 pieces of dough.

Line a rimmed baking sheet with a wire rack or paper towels. Fill a wok or large Dutch oven with 2 inches (5 cm) of oil; it should come no more than halfway up the vessel. Heat the oil over medium-high heat to 300°F (150°C).

Working in batches, if needed, add the shaped dough to the hot oil. Cook on one side for about 1 minute, then flip, and repeat until fried, about 4 minutes total. You may see some moist patches as you fry, but they should disappear once this round of cooking is completed. Use a slotted spoon to transfer the cookies to the prepared baking sheet. Let them sit for a minute, then transfer them to the rack to cool completely. Repeat with the remaining cookies,

clearing broken bits from the oil and allowing the oil to return to temperature between batches.

Transfer the cooled cookies to an airtight container and set aside at room temperature for 8 hours or overnight.

The next day, preheat the oven to 300°F (150°C).

Transfer the cookies to a rimmed baking sheet. Bake for 10 minutes, until heated through. Remove from the oven and transfer the cookies to a rack to cool completely. (Alternatively, you can refry the cookies in hot oil at 300°F/150°C for 3 to 4 minutes, until heated through.)

Store in an airtight container in the refrigerator for up to 8 weeks or in the freezer for up to 6 months.

DAKŪWA

SOFT GROUNDNUT AND CORN FLOUR SWEETMEAT

1¼ cups (155 g) yellow corn flour, sifted

1 cup (150 g) Roasted Groundnuts (page 200), skinned

½ teaspoon ground ginger

½ teaspoon ground cloves

½ teaspoon dry pepper (see page 22)

½ teaspoon ground alligator pepper (see page 235; optional)

¼ cup (50 g) sugar

½ teaspoon fine sea salt

Up to 3 tablespoons peanut oil or other neutral oil

COMBINATIONS OF DAKŪWA

Groundnuts (peanuts) are always used in dakūwa, but in variations, the ratios of groundnuts to the other ingredients differ. Dakūwar aya is made with tiger nuts, dakūwar waken soya uses soybean flour, and dakūwar dāwa incorporates Guinea corn (sorghum). Southern versions called kayan or tanfiri use rice or garri in a 2:1 ratio with groundnut butter.

These nutty truffles feature a key ingredient in the kitchens and stores of the Nupe people—groundnuts. Dakūwa are soft and spiced, perfect for enjoying on their own or with drinks. Made from a mixture of groundnut (peanut) butter and toasted corn flour, they are easy to pull together. The mixture is typically pounded in a mortar, but you can achieve similar results with a food processor. You can adjust the amount of spices, if you like, and use your favorites to create your own blend.

Enjoy on its own or crumbled over Àkàmù (page 76).

Place the corn flour in a large pan, shaking the pan to spread it evenly over the bottom. Cook over medium heat, stirring continuously and being careful not to inhale flour as you stir, until the flour is toasted, about 8 minutes. Turn the corn flour out onto a large plate, spread it evenly, and let cool.

In a food processor, combine the groundnuts, ginger, cloves, dry pepper, and alligator pepper (if using). Process until the groundnuts become pasty, stopping to scrape down the sides so the resulting mixture is uniformly smooth.

Spread 2 tablespoons of the toasted corn flour on a plate. Add the remaining toasted corn flour, the sugar, and the salt to the food processor and process until well incorporated. The mixture should be stiff and hold its shape. Add 1 tablespoon of the oil and process until well incorporated. Add another tablespoon of oil if you need it to bind, then transfer the mixture to a plate or bowl. Using a 1-tablespoon cookie scoop, create 20 portions.

Grease your (clean) hands with oil, then roll each portion of dough into a ball and place it on the plate with the toasted corn flour as you work. Roll the balls in the toasted corn flour (it helps them hold their shape). Serve immediately, or store in an airtight container in the refrigerator for up to 1 month.

COCONUTS AND GROUNDNUTS

Coconuts and groundnuts (peanuts) are popular in Nigerian cuisine, versatile, and beloved. Both ingredients have long histories, from the first coconut plantation established in Badagry (in Lagos state) in 1876 to the groundnut pyramids of the 1940s and '50s in Kano, in the north of Nigeria. The pyramids were built of burlap and jute sacks of groundnuts, bagged and ready for export.

I first became aware of the groundnut pyramids when my dad passed away in 2001. I found a photo album with a variety of postcards depicting life in 1950s and '60s Nigeria. They were mostly black-and-white photos of Broad Street in Lagos, men and women dressed up, fishing boats on the shore in Elegbata, and masquerades, but there was one color postcard, which showed the groundnut pyramids—geometrically arranged sacks of groundnuts. The pyramids were a tourist attraction celebrating "Made in Nigeria," something of national pride and value.

Located right in the heart of Kano, the groundnut pyramids were set up primarily as a way to store the groundnuts once they were ready for distribution. They were conveniently stacked near rail lines, for ease of access to coastal regions for local distribution and to the ports for export. Today, the pyramids are gone, for many reasons, from changes in the railway system to a shift in focus from agriculture to oil and gas, and more, but groundnuts are still revered across the country.

While groundnuts thrive in the north, coconuts flourish along the southern coast, where they are enjoyed for their refreshing water and milk, soft jellied fruit, as a snack on their own with roasted or boiled corn, shredded, and as coconut meal and oil.

Every year in May, the Odun Agbon Osara festival celebrates fertility, religion, history, and culture in the South West city of Ile-Ife. People dance and celebrate, wearing anklets and wristlets made from coconut in memory of the wishes of Osara, one of the two wives of Oduduwa (considered the father of the Yorùbá).

Since 2009, a coconut festival called Agunkefest has been held in the ancient town of Badagry, on the southwestern coast of Nigeria, where the first coconut plantation was established. It is a celebration of history and heritage, and a look toward the future of the coconut and its cultivation.

SWEET MOUTH

CANDIES AND DESSERTS

"You too get sweet mouth."

"SWEET MOUTH" HAS MULTIPLE MEANINGS IN NIGERIA.
It's someone who loves sweet things, whether candy, fruits, or snacks, but it's also someone who is a sweet talker and has a way with persuasive and endearing words.

Nigerians don't have a huge dessert culture as part of the daily meal ritual at home. If you feel peckish after a meal, fresh seasonal fruits and vegetables like carrots and cucumber, or cookies, cakes, and ice cream tend to fill the gap. When I was younger, desserts at parties were fairly simple confections; today, you see baked cakes, layered fruit and cream desserts, cheesecakes, and more.

Candies, on the other hand, both imported and homemade, were plentiful, and remain so. Sugar-based sweets are melted, spun, pulled, and caramelized. In Hausa, "candy" is *alawa* or *alewa*; both words have roots in Arabic *halva*. The pulled sugar is flavored with vanilla, lemon, peppermint, or ginger, and often twisted to become airy, chalky, and crunchy.

Caramels are popular—on their own, shaped into little golden cones with short sticks that resemble Christmas trees and lollipops at the same time, but also combined with nuts in brittles and in coconut candy, where shredded fresh coconut is cooked in caramel and shaped into truffle-size treats. Making caramel at home can be easier if you use light-colored pots and pans; it'll help you see when the caramel is ready.

Beloved treats are made from and with milk, too. There are those made with powdered milk doughs like a̱lēwa̱r madara, and others made with condensed milk.

CLOCKWISE FROM LEFT: *A kiosk with snacks and more; a fruit and veg stall; a gentleman eating corn; watermelon wedges*

FEATURED IN THESE RECIPES

1. **Amoriri.** A syrup made from a Nigerian variety of black plums, *Vitex doniana*, and often called "local honey."

2. **Brown coconut.** A hard-shelled, mature coconut.

3. **Coconut milk.** Can be homemade or canned. Though similar in flavor, there is a difference in consistency; homemade contains no preservatives and is often thinner than the canned (store-bought) milks, some thickened with gums.

4. **Coconut pieces.** Flakes and shavings, available sweetened and unsweetened.

5. **Honey.** This comes in a variety of colors and flavors, from dark wildflower varieties to those with a fermented profile, the latter often the product of beehives that are close to wine-producing palm trees.

6. **Mazarkwaila.** Heavy, compact discs of brown sugar, cooked down from sugarcane juice and processed in a similar manner to piloncillo or jaggery. In the north of Nigeria where it's made, it's a popular addition to drinks and enjoyed like candy.

7. **Milk powder.** Known in Nigeria as powdered milk. You'll find full-fat, semi-skimmed, and nonfat versions.

8. **Mortar and pestle.** The historic food processor. Used for processing cereals and grains, cracking hulls, bruising skins like for palm nut cream, removing skins, and pounding cooked foods like pounded yam and other swallows.

9. **White sesame seeds.** Also known as rīdī.

10. **Tapioca granules.** Dried granules that come in a range of sizes from less than ⅛ inch (3 mm) to up to 1 inch (2.5 cm). Check Brazilian grocery stores for tapioca granulada or use small pearl tapioca or cassava sago (4 to 6 mm).

ALĒWAR MADARA

MILK CANDY

3 tablespoons unsalted butter, at room temperature, or neutral oil, plus more for greasing

¼ cup (50 g) sugar

1 teaspoon vanilla extract (see Note)

¼ teaspoon fine sea salt

¼ teaspoon liquid or gel food coloring (optional)

3 cups (375 g) full-fat powdered milk

NOTE: *You can swap out the vanilla extract for strawberry, mint, toffee, or other flavorings.*

These sweet, soft, creamy candies of cooked powdered milk are from the North West, commonly associated with the city of Kano. To make them, begin as though you are making a swallow and end as a treat—cut or shaped. Though they are often left cream-colored, a touch of food coloring can be added. You decide.

Lightly grease a small rimmed baking sheet with 1 tablespoon of the butter.

In a medium pot, combine the remaining 2 tablespoons butter, the sugar, vanilla, salt, food coloring (if using), and ¾ cup (180 ml) room-temperature water. Bring to a boil over medium-high heat, stirring, until the sugar has dissolved and the mixture turns syrupy, about 7 minutes.

Reduce the heat to low. Evenly sprinkle 2 cups (250 g) of the powdered milk into the pot. With a wooden spoon or sturdy spatula, stir the mixture, adding the remaining powdered milk ¼ cup (about 32 g) at a time, until it is all incorporated and a soft dough forms, pulls away from the sides of the pan, and becomes shiny, about 8 minutes.

Transfer the mixture to the center of the prepared baking sheet. With a spatula or rolling pin, gently and evenly spread the dough to a thickness of about ⅓ inch (8.5 mm). Let cool completely.

Carefully grease a large, sharp knife with butter and cut the candy into 25 to 30 squares, rectangles, or diamonds. Alternatively, cut it into shapes using cookie cutters. Put the milk candy in an airtight container and refrigerate for an hour to set before serving.

Store in the refrigerate for up to 2 weeks or in the freezer for up to 4 weeks.

MAKES 35 TO 40 CANDIES

COCONUT CANDY

1 to 2 tablespoons coconut oil, plus more for oiling your hands

1 teaspoon fresh lime juice or lemon juice

¼ cup (60 ml) coconut water or water

1 cup (200 g) sugar

½ teaspoon fine sea salt

3 cups (300 g) grated fresh coconut (see Note) or thawed frozen coconut

NOTES: *To get long shreds of coconut, which hold better and are a touch chewier, use the large or coarse grating holes on a box grater.*

For a firmer version of this coconut candy, use dry unsweetened shredded coconut instead of fresh or frozen.

These golden to dark brown balls of grated coconut caramelized in sugar are a childhood favorite. Sweet, sticky, and full of delicious coconut flavor, they can be made plain or with added citrus or spice.

If you don't have access to fresh coconut, use frozen coconut. Defrost it and press out excess liquid before using.

Lightly grease a medium baking sheet with 1 to 2 tablespoons of the coconut oil, as needed.

Fill a cup with room-temperature water and set it within easy reach of the stovetop.

In a medium heavy pan, combine the lime juice, coconut water, and sugar. Stir well. Dip a heat-safe pastry brush into the cup of water to wet it and use the wet brush to push any sugar crystals that cling to the sides of the pot into the mixture.

Set the pan over medium-low heat. Cook, stirring occasionally, until the sugar dissolves and a clear syrup forms, 4 to 5 minutes. If any sugar crystals accumulate on the sides of the pot, dip your pastry brush into the water again and gently nudge them into the syrup. Increase the heat to medium and continue to cook, occasionally stirring with a metal whisk, until the syrup begins to caramelize and turns golden brown, 6 to 7 minutes more.

Sprinkle in the salt and stir to combine, then add the coconut in three or four additions, stirring well after each to ensure it is evenly incorporated before adding the next. Cook, stirring often, until the coconut pieces are translucent and the mixture is brown and sticky and smells like toasted coconut, up to 10 minutes. Transfer the mixture to a clean heatproof surface to cool for about 5 minutes.

With a 1-tablespoon cookie scoop, spoon mounds of the mixture onto the greased baking sheet. Let cool until warm enough to handle safely, about 10 minutes, then portion into 35 to 40 pieces. With lightly oiled hands, roll each portion into a ball, placing them back on the baking sheet as you work. Let cool completely.

Store in an airtight container for up to 1 week at room temperature and up to 4 weeks in the freezer.

CANDIED GROUNDNUTS

1 cup (200 g) sugar

¼ teaspoon fine sea salt

1 cup (175 g) raw, red, skin-on groundnuts (peanuts), picked and rinsed

These sugar-coated nuts, similar to Thai tua krob kaew, feature red skin-on groundnuts (peanuts) and cook like magic: The sugar goes from crystals to syrup to caramel to sandy-textured sugar, back to caramel, and then to sandy-textured again. It is this cycle that creates the crunchy, candied shell around the nuts.

Skin-on raw groundnuts are essential to the success of these candies because the skins protect the peanuts from overcooking and give the sugar-caramel something to latch on to as it goes through the crystallization cycle, creating nuts that stay whole with a perfect layer of coating.

Be careful when working with hot sugar. Do not use your bare hands, and do not taste the candy before it has cooled completely.

Line a large baking sheet with parchment paper.

In a large heavy-bottomed saucepan or nonstick wok, combine the sugar, 1 cup (240 ml) room-temperature water, and the salt. Stir well and bring to a boil over medium-high heat, stirring continuously, until the sugar has dissolved, 4 to 5 minutes.

Reduce the heat to low, stir in the peanuts, and cook until the syrup thickens, reduces, and then evaporates, 15 to 20 minutes. Continue stirring until the syrup crystallizes and breaks down into moist sandy sugar, then dry sandy sugar, coating the nuts in a hard candied shell. Some loose crystallized sugar will remain. Try to incorporate as much as you can—continue cooking, still on low heat.

Beads of caramel will appear on the peanuts and at the bottom of the pan. Stir vigorously until there's a very minimal amount of loose caramel. Remove from the heat immediately and transfer the nuts to the prepared baking sheet so that the crunchy sugar coating doesn't begin to liquefy. Spread the nuts into a single layer, separating them so they don't form clusters. Let cool completely before tasting.

Store in an airtight container or jar at room temperature for up to 3 weeks.

AROSIDOSI
RICE PUDDING

1 teaspoon coconut oil

1 cup (235 g) short-grain rice, rinsed well and drained

4 or 5 whole cloves

½ teaspoon fine sea salt

½ cup (100 g) sugar

4 cups (about 1 L) coconut milk, plus more as needed

2 teaspoons vanilla extract

2 or 3 wide strips of lemon zest (no pith; optional)

1 teaspoon freshly grated nutmeg

White sesame seeds, raw or toasted (optional)

NOTE: *Stir in a few tablespoons of chopped chocolate or malted chocolate powder (such as Milo) for another version.*

Arosidosi is a creamy, coconutty rice pudding connected in name and concept to Portuguese arroz doce via the Afro-Brazilian community.

For the creamiest results, use short-grain rice like sushi, risotto, or paella rice. Though we use coconut milk, dairy and unsweetened nondairy milks work, too.

In a medium pan, warm the coconut oil over low heat until shimmering and fragrant. Stir in the rice, whole cloves, and salt. Cook, stirring continuously, until some grains of rice are toasted, 8 to 9 minutes.

Add ¼ cup (50 g) of the sugar and stir for about 30 seconds; it will begin to caramelize. Slowly stir in 2 cups (480 ml) of the coconut milk. Add the vanilla and the lemon zest (if using). Reduce the heat to low, cover, and cook, stirring every few minutes and making sure to scrape the bottom to avoid scorching, until the liquid has been absorbed, the mixture is creamy, and the rice has softened a bit, 10 to 12 minutes.

Add the remaining 2 cups (480 ml) coconut milk. Stir well and taste; add some or all of the remaining ¼ cup (50 g) sugar as needed. Cover and cook until the rice is al dente, checking it now and again, 40 minutes more. The rice pudding should still have some liquid, as it will thicken as it stands. If you want it softer, add ½ cup (120 ml) more water or coconut milk, sweeten accordingly, and cook until the consistency is to your liking. Remove from the heat, discard the cloves, and let rest for 15 minutes before serving.

Just before serving, sprinkle ½ teaspoon of the nutmeg over the top and stir it in. Serve warm or cold, on its own, sprinkled with some or all of the remaining ½ teaspoon nutmeg and some sesame seeds, if desired.

FRESH FRUIT SALAD

3 ripe large oranges, rinsed

1 cup (165 g) chopped (½-inch/1.3 cm pieces) ripe pineapple

½ cup (75 g) chopped (½-inch/1.3 cm pieces) firm but ripe papaya

½ cup (75 g) chopped (½-inch/1.3 cm pieces) watermelon

½ sweet apple, peeled, cored, and cut into ½-inch (1.3 cm) pieces

1 large ripe banana

Fresh mint leaves, for garnish (optional)

This staple of my childhood celebrates all that is beloved about tropical fruit: color, flavor, and juice. When my family had gatherings at our house, the meal of jollof rice (page 143), Dòdò (page 120), and other savory delights would be followed by a spread of huge bowls of fresh fruit salad, diced strawberry or orange jelly, evaporated milk, sweetened condensed milk, and sometimes ice cream.

With the exception of the oranges to be sectioned and the bananas to be cut just before serving, you can prepare this salad up to 2 hours before you need it, so it chills properly and the flavors meld. Cut all the other fruits to about the same size.

On a cutting board, use a small, sharp knife to cut 1 of the oranges in half; juice the orange into a large bowl. Reserve the orange peels for another use or discard them.

Cut the remaining 2 oranges into suprêmes: Cut off the top and bottom of one orange and stand it on one of its cut sides on the cutting board. Starting from the top and following the curve of the orange, cut away the peel and any white pith in strips to expose the orange flesh. Holding the peeled orange over the large bowl with the orange juice, cut along the sides of each membrane to release the orange sections, letting them fall into the bowl as you work. Squeeze any juice from the membrane into the bowl as well, then discard the membrane. Repeat with the remaining orange.

Add the pineapple, papaya, watermelon, and apple to the bowl and stir well to incorporate. Cover and refrigerate for at least 2 hours and up to 8 hours. Uncover and let the fruit salad rest at room temperature for 10 minutes before serving.

Meanwhile, peel the banana and slice it lengthwise, then into ⅓-inch (8.5 mm) chunks. Gently fold the banana into the salad. Finish with fresh mint, if you like, and serve. Store leftovers in an airtight container in the refrigerator for no more than 2 days.

STREET FRUIT SALAD

1 cup chopped (165 g) ripe pineapple

½ cup (75 g) chopped firm but ripe papaya

½ cup (75 g) chopped watermelon

1 medium (orange) carrot, cut

1 small cucumber, chopped

¼ cup (35 g) fresh coconut chunks or shavings

½ cup (120 ml) sweetened condensed milk, for serving

½ cup (75 g) Roasted Groundnuts (page 200), skinned, for garnish

This street food take on fruit salad, sold in transparent packs accompanied by toothpicks and cutlery, combines sweet, fresh produce with toppings of condensed milk and skinned roasted groundnuts (peanuts). Sweetness comes by way of the pineapple and papaya, freshness from cucumber, and crunch from strips of carrot and fresh coconut.

For this salad, the fruit is cut into slightly larger pieces (about an inch/2.5 cm) that are often eaten one at a time, rather than mixed together. Feel free to make an American-style fruit salad of it by cutting the fruit smaller and combining.

In a large serving bowl, combine the pineapple, papaya, watermelon, carrot, cucumber, and coconut. Stir well to combine. Cover and refrigerate for at least 2 hours and up to 8 hours before you plan to serve it.

Uncover and let the fruit salad rest at room temperature for 10 minutes before serving.

Spoon the salad into individual bowls, drizzle condensed milk over the top of each portion, and sprinkle with the groundnuts. Store leftovers in an airtight container in the refrigerator for no more than 2 days.

MINGAU DE TAPIOCA
TAPIOCA AND COCONUT PUDDING

¾ cup (85 g) tapioca granules or pearled tapioca (see Note), rinsed

2 cups (480 ml) coconut milk

¼ cup (50 g) granulated sugar, or more as needed

½ teaspoon fine sea salt

1 (3-inch/7.5 cm) cinnamon stick

4 to 6 whole cloves, or ½ teaspoon ground cloves

½ teaspoon freshly grated nutmeg, plus more for serving

¼ cup (35 g) chopped fresh coconut (optional)

Nondairy milk(s), for serving

Mazarkwaila, amoriri, or granulated sugar, for serving

Ground cinnamon, for serving

NOTE: *If you can't find Nigerian tapioca granules, which come in a range of sizes from small (less than ⅛ inch/3 mm) to medium (up to 1 inch/2.5 cm), check Brazilian grocery stores for tapioca granulada. Alternatively, use small pearl tapioca or cassava sago (⅛ to ¼ inch/4 to 6 mm).*

On Lagos Island, mingau de tapioca is a creamy pudding of soft, chewy tapioca granules, cooked in coconut milk and finished with a grating of fresh nutmeg. It is similar in some ways to North American tapioca pudding, but without the eggs. In Brazil, where its roots lie, mingau is similar to everything from "thin gruel" to "infant food and drink." As a drink, it reminds me of warm, coconutty bubble tea.

The presence of mingau in Lagos is one anchor of several brought by returnees at the end of chattel enslavement who settled in Ìsàlẹ̀ Ẹ̀kọ, the "lowlands" of Lagos. It is popular for breakfast with Àkàrà (page 64).

When it is made ahead, refrigerated, and reheated, the granules of tapioca become firmer and chewier, like boba. Serve with more sugar or sweetener and (warm) coconut milk. Some people create a tres leches topping with coconut milk, evaporated milk, and sweetened condensed milk. You can also use other nondairy milks, such as Madarān Ayā tiger nut milk (page 310), or your favorite.

In a medium bowl, combine the tapioca, coconut milk, and 2 cups (480 ml) cold water. Stir, cover, and refrigerate until the granules absorb the liquid and soften, about 6 hours or up to overnight.

In a medium pot, stir together 2 cups (480 ml) cold water, the granulated sugar, salt, cinnamon stick, cloves, nutmeg, and chopped coconut (if using). Bring to a boil over medium heat, cover with the lid ajar, and cook for about 8 minutes.

Add the soaked tapioca and any remaining liquid in the bowl, stir well, and cook for 10 minutes, at which point the mixture should be at a boil. Reduce the heat to low and cook, whisking often to break up any clumps, until the tapioca swells, thickens, and becomes translucent, about 5 minutes. Remove the cinnamon stick and cloves.

Ladle into bowls and top with the chopped coconut, if using. Serve with the milk or milks of your choice. Sweeten with mazarkwaila and finish with a sprinkling of nutmeg and cinnamon.

BELOVED CORN

Though not native to Nigeria, corn is popular in our cuisine and celebrated—probably due to the fact that it resembles the indigenous grain sorghum, also known as Guinea corn. The most common type is waxy, glutinous field corn, not sweet corn, and is mostly white or yellow. Overall, field corn is starchier than sweet corn, and not as sweet. Though soft and tender right after harvest when the sugars are fresh and not yet converted to starch, it becomes starchier with time.

When corn is in season from April to August, we eat it boiled, roasted, blended, made into steamed puddings, and added to pottages like adalu (stewed beans cooked with corn). The kernels are also dried and used in a variety of ways, such as boiled, and fermented for Àkàmù (page 76).

In the rainy season, many fruits and vegetables are celebrated, but corn comes first, followed by yam. The Agẹmo festival in the South West is traditionally celebrated in the harvest months between June and August. It features omo alagemo merindinlogun, children of the sixteen Agẹmo masquerades, specifically in the city of Ijebu Ode.

As part of the Umatu festival in the South East of Nigeria, the first corn harvest is celebrated in Onitsha Ado N'idu. The people, the king, and his leaders celebrate the success of the corn crop, especially as it precedes the coming of new yams and the New Yam Festival (see page 15). Nni oka, a corn flour swallow like Tūwōn Masàřā (page 221), served with draw soup (see page 245), is the celebratory meal of the festival.

Corn is a popular street food in Nigeria. You'll find it parched, where the grains are toasted until cooked through. Because the variety cooked is not popcorn, it ends up mostly as toasted kernels, but not popped, though some attempt to pop. You can often buy what I call "Lagos Island trail mix," with parched corn, popcorn, and skinned roasted groundnuts (peanuts).

Roasted corn on the cob is jokingly called "mouth organ" (referring to the instrument also known as the harmonica or French harp) because the action of eating it is likened to moving up and down the harmonica, sometimes blowing to cool it down, and because it is held in both hands like a harmonica. Eating it is also considered a workout, like playing the harmonica.

At home, fresh corn kernels are handpicked off their cobs rather than sliced off, then blended and used in dishes like sapala, similar to a corn tamale; and iyan gidi, a swallow made of cooked yam and steamed ground fresh corn; the ground corn is wrapped in leaves, steamed until cooked through, then pounded with cooked yam. Corn flour is used as a soup thickener—whisked into the broth in ntime abakpa, a dish from the Ibibio people in the South South.

QUENCH YOUR THIRST

DRINKS

THERE ARE DRINKS FOR DRINKING; DRINKS FOR EATING; hot and cold drinks for the morning; drinks for afternoons and evenings, like Aba Punch; drinks for celebration, like palm wine (see page 323); and those to enjoy just because—a Shandy, anyone?

Both robusta and arabica coffee are grown across the country, robusta across all regions and arabica on the plateaus—Obudu in the South South, Vom in the North Central, and Mambilla in the North East, where highland tea farms are also located. Fresh milk, nono (similar to buttermilk), and nondairy "milks" are staples in the north.

From juice and smoothies to sap, drinks are sweet, sour, and fermented. Expect bright flavors of fruit, spice, and herbs, as in pineapple skin drink, which uses the often discarded skins and cores of pineapples; or the sweet, sour, and tangy pulp/covering of fruits like tamarind and baobab; or infusions from calyxes, like Zōbò, with its warm and spicy notes from dried ginger and cloves.

Sodas, also known as minerals or soft drinks, are popular, as are nonalcoholic malt drinks of barley and hops sweetened with dark caramel.

Bitter is a flavor embraced by Nigerians. Agbo, a group of botanical tonics and elixirs, is like medicine, with specific "cures" for a range of ailments. Brewed by specialists, considered primary health caregivers, these beverages are in plentiful supply, available on every street corner. Buy only from trusted sources.

Here's a tip to enjoy the full flavors of your drinks: Make ice cubes of the ingredients—freeze the prepared drink. That way, you can chill the drink without diluting its flavors.

CLOCKWISE FROM LEFT: *A selection of drinks; at a fruit and vegetable store, Lekki 1, Lagos; cradling ginger; tangerines and pineapples*

FEATURED IN THESE RECIPES

1. **Angostura bitters.** Aromatic bitters of herbs, roots, and other botanicals that impart a unique taste to Nigerian Chapman (page 314).

2. **Beer & Wine**
   - » **GULDER.** A golden lager of barley and Guinea corn (sorghum).
   - » **PALM WINE.** A creamy-gray drink prized in Nigerian cuisine.
   - » **STAR.** A pale lager. The first beer to be commercially brewed in Nigeria, starting in 1949 (eleven years before Nigeria's 1960 Independence). Known as Shine Shine Bobo, in reference to a cool person with glitz and glam.
   - » **STOUT.** Guinness stout, simply known as Guinness. A dark, dry stout from Ireland, adored for its bitterness. It comes in cans and bottles—large bottles are called Odeku.

3. **Dates.** Popular across the country, especially in the northern regions.

4. **Ribena.** Black currant cordial. A common addition to Chapman (page 314). Substitute cassis syrup or cordial, or grenadine.

5. **Tamarind.** Also called tsamiya. Sticky pulpy fruit in brittle shells, eaten out of hand and used as a souring agent.

6. **Tiger nuts** (*Cyperus esculentus* var. *sativus*). Not an actual nut, tiger nuts are starchy sedge tubers, sold fresh and dried. They come in yellow, brown, or black varietals, and are generally smaller than hazelnuts, between 0.2 and 0.6 inch (0.5 to 1.5 cm) in diameter. They can be enjoyed out of hand and have a crunch akin to water chestnuts, though they're heftier and less watery with a coconutty flavor. They can also be candied, like groundnuts (page 295).

7. **Zōbò calyxes.** From *Hibiscus sabdariffa*, a variety of wild hibiscus. Commonly sold and used dried.

MADARĀN AYĀ
TIGER NUT DRINK

2 cups (340 g) dried tiger
nuts, rinsed

Sugar or your favorite
sweetener (optional)

Wheelbarrows are used as street food carts in Nigeria; think of
them as mobile marketplaces showcasing seasonal produce. You'll
find them laden with fresh, dried, and baked tiger nuts (*Cyperus
esculentus*), sold by the cup. They can be eaten out of hand or
blended and strained to create cooked porridges and (sometimes
thick) milky drinks with notes of vanilla and the nuttiness of coconut
and almonds, like Spanish horchata de chufa.

Pick over the tiger nuts and discard any odd bits. Place the nuts in a
strainer and rinse two or three times. Transfer to a large bowl, add
water to cover by 2 to 3 inches (5 to 7.5 cm), cover, and refrigerate for
8 hours or overnight. Drain and rinse the soaked tiger nuts.

Line a fine-mesh strainer with a few layers of cheesecloth and set it
over a large container. In a blender, combine 1 cup (170 g) of the
soaked tiger nuts and 2 cups (480 ml) room-temperature water. Puree
until smooth and creamy. Strain the pureed mixture, gathering the
overhanging cheesecloth and twisting to help squeeze out as much
liquid as possible. Reserve the solids in the strainer. Repeat with the
remaining tiger nuts and 2 cups (480 ml) room-temperature water.

Transfer the solids from the strainer to the blender and add 3 cups
(720 ml) water. Puree, then strain. Discard the solids.

Transfer the tiger nut drink to airtight containers. Refrigerate until
well chilled, an hour or two, or store in the fridge for up to 3 days
(any longer and it will begin to ferment) or in the freezer for up to
1 month.

Before using, shake to reincorporate any starch that has settled at the
bottom, or decant and discard the starchy dregs. Taste and sweeten as
you like.

VARIATION

The addition of dates and/or coconut is also popular. Combine
½ cup (88 g) pitted dates with 1 cup (150 g) fresh coconut chunks
or shredded coconut. Add the soaked tiger nuts. Blend and strain as
directed.

TAMARIND DRINK

2 heaping cups (400 g)
shelled unseeded sour
tamarind pods

4 cups (about 1 L) boiling
water

⅔ cup (100 g) sugar, or more
to taste

Sparkling water, soda water,
tonic water, or ginger ale, for
serving

¼ teaspoon fine sea salt
(optional)

NOTE: *You can find packages
of tamarind in regular
grocery stores as well
as Asian and Caribbean
markets. If you buy it
packaged, look for varieties
that list only tamarind in the
ingredients, without salt.*

There are two popular types of tamarind in Nigeria: small ones
known as icheku, awin, or licky licky, with velvety black shells
covering powdery peach-orange pods, and longer, dark brown pods
(resembling groundnuts) with brittle shells, sticky pulp, multiple
seeds, and sweet-sour notes—these are a staple in the Arewa
kitchen, where they are used as souring ingredients.

You will need sour or sweet-sour tamarind, not sweet (ripe)
tamarind, which ends up being too sweet.

In a nonreactive heatproof medium bowl, combine the tamarind
pods with the boiling water. Cover and let stand until completely
cooled and the pulp has softened, about 1½ hours.

Set a fine-mesh strainer over a large pot. Working in batches, scoop
the tamarind mixture into the strainer. With a spatula or whisk, or
wearing food-safe gloves, work the mixture through the strainer,
massaging the pods until the seeds are shiny and the pulp has been
released. Pour 1 to 2 cups (240 to 480 ml) room-temperature water
through the strainer to rinse the pulp into the pot. Discard the solids
in the strainer, then use 1 to 2 cups (240 to 480 ml) more water to
rinse any last bits of pulp into the pot.

Add the sugar to the pot. Cook over medium heat, stirring, until
the sugar has dissolved and the mixture comes to a boil, about
10 minutes. Don't worry about the froth; just stir it back in. Reduce
the heat to low and cook for 5 minutes. Remove from the heat and
let cool to room temperature, about 2 hours.

Transfer to airtight containers and refrigerate until ready to serve, up
to 5 days, or freeze for up to 3 months.

Shake the container to mix the drink, as it tends to settle. Pour into
glasses over ice, filling them about three-quarters full, then top with
sparkling water and salt (if using) and stir well.

VARIATION

To make Kankaran tsamiya, fill ice pop bags or molds with the
tamarind drink and freeze until solid. Enjoy as ice lollies.

CHAPMAN

4 ounces (120 ml) black currant cordial or syrup, such as Ribena, plus more as needed

About 24 ounces (720 ml) orange soda, such as Fanta orange, chilled

About 24 ounces (720 ml) lemon-lime soda, such as Sprite, chilled

Angostura bitters (see Note)

Juice of 1 lemon

Juice of 2 limes

4 lemon slices, for garnish

4 lime slices, for garnish

4 thin slices skin-on cucumber, for garnish

NOTES: *Some people consider this drink alcoholic because Angostura bitters are 44% alcohol by volume. However, only a little is used, and Chapman is not the same without the complexity of bitters. If you'd like, use nonalcoholic bitters instead, or skip if you must.*

Though garnishes today mostly consist of cucumber and citrus, historically one might have encountered other fruits, like candied cherries or sliced bananas, and herbs such as mint.

The beauty of Chapman is how refreshing and balanced it is. The combination of soda, bitters, and black currant cordial with cucumber and citrus slices is more than the sum of its parts.

Chapman is said to have been created in the 1960s by Sam Alamutu, a hotelier and manager of Nigerian Hotels Limited, for his wife, who loved soft drinks. It debuted at Ikoyi Hotel, then Ikoyi Club, a country club on Lagos Island, and spread across the country. It remains a favorite of bartenders, and you'd be hard-pressed to find a Nigerian drinking spot or party where Chapman isn't on the menu, for both children and adults.

Make it to order in individual servings, or in small punch bowls. Chapman served in dimpled beer mugs was popular in the 1980s and '90s, and though this mug isn't as popular today, whatever glass you use will hold the essence of the ruby-red drink: always served with ice, not too sweet, fresh, with hints of mystery from the Angostura bitters. Adjust the black currant cordial if need be. Enjoy it on its own, spiked with Campari, gin, or crème de cassis, or with your favorite eats.

Set out four beer mugs. Pour 2 tablespoons of the black currant cordial into each glass. Add ¾ cup (175 ml) each of the orange soda and lemon-lime soda to each glass, then sprinkle each with 3 or 4 drops of bitters. Stir, taste, and add more cordial if you like.

Distribute the lemon and lime juices evenly among the glasses. Add 3 or 4 ice cubes to each glass and stir well.

Top each glass with a slice of lemon, lime, and cucumber. Finish with straws and serve immediately.

SEVEN UNCOMMON VERSIONS OF CHAPMAN

1. Lemon-lime soda, orange soda, black currant cordial, Campari, Angostura bitters
2. Lemon-lime soda, ginger beer, lemon or lime cordial, Angostura bitters
3. Lemon-lime soda, lemon or lime cordial or orange syrup, Angostura bitters
4. Lemonade, orange soda, tonic water, Angostura bitters
5. Ginger beer, lemon or lime cordial, Angostura bitters
6. Ginger beer or lemon-lime soda, orange syrup, Angostura bitters
7. Orange soda, tonic water, orange syrup, Angostura bitters

MAKES 1½ QUARTS (1.4 L);
SERVES 6 TO 8

ZŌBÒ
RED SORREL DRINK

2 cups (100 g) deep red zōbò calyxes (see Notes)

4 to 6 slices dried ginger, or 2 thumb-size pieces fresh ginger, peeled

10 to 12 whole cloves

Ginger Simple Syrup (recipe follows)

NOTES: *You'll find dried zōbò calyxes in the tea, drinks, or edible flower sections of African, Central and South American, and other grocery stores, or online.*

Sometimes the calyxes are sandy—swish them well in a lot of water to release any residual sand and grit, and carefully lift the calyxes rather than pour them out.

This recipe calls for steeping the calyxes in water for 8 hours to soften them, which also allows the nuances in flavor and color to come through. Though recommended, this is not necessary. To save time, you can go ahead and make the infusion after the calyxes are washed.

Drunk year-round, hot, cold, or frozen into ice pops (Kankaran zōbò rodo), zōbò is made from the dried calyxes of a wild hibiscus plant. You might have encountered some version of it as hibiscus tea or agua de Jamaica. This version tends to be more nuanced with a deeper flavor.

About that flavor: Dried ginger slices (or a bashed piece of fresh ginger) and whole cloves are common. Baking spices, herbs, the flesh or skins of citrus and other fruits, extracts, and cucumber are also used. Some people even include cloves of garlic!

When it comes to adding sweeteners, options include very ripe pineapple and honey, but my recommendation is: Don't. It will cause the drink to ferment much faster. Instead, use ginger simple syrup.

This deep purple-burgundy drink can stain, so watch your whites.

In a 4- or 5-quart (4 to 5 L) nonreactive pot or Dutch oven, combine the zōbò calyxes, ginger, cloves, and 2 quarts (1.9 L) water. Cover and let steep and rehydrate for 8 hours, or overnight if you can (see Notes).

Set the pot over medium heat, cover with the lid ajar, and bring to a boil; cook for about 10 minutes, then reduce the heat to low and cook until the liquid is deep in color and somewhat fragrant, 15 minutes more. Remove from the heat and let stand until cool, about 2 hours.

Line a fine-mesh strainer with a few layers of cheesecloth and set it over a large container. Working in batches, strain the zōbò, gathering up the overhanging cheesecloth and twisting to squeeze out as much liquid as possible. Reserve the solids to make another batch of zōbò (bag, seal, and freeze them). Transfer the zōbò infusion to airtight containers and refrigerate until ready to serve, up to 2 weeks.

When ready to serve, pour the zōbò infusion into a pitcher or punch bowl and sweeten to taste with the ginger syrup. Serve over ice.

RECIPE CONTINUES →

To make a punch version, add fresh fruit such as chopped pineapples, watermelon, cucumbers, and citrus, to taste, or make cocktails with rum, cachaça, or vodka.

Ginger Simple Syrup

MAKES 4 CUPS (1 L)

2 thumb-size pieces fresh ginger, peeled and chopped

3 cups (600 g) sugar

6 to 8 whole cloves

This ginger simple syrup packs a punch that works well for zōbò. It also makes a great sweetener for Àkàmù (page 76), Ibyer (page 78), or as you wish.

In a blender, puree the ginger with 1 cup (240 ml) water until creamy and the ginger fibers are broken down. Transfer the puree to a medium pot (do not strain it). Add the sugar, cloves, and 2 cups (480 ml) room-temperature water and stir well to incorporate. Cook over medium heat, stirring now and again, until the sugar has dissolved, the mixture turns golden, the aroma of ginger fills your house, and the flavor of the ginger comes through, 8 to 10 minutes. Remove from the heat and let cool for about 30 minutes—it will thicken as it cools. Strain through cheesecloth and store in a bottle or jar. Seal and refrigerate for up to 2 weeks, or store in the freezer for up to 3 months.

SHANDY

24 ounces (720 ml) pale lager, chilled

24 ounces (720 ml) sweetened apple juice, chilled

Juice of 2 to 4 limes

4 lime slices, for garnish

This refreshing drink has, in balance, the effervescence of lager, the sweetness of fruit juice or soda, and the fragrance of citrus. Make it on a hot summer's day.

Green Sands Shandy was a popular brand in Nigeria in the 1980s. Anyone could buy and drink it, even though it contained a small volume of alcohol, from 1 to 5 percent. This drink introduced my teenage self to the sweet wonders of lager and soda. The commercial shandy disappeared from the markets a few years later, rumor has it because of alcohol laws, so many bars and restaurants began making it from scratch. They would pour the drink tableside, and you got to choose your ratios, beyond the standard equal amounts. More bitter? Add more lager. Not sweet enough? Pour a touch more soda.

To make a shandy at home, use sweet, clear apple juice (this is not the place for thick, cloudy apple cider) and a lager with a light, clean flavor. The result is clean, fruity, and refreshing, and should taste of freshly pressed apple juice.

Because of the carbonation, this drink is best made by the glass.

Fill four highball glasses with about 6 ounces (180 ml) of lager each, tilting the glass as you pour to limit the froth. Top each with 6 ounces (180 ml) of the apple juice, and finish with the juice of ½ to 1 lime per glass. Garnish with lime slices and serve.

VARIATION

Use lemon-lime soda instead of the apple juice. Dial back on the lime juice, if you like, or swap in lemon juice.

MAKES 2 QUARTS (1.9 L); SERVES 6 TO 8

PINEAPPLE SKIN DRINK

Cleaned pineapple skin and core (about 1.1 pounds/500 g total; see Notes)

2 thumb-size pieces fresh ginger, peeled and grated

½ cup (100 g) sugar, plus more as needed

1 (3-inch/7.5 cm) cinnamon stick

8 whole cloves

Lime wedges, for garnish

Fresh mint or basil leaves, for garnish

NOTES: *Prepare your pineapple by rinsing it under running water, then soaking it in a solution of baking soda and water. Use 2 teaspoons baking soda for every 4 cups (1 L) of water, and soak for 15 to 20 minutes. Finally, rub some salt over the exterior and rinse it off. Pat dry, and use as desired.*

Freeze your pineapple skins until you have enough to double, triple, or even quadruple the recipe.

The amount of sugar in this recipe is a guide; adjust to suit your taste.

Freeze some of the drink in ice cube trays, then use them to cool your drink for double the flavor.

For a clearer drink, pour the finished drink into bottles and let stand on the counter overnight, undisturbed, then refrigerate.

Pineapple skins are an essential part of herbal remedies in Nigeria. My dad taught me to make this drink with the inedible, often-discarded skin and the fruit's core; it was part of his waste-not philosophy. Every time we prepared pineapples, we would bag and freeze the skins and cores, saving them until we had enough to make lots of pineapple drink.

Among the many varieties of pineapple in Nigeria, Queen is my absolute favorite—it is sweet, with flesh that is rich yellow, full flavored, and not at all acidic. The fruit makes for great eating and the skins make a lovely, fruity drink. For an additional layer of fruitiness, you can be a touch generous with the amount of flesh left on the skins as you remove the eyes.

In a large pot, combine the pineapple skin and core, ginger, sugar, cinnamon stick, cloves, and 2½ quarts (2.4 L) water. Cover and bring to a boil over medium-high heat, 12 to 15 minutes from the time the pot is covered. Reduce the heat to low and cook until the skins have softened and become translucent, about 20 minutes.

Uncover and gently press down on the mixture with a wooden spoon or spatula, releasing even more pineapple flavor. Cover and cook for 15 to 20 minutes more. Taste and adjust the sweetness with more sugar, if desired, stirring to incorporate it. Remove from the heat and let cool to room temperature, about 1 hour.

Line a fine-mesh strainer with a few layers of cheesecloth and set it over a large container. Working in batches, strain the cooled pineapple drink, gathering the overhanging cheesecloth and twisting to help squeeze out as much liquid as possible. Discard the solids and repeat with the remaining drink.

Serve warm, or over ice, garnished with lime wedges and mint or basil leaves. Store leftovers in an airtight container in the refrigerator for up to 5 days or in the freezer for up to 3 months.

ABA PUNCH
PALM WINE AND STOUT

About 21 ounces (620 ml) chilled palm wine

About 21 ounces (620 ml) chilled stout, preferably Guinness Foreign Extra

NOTES: *There are several ways to layer the drink: with the stout first, then palm wine on top; or palm wine first, then stout on top, the version I've had the most success with. You'll need more palm wine than stout; a ratio of 2:1 instead of equal amounts.*

Make the drinks one at a time. Fill a glass two-thirds of the way with palm wine. Set a tablespoon inside the glass, angling it as though you were going to lift it up, with the front of the spoon at the lowest point, just touching the glass above the surface of the palm wine. Slowly pour the stout into the spoon, lifting up as you pour, until you get to the top. Remove the spoon and enjoy your layered creation.

Nigerians have a love-love relationship with bitter flavors in everything from botanical brews and bitters to stout—Guinness Foreign Extra Stout in particular, sold in two sizes, big (640 ml, also known as Odeku) and small (330 ml). Nigerians consider the stout produced here to be the best in the world for its particular taste and quality. It's no wonder that in 1962, Nigeria was the first country outside Ireland and Great Britain to have a Guinness brewery.

My friend Miss Jayla calls this traditional combination of sweet palm wine and stout (most commonly Guinness) aba punch. It is similar to many layered beer cocktails like the Irish Half and Half, which combines a pale beer (or ale) with stout (or dark beer), and the Black Velvet, a combination of sparkling white wine (usually Champagne; cider and perry are sometimes used) and stout. The result, though not always layered, is an earthy brew with bitter, sweet, slightly sour flavors. Combine, stir gently, taste and, adjust with more palm wine or stout to suit your palate. The drink goes well with Nkwobi (page 179).

Divide the palm wine evenly among four highball glasses. Top each evenly with the stout, tilting the glass as you pour to limit the froth. Stir and serve.

VARIATIONS

Cocktail of cola and stout: If bittersweet were a drink, it would be this combination of dark, malty stout tempered by sweet cola instead of palm wine, preferably Nigerian or Mexican cola made with cane sugar rather than corn syrup.

Divide the Guinness evenly among four highball glasses, tilting the glass as you pour to limit the froth. Top each evenly with the cola and serve.

Other combinations are common—replace the cola with orange soda, lemon-lime soda, malt drinks, or even yogurt!

PALM WINE

Palm wine is made with the sap from various palms (oil, coconut, date, raffia, and palmyra), tapped from the trunks like maple syrup. It is one of the most esteemed drinks across Nigeria, an essential part of traditional celebrations, where it is served in long, slim gourds or calabash bowls.

Freshly tapped palm sap is sweet and light gray or off-white in color. It begins to ferment immediately, and within a few hours, its alcohol content increases, and it becomes creamier and acidic, with notes of vinegar and/or beer. This rapid fermentation occurs thanks to natural yeasts in the environment. In fact, for many years before commercial yeast was widely available, palm wine was used as a leavener in everything from bread to Puff Puff (page 39).

There are popular distillates of palm wine like ògógóró (which also goes by the names Sapele water, akpeteshie, kai-kai, Push-Me-I-Push-You), which play a role in traditional belief systems where they are poured out as libations to the ancestors. Today you'll find bottled brands of ògógóró in stores.

In *The Palm Wine Drinkard* by Amos Tutuola (one of my favorite novels), a man goes on a long journey to find his beloved palm wine tapper and bring him back from the dead. And not only has palm wine inspired literature, it also fueled a musical genre across West Africa, from Sierra Leone to Nigeria. Palm wine music is a blend of guitars and a variety of rhythms and melodies, local and diasporic. In its early history, musicians would come together to play in local bars and other spaces where palm wine was served.

In the East, the Igbos call their traditional marriage ceremony Igba Nkwu, "Wine Carrying." As part of the ceremony, the bride receives a cup of palm wine from her father and goes on a journey to find her husband. When she finds him, she takes a sip of the drink, gives him a sip, and then leads him to her family. The circle of love, joy, and familial connection is now established. Outside of events and festivals, palm wine is enjoyed on its own, with Chicken Pepper Soup (page 239), àbàchà (see page 103), Nkwobi (page 179), and more.

In Nigeria, you will find palm wine for sale on the street, but be sure to buy it only from a trusted source or in sealed bottles. Although you can't make palm wine at home, you will find it sold in bottles in Nigerian and African supermarkets around the world. Bottled palm wine is often young and sweet, pasteurized to stop further fermentation, sometimes with added sweetener. Keep palm wine chilled and shake it well before you drink it, as some bottled wines tend to separate.

GUINEA CORN, MILLET, AND ACHA

Sorghum, known locally as Guinea corn (dawa in Hausa); millet (gero in Hausa); and fonio (acha in Hausa) are important grains across Nigeria, particularly in the North West, North East, and North Central regions. There are several varieties of all three grains.

These grains continue to thrive across the African continent, one of the earliest sites of domestication, and feature in dishes in a variety of ways. They are dry, ground, and malted to make thin and thick porridges and pottages, and are incorporated into fresh, milky, boozy, and fermented drinks. The grains can be processed into traditional beer and wine, too. They can be popped like popcorn, boiled, fried, ground into flour to be used in dishes like swallow, and more.

Across Nigeria, there are many planting and harvest festivals that feature Guinea corn. Because of the different geographies and climates, the planting and harvest dates vary from place to place, as do the celebratory food and drinks.

In my hometown of Igarra, in the South South of Nigeria, Ireshiobani is a traditional rite that celebrates the release of Guinea corn for planting in June. Like the Agẹmo festival of Ijebu (see page 302), it marks the start of the Guinea corn planting season and precedes the harvest of yams and New Yam festivals. On the appointed day, the festivities begin with the sounds of drums to announce the event. Then a procession of farmers head to their farms to plant the Guinea corn, while new yams are being harvested. The yams are gifted to family members and neighbors in gratitude for the abundance the farmers have received from their Maker.

CUISINE
BASICS

PASTE FOR ÀKÀMÙ

3 cups (375 g) white corn flour

3 to 4 quarts (2.8 to 4 L) filtered water

NOTE: *The liquid that separates from the starch is known as omi-eko, omikan, or omidun, and can be used as a probiotic drink, added to herbal tonics, or stirred into the paste when making Àkàmù.*

For Àkàmù (page 76), you can make the paste from any color corn, millet, Guinea corn (sorghum), fonio, or a combination. In Nigeria, skin-on corn kernels are the starting point. (Corn yields a starchier paste than millet or sorghum and cooks slightly thicker.) Typically, in hot climates, the grains are soaked for 2 to 3 days until soft and fermented, then processed to make the starchy paste. In colder temperatures, it may take up to 5 days for this to happen. In either case, telltale signs of fermentation are cloudy water with frothy bubbles, a slight, sometimes sweet yeasty smell, and softened grains. The longer the grains soak, the stronger the ferment.

In Nigeria, people typically take the fermented grains to commercial grinders in the neighborhood or market. These high-powered grinders make light work of turning the corn into a smooth slurry, increasing its overall yield once it is "washed" and separated from the chaff. For best results at home, you will need a high-powered blender.

Finding Nigerian-style dried corn was difficult for me in Ontario, so after fermenting a variety of corn types—cracked corn, cornmeal, and corn flour, both white and yellow—I settled on white corn flour (farine de mais blanc, farinha de milho branca), which gives the most consistent results in texture and taste.

Place the corn flour in a large bowl and add filtered water to cover by 3 to 4 inches (7.5 to 10 cm). Stir well and cover the bowl with a lid and set aside to soak.

Soak the flour for 4 days, changing the water daily. On day 3, you should see bubbles. The mixture will smell yeasty, a bit like yogurt.

To process the blended corn flour, set a nut-milk bag over a jug or bowl. Working in batches, transfer the blended corn flour into the nut-milk bag to strain. Squeeze until all of the corn liquid is extracted and the bag has corn flour bits. Pour the corn liquid into a 5-quart (4.7 L) or larger bowl.

Add filtered water to the bag of corn flour bits, which will still have a bit of starch. Massage the bag to release the starch and repeat the squeezing to extract the corn liquid. Add to the 5-quart (4.7 L) bowl. Repeat with the remaining blended corn flour.

PREVIOUS: *Kilishi, Nigerian beef jerky, here as street food displayed in a showglass*

Cover the bowl and let rest until the paste settles at the bottom of the bowl, at least 2 hours and up to 8 hours.

Carefully pour off the water into an airtight container, leaving the paste behind in the bowl, and refrigerate or freeze the liquid for another use (see Note).

Transfer the paste to an airtight container, top with 2 to 3 inches (5 to 7.5 cm) of filtered water, and cover. Refrigerate for up to 4 weeks, changing the water every few days.

SARDINE BUTTER

MAKES ½ TO 1 CUP (100 TO 200 G)

1 (4.4-ounce/125 g) can of sardines in oil, drained

1 tablespoon unsalted butter, softened

½ teaspoon dry pepper (see page 22) or ½ small red Scotch bonnet or habanero pepper, finely diced

¼ teaspoon fine sea salt, plus more as needed

1 small red onion or shallot, finely chopped (optional)

½ small green bell pepper, diced (optional)

½ small red bell pepper, diced (optional)

In my childhood in Nigeria, sardine butter and other compound butters were staples, especially for lunch boxes, parties, and road trips. Make them as simple or as complex as you want—combine mashed butter, margarine, or mayonnaise with anything from sardines to chopped vegetables, from onions to bell peppers, chiles and more. The spread keeps refrigerated for 2 to 3 days.

In a small bowl, mash the sardines until they form a paste. Add the butter, dry pepper, salt, and, if using, the onion and bell peppers. Stir well to combine. Taste and add more salt if needed.

Serve as desired. My favorite use is as a sandwich spread.

VARIATION

Corned beef butter: Replace the sardines with canned corned beef and skip the salt, or adjust according to your taste.

FRIED MEAT

Neutral oil, for frying

2 pounds (900 g) cooked meat (from Curry Stock, page 333)

I daresay no Nigerian gathering is complete without golden brown fried meat, made with beef, chicken, goat, ram, or turkey wings. The best fried meat has a chewy exterior and soft interior. The meat should be seasoned and cooked until soft but not falling apart; otherwise, it will end up in shreds. Adjust the cooking times depending on the size and type of meat you choose.

Enjoy fried meat on its own as a snack, with Soaked Garri (page 72), jollof rice (page 143), Nigerian Fried Rice (page 149), in stew, and more.

Fill a wok, large pan, or Dutch oven with 2 inches (5 cm) of oil and heat over medium heat to 350°F (175°C). Line a strainer with paper towels.

Working in batches, add the meat to the hot oil, being careful not to overcrowd the pan. Fry on one side until golden around the edges, about 4 minutes, then carefully flip the meat and cook on the second side until evenly golden brown, 3 to 4 minutes more. Transfer the fried meat to the paper towel–lined strainer to drain. Repeat with the remaining meat, allowing the oil to return to temperature between batches.

Serve hot, warm, or cold. Store any leftovers in an airtight container and keep in the refrigerator for up to 7 days or the freezer for up to 2 months.

VARIATIONS

To air-fry the meat: Arrange the meat in a single layer on the air fryer tray. Air-fry at 390°F (200°C) for 8 minutes, give it a shake, then cook for 6 minutes more, or until just browned all over.

To roast the meat: Arrange the meat in a single layer on a rimmed baking sheet. Roast at 400°F (205°C) for about 15 minutes, until browned all over.

ATA DINDIN

1 large red or white onion,
coarsely chopped

2 red tatashe peppers or
Hungarian Beaver Dam
peppers, or 1 Italian sweet
pepper or medium red bell
pepper (240 g), coarsely
chopped

20 dried bird's-eye chiles
(5 g), or 10 dried Thai chiles,
stemmed

3 red Fresno peppers,
coarsely chopped

2 Scotch bonnet or
habanero peppers, coarsely
chopped

1½ cups (360 ml) peanut oil
or other neutral oil

2 teaspoons fine sea salt

This spicy pepper sauce is popular as a dip or side. There are a variety of options for seasoning: with crayfish or dry fish (or both) and irú, traditional Nigerian flavors; or with curry powder and thyme, colonial-inspired additions.

Serve it with small chops or prepared vegetables, or anywhere you want a kick of spice.

In a blender or food processor, combine the onion, tatashe peppers, dried chiles, Fresnos, and Scotch bonnets. Pulse until the vegetables are broken down and form a chunky puree.

Set a wide pan or wok over medium-high heat and add 1 cup (240 ml) of the oil. Once warm, reduce the heat to medium-low and gradually add the blended mixture. Season with 1 teaspoon of the salt, stir well, cover with the lid ajar, and cook until the onion and peppers soften and the mixture reduces a touch, stirring often and scraping the bottom to avoid scorching, about 35 minutes.

Taste and season with some or all of the remaining 1 teaspoon salt. Add the remaining ½ cup (120 ml) oil. Cover with the lid ajar and cook until the oil rises to the top and the mix underneath has a "fried" or dimpled texture, 10 to 15 minutes more. Remove from the heat and let cool completely before serving or storing. It will keep in an airtight container in the refrigerator for up to 2 weeks or in the freezer for up to 3 months.

CURRY STOCK

2 pounds (900 g) raw bone-in beef and chicken pieces

1 large red onion, coarsely chopped

1 medium green bell pepper, coarsely chopped

1 Scotch bonnet or habanero pepper (optional)

1 tablespoon plus 1½ teaspoons Curry Powder (page 25)

1 tablespoon dried thyme leaves

3 large dried bay leaves

2 teaspoons fine sea salt, plus more as needed

½ teaspoon freshly ground black pepper

4 thumb-size pieces fresh ginger, peeled and cut into chunks

4 medium garlic cloves, peeled

Typically seasoned with curry powder, dried thyme, ginger, red onion, and garlic, curry stock can include more than one type of meat (beef, chicken, turkey, or goat) and often uses two in combination. When using meats with different cooking times, start with the one that takes the longest to cook, then add the others later so they will be cooked through at about the same time. After making the stock, reserve the meat for Fried Meat (page 330).

In a stockpot, combine the meat, onion, bell pepper, Scotch bonnet (if using), curry powder, thyme, bay leaves, salt, and black pepper. Cook over high heat, stirring, until the meat loses its raw look, 5 to 8 minutes. Reduce the heat to low, cover, and cook until the meat begins to yield juices, 5 minutes more. Stir with a wooden spoon, scraping the bottom of the pot to dislodge any toasty bits, cover, and cook for 10 minutes more.

In a blender, combine the ginger, garlic, and 2 cups (480 ml) water; blend until thoroughly combined. Strain the ginger-garlic mixture through a fine-mesh strainer directly into the pot, pressing on the solids to extract as much liquid as possible, then discard the solids.

Add enough water to the pot to just cover all the solid ingredients (about 2½ quarts/2.4 L) and stir well to incorporate. Cover and bring to a boil over high heat, about 12 minutes, then reduce the heat to medium-low and cook until the stock is aromatic, the vegetables are soft, and the meat is tender but retains some resistance, 40 to 45 minutes.

Set a fine-mesh strainer over a large bowl. With tongs, transfer the meat to the strainer. Let it drain and cool for about 15 minutes.

With a spider or slotted spoon, transfer the cooked vegetables and bay leaves to the blender with 1 cup (240 ml) of the stock and puree until homogeneous and smooth. Strain through a fine-mesh strainer back into the pot with the remaining stock, pressing on the solids to extract as much liquid as possible; discard the solids. Stir well to incorporate.

RECIPE CONTINUES →

There will be some fat, which you can skim off immediately with a ladle or large spoon, or let the stock cool completely and refrigerate in an airtight container until the fat solidifies on the surface, then remove it and reserve it for other uses or discard it.

The stock can be portioned into freezer-safe containers, refrigerated for 5 days and frozen for up to 3 months.

ALKALINE WATER

MAKES 1 CUP (240 ML)

¼ cup (60 g) akaun (see page 95), ground to a powder

1 cup (240 ml) filtered water, at room temperature

This alkali-rich liquid is used as an emulsifier for sauces and salad dressings like Àbàchà Ǹcha (page 103).

In a 2-cup (480 ml) bottle or jar with a lid, combine the akaun and the water. Cover and shake to combine, then set aside until the liquid turns light gray and the akaun sediments settle to the bottom, about 30 minutes.

Shake the bottle again and set aside until the akaun sediments separate out again, 30 minutes more. Repeat this process of shaking and leaving to separate out two more times. The column of liquid should be evenly colored and somewhat golden. Carefully decant the golden liquid and reserve. If need be, pass through a fine-mesh strainer or coffee filter. Discard the sediment. Store leftovers in an airtight container away from light and heat, for up to 12 months.

VARIATION

Baking soda is a suitable replacement for akaun when making alkaline water, though the "when" differs—you make this version as you need it, not ahead of time.

Stir ⅛ to ¼ teaspoon baking soda into 2 tablespoons filtered water. Use immediately.

PEPPER STEW BASE

1 large red or white onion,
coarsely chopped

2 red tatashe peppers or
1 red shepherd pepper,
coarsely chopped

¼ Scotch bonnet or
habanero pepper, or more
as needed, stemmed

This base is perfect for palm oil–based sauces.

In a blender, combine the onion, tatashe peppers, Scotch bonnet
(to taste), and 1 cup (240 ml) water. Puree on high to form an even,
creamy mix. Pour the puree into a medium saucepan. Rinse out the
blender with ½ cup (120 ml) water and add that to the pot.

Cover with the lid ajar and cook over medium-high heat, stirring as
needed, for about 15 minutes, to thicken and reduce the mixture.
The color will deepen and the flavors will smooth out.

Use immediately, or let cool. Transfer to an airtight container and
refrigerate for up to 5 days or freeze for up to 3 months.

TOMATO STEW BASE

1 pound (450 g) Roma (plum)
tomatoes (about 3 medium),
coarsely chopped

2 red tatashe peppers or
1 red shepherd pepper,
coarsely chopped

1 large red onion, coarsely
chopped

¼ Scotch bonnet or
habanero pepper, stemmed

1½ cups (360 ml) Curry
Stock (page 333)

Tomatoes, onions, and peppers are the "holy trinity" of Nigerian
cooking. Skinning fresh tomatoes is not common, but you can do it.
If using frozen whole tomatoes, peel them before use, as the skins
become tough and gritty.

In a blender, combine the tomatoes, tatashe peppers, onion, Scotch
bonnet, and stock. Puree until smooth, about 2 minutes. You should
have just shy of 5 cups (1.2 L).

Transfer the stew base to a 3-quart (3 L) saucepan, cover with the lid
ajar, and bring to a boil over medium-high heat. Reduce the heat to
medium-low and cook, stirring and scraping the bottom occasionally
to avoid scorching, until reduced, about 30 minutes.

Use immediately, or let cool. Transfer to an airtight container and
refrigerate for up to 5 days or freeze for up to 3 months.

FURTHER READING

◇◇◇◇◇◇◇◇

This is a list of resources—mostly cookbooks and culture books, a couple of memoirs, even a few textbooks—that trace the food history and personal experiences of the authors, as well as give insight and context into Nigerian cuisine and related histories.

Afolabi, Niyi, and Toyin Falola, eds. *The Yoruba in Brazil, Brazilians in Yorubaland.* Durham, NC: Carolina Academic Press, 2017.

Anthonio, H. O., and Miriam Isoun. *Nigerian Cookbook.* London and Basingstoke: Macmillan Education, 1982.

Aríbisálà, Yẹ́misí. *Longthroat Memoirs: Soups, Sex and Nigerian Taste Buds.* Abuja and London: Cassava Republic Press, 2017.

Bascom, W. "Yoruba Cooking." *Africa: Journal of the International African Institute* 21 (no. 2; April 1951): 125–137.

———. "Yoruba Food." *Africa: Journal of the International African Institute* 21 (no. 1; January 1951): 41–53.

Crowther, Samuel Ajayi, and Emeric Owen Vidal. *A Vocabulary of the Yoruba Language.* London: Seeleys, 1852.

Dalziel, J. M. *A Hausa Botanical Vocabulary.* London: T. Fisher Unwin Ltd., 1916.

———. *The Useful Plants of West Tropical Africa.* London: The Crown Agents for the Colonies, 1937.

Edet, Laura. *Classic Nigerian Cook Book.* London: Divine Grace Publishers, 1996.

Eyeoyibo, Mac. Oma. *Cookery Book in Itsẹkírì (Warri Kingdom).* Benin City: Mofe Press, 1993.

Falola, Toyin. *Culture and Customs of Nigeria.* Westport, CT: Greenwood Press, 2001.

Isichei, Elizabeth. *A History of Nigeria.* Oxford, UK: Oxford University Press, 1987.

Jackson, Elizabeth A. *South of the Sahara—Traditional Cooking from the Lands of West Africa.* Hollis, NH: Fantail, 1999.

McCall, Ian. *Sweet Pass Kerosene.* Eyemouth, Scotland: Cross Border Consultants, 2011.

National Research Council. *Lost Crops of Africa, Volume I: Grains.* National Academies Press, 1996. Available as a free online resource.

———. *Lost Crops of Africa, Volume II: Vegetables.* National Academies Press, 2006. Available as a free online resource.

———. *Lost Crops of Africa, Volume III: Fruits.* National Academies Press, 2008. Available as a free online resource.

Observatory of Economic Complexity. *Rice in Nigeria.* September 8, 2021.

O'Reilly-Wright, Enid. *The Student's Cookery Book.* Oxford, UK: Oxford University Press, 1964.

Plummer, Gladys. *The Ibo [sic] Cookery Book*. Lagos: C.M.S. Bookshops, 1937.

Politis, Victor. *Festivals of Nigeria—Through the Eyes of a Passerby*. Nigeria: Voyager Media, 2011.

Reddy, Deepa. "The Last Word on Curry." May 13, 2023. Blog post. www.paticheri.com/2023/05/13/the-last-word-on-curry.

Segun, Mabel. *Rhapsody: A Celebration of Nigerian Cooking and Food Culture*. Lagos: Mabelline Publications, 2007.

Smith, Ifeyironwa Francisca. *Foods of West Africa—Their Origin and Use*. Ottawa: printed by the author, 1998.

Sparks, Lacey. "'Something a Little Bit Tasty': Women and the Rise of Nutrition Science in Interwar British Africa." PhD diss., University of Kentucky, 2017. DOI: 10.13023/ETD .2017.414.

Tooley, E. M., and J. A. Mars. *The Kudeti Book of Yoruba Cookery*. Lagos: C.M.S. Bookshops, 1934.

Williams, Rhoda Omosunlola. *Miss Williams' Cookery Book*. London: Longmans, 1957.

STOCKISTS

◇◇◇◇◇◇◇◇◇

It is easy to access Nigerian ingredients across many parts of the world these days. You can find many of the basic ingredients at regular grocery stores, and in stores that cater to South and Central American, South Asian, and Southeast Asian communities; there are many commonalities in the ingredients. The range of available products, from individual ingredients to ready-to-eat meals, seasonings, spices, and even seeds to start your own Nigerian garden, have changed, as well as the possibilities for delivery. Here are some of my favorite sources.

Ingredients

MY CHOPCHOP

mychopchop.ca

A great online and physical retail store, with quality African groceries, healthy snacks, and more. Based in Canada; delivery is available all over North America.

OSI AFRIK

osiafrik.com

A great destination for Nigerian groceries in the United States. Delivery is quick and efficient. In addition to groceries, they have a seed collection so you can grow your own Nigerian ingredients.

Ready-Made Nigerian Food

ADUN

getadun.com

For African flavors in an instant, this US-based company ships prepared and packaged foods everywhere in the continental US. They have a range of products, from sides to main meals, soups, stews, and more, including puff puff, pepper soup, stew, ẹ̀gúsí, èfọ́ rírò, beef pies (meat pies), native rice (palm oil jollof), and okro.

ATARE FOODS

atarefoods.com

This Canada-based company has a couple of great jarred sauces, Jollof Now (for jollof rice and stews) and Atasu (a seafood-based condiment), and delicious plantain chips.

CHEF LILIAN OF NAIJA BUKA SEATTLE

cheflilian.com

Naija Buka produces meal kits, ready-to-eat meals, frozen favorites, sauces, and seasonings.

EGUNSI FOODS

egunsifoods.com

This New York–based company produces classic West African foods, including ọbẹ̀ ata, gbẹ̀gìrì, egunsi (ẹ̀gúsí), and groundnut (peanut) soup.

Spices and Seasonings

INDEEGENUS FOODS

indeegenus.com

This US-based West African company sources treasured ingredients used across the African diaspora.

POKS SPICES

poksspices.com

Their range of seasonings deliver the flavors of West Africa.

Nigerian Seeds and Plants

JOLLOF CODE

jollofcode.com

For seeds, classes, tutorials, and resources on everything about setting up a Nigerian garden outside Nigeria, turn here; from the founder of Atare Foods.

OKO FARMS

okofarms.org

This urban farm in New York is focused on sustainable farming methods through aquaponics. They cultivate a wide variety of vegetables, herbs, fruits, medicinal plants, and flowers, including cabbage, sweet potatoes, lemongrass, millet, sorghum, okra, peppers, tomatoes, indigo, and more.

TRUE LOVE SEEDS

trueloveseeds.com

They have a collection of African diaspora seeds including callaloo (amaranth greens), sorghum, garden eggs, okro, ẹ̀fọ́ sọkọ, waterleaf, sesame seeds, roselle (zòbò), ẹ̀gúsí, waxy African corn, and more. They also sell a cute gift set of seeds and postcards.

ACKNOWLEDGMENTS

◇◇◇◇◇◇◇◇

I'm grateful to God for this dream come true. From the point when I started enjoying food, my dream has been to write a cookbook. Though the what, how, and why has changed over the last two decades, the dream has stayed constant. Today, the why centers on legacy, celebration, and broadening the definition of *global*.

My thanks and gratitude to:

My family—my mum, Florence Ehinlaiye; my uncle Kenny and aunt Tayo Ladipo for everything and lots of beautiful fabric; my uncle Charles and auntie Jumoke Ehinlaiye; my uncle Kayode James. All my siblings and cousins.

James Ransom, friend and photographer who did everything possible to help me get started with the process, from book proposal all the way to the gorgeous photography, with stops in Lagos and Mississauga. Special thanks to our fixers, Logor Oluwamuyiwa and Adetolani Akinbo-Michaels.

Caro Lange for her work with me on the book proposal. Michael Adé Elégbèdé, Lopè Ariyo, Yemisí Aríbisálà, Abby Williams, Kachi Tila-Adesina. Early believers.

While all the groundwork was being laid, I met Anne E. McBride. This book would not exist without Anne's kindness and generosity. She introduced me to her (now also my) agent, Jonah Straus. Jonah's thoughtful direction and support from the start have been invaluable.

The experts, with a variety of cookbook experience—Iquo Ukoh, Flo Madubike, Yewande Komolafe, Hawa Hassan, Naomi Duguid, Nana Araba Wilmot, Erin Jeanne McDowell, Kathryn Pauline, Sho Spaeth—thank you for your thoughtful guidance and direction. Special thanks to Hauwa Datti-Garba and Naomi Duguid for expertise, knowledge, guidance, and friendship, over countless hours.

There's no way I could have done it without my loves—Jedidiah, Riobo, and Daniel. They have stretched my capacity for love, hope, and, importantly, the courage to keep going. And helped with my recipe list, tasting and testing and mostly enjoying the dishes.

For translating words and bringing my vision to life, James Ransom, Lindsay Guscott, Andrea McCrindle, Dami Dokunmu, and Jacquie Matthews.

Ngozi Christiana Ebegbulem, Fatima Mamman Kazure, Bolatito Alawode of My Chop Chop, Ayo Sokefun of Go Chips, Victor and Angela Ugwueke of Afrobeat Kitchen in Toronto, Dayo Oluwole, Sanusi and Tomi Ismaila, Toun and Lumi Morgan, and Bunmi Kusimo for the support and gifts.

For the warm answers to the never-ending questions, and for reasoning with me—Adebola Falade, Jite Efemuaye, Ronke Edoho, Neema Syovata, my big sis Bo Ebuehi and her cousin Beauty Awe aka MamaBee, Danielle Ogwo, Deepa Reddy, Oreoluwa Olaolu, Rahama Aliyu-Yelwa, Nicole Rufus, Maryam Ahmed, Ameena Abubakar, Atim Ukoh, Eromo Egbejule, Irina Mihalache, Funmilade Taiwo, Maureen Celestine, Patricia Ezewoko, Isioma Afuberoh, Chinwe Ifeonye, Biola Odanye, Okhai Okojie, Sabirah Oniyangi, Sweety Bassey, and so many others.

And to the wonderful, amazing team who made this beauty possible. Under the thoughtful guidance and listening ears of Judy Pray and the team at Artisan, including Laura Cherkas, Brooke Beckmann, Nina Simoneaux, and Nancy Murray; Bonnie Benwick; the team at Appetite by Random House, including Robert McCullough, Zoe Maslow, Katherine Stopa, Adria Iwasutiak, Aakanksha Malhotra, and Charlotte Nip; and the team at Narrative Landscape especially Eghosa Imasuen, Anwuli Ojogwu, and Joy Chime, this book emerged. You have my gratitude.

INDEX

◇◇◇◇◇◇◇◇◇

Note: *Italic* page numbers indicate photos. **Bold** page numbers indicate recipes.

Ozoz Sokoh is a Nigerian food writer, educator, budding curator, and traveler by plate. A geologist by training, she began documenting her food journey on her blog, *Kitchen Butterfly*, in 2009. Central to her work is exploring connectedness through food, food sovereignty, cultural identity, reclamation of Nigerian cuisine, and the joy of eating. Her research and documentation explore the roots of Nigerian and West African cuisine and their connection to the African diaspora, as well as the impact of West African intellectual contributions on global development across the world.

Her ongoing project, "Coast to Coast: From West Africa to the World," documented on FeastAfrique.com, traces the histories and edible trails of West Africa and its diaspora through ingredients. It includes an open-access digital library of 250-plus cuisine and cookbooks from the 1800s to the present, a hall of fame, data-driven work on the role of food media in marginalizing West African voices, and a series of short films available for screening.

Ozoz has spoken at TEDx and at conferences hosted by the Culinary Institute of America. Her work has been featured in *Brittle Paper*, *Smithsonian* magazine, Gastro Obscura, CNN's *African Voices*, *Anthony Bourdain: Parts Unknown*, and others.

She is a professor of food and tourism studies at Centennial College, Ontario-Canada, where she teaches a variety of courses, including Exploration of Foodways. She makes her home with her three teenage children in Mississauga, part of the Treaty Lands and Territory of the Mississaugas of the Credit First Nation. Find her online at @KitchenButterfly.